A Gendered Collision

A Gendered Collision

Sentimentalism and Modernism
in Dorothy Parker's
Poetry and Fiction

Rhonda S. Pettit

Madison • Teaneck
Fairleigh Dickinson University Press
London: Associated University Presses

Associated University Presses
440 Forsgate Drive
Cranbury, NJ 08512

Associated University Presses
16 Barter Street
London WC1A 2AH, England

Associated University Presses
P.O. Box 338, Port Credit
Mississauga, Ontario
Canada L5G 4L8

The paper used in this publication meets the requirements of the American National Standard for Permanence of Paper for Printed Library Materials Z39.48–1984.

Library of Congress Cataloging-in-Publication Data

Pettit, Rhonda S., 1955–
    A gendered collision : sentimentalism and modernism in Dorothy Parker's poetry and fiction / Rhonda S. Pettit.
        p. cm.
    Includes bibliographical references (p.) and index.
    ISBN 0-8386-3818-X (alk. paper)
    1. Parker, Dorothy, 1893–1967—Criticism and interpretation. 2. Women and literature—United States—History—20th century. 3. Modernism (Literature)—United States. 4. Sentimentalism in literature. I. Title.

PS3531.A5855 Z83 2000
818'5209—dc21

                                                        99-051766

PRINTED IN THE UNITED STATES OF AMERICA

To
the memory of
Gora Franklin "Pete" Pettit

and to
Opal Katherine (Anderson) Pettit

Contents

Preface

By coincidence, 1994—the year I began writing this book—marked a celebratory year of sorts for Dorothy Parker. The seventy-fifth anniversary of the Algonquin Round Table, a luncheon and cocktail coterie of New York writers, critics and actors that included Parker as one-of its few female members, was celebrated in New York City. The Algonquin Hotel, headquarters for the group, offered tours. Random House published its Modern Library edition of *The Poetry and Short Stories of Dorothy Parker*, and sponsored a breakfast panel focused on Parker at Mad 61, an uptown restaurant. Finally, Alan Rudolph's film *Mrs. Parker and the Vicious Circle* appeared in theaters across the country. As Margo Jefferson wrote in the *New York Times*, "Dorothy Parker always made good copy."[1] However, "good copy" often had—and still has—unfortunate consequences for Parker's literary reputation.

The activities described above did little to alter the conventional wisdom about Parker and her work. While a tour of the Algonquin might offer an historical sense of time and place that is valuable, it not surprisingly says more about the hotel than it does about Parker, who was associated with the hotel for less than ten of her seventy-four years. The Modern Library edition of Parker's work may possess, among other things, nostalgic value, but it fails to provide a complete collection of her fiction and poetry. The panel discussion led by Random House president Harold M. Evans to mark the event is even more problematic. Admirers of Parker, including opera star Beverly Sills, dance writer Joan Acocella and actress Lauren Hutton, were present and vocal. But, according to a *New York Times* account by Wil-

liam Grimes, the discussion, ostensibly targeted at the value of Parker's
work, quickly degenerated into a gab session about Parker's caustic
and paradoxical personality. Actress Kitty Carlisle Hart complained
about Parker's insensitivity to her career struggles, and concluded,
"'She was extraordinarily malicious and difficult. She had a real mean
streak.'" Parker, who, according to former *New Yorker* writer and pan-
elist Brendan Gill, "'turned whining into a form of high art,'" evidently had little tolerance for the self-indulgent whining of others.
This suggests that more than autobiography lay behind Parker's "high
art," but the panel—or Grimes's account of it—failed to consider this
possibility. Gill offered another familiar critique of Parker's verse and
fiction: "'She represents accurately a civilization that has vanished
without a trace . . . as remote from us as ancient Egypt,'" he said,
referring to the Roaring Twenties in New York City. It is difficult to
stamp Parker as a period writer, however, when many of her topics—
abortion, divorce, family discord, war, racism, economic disparity—
have relevance beyond (and certainly before) the 1920s. Again, this
observation was not raised in the discussion.[2]

Receiving much broader circulation is Alan Rudolph's film, *Mrs.
Parker and the Vicious Circle*, starring Jennifer Jason-Leigh as Dorothy
Parker.[3] Rudolph gives us a Parker largely identified with her
Algonquin Round Table friends of the 1920s, focusing on her depression, alcoholism, and unhappy love life. A number of biographical accounts validate these aspects of Parker's life, so in a sense,
Rudolph's portrayal is "accurate." What Rudolph fails to give us, however, is an accurate dramatization of Parker's political life, a life
concerned with economic inequity, racial injustice, xenophobia,
and political freedom in the face of fascism both at home and
abroad—a life reflected in her work. Instead we get black and
white flashes forward into Parker's future, where her involvement
with the writers' union in Hollywood and her concern about seg-
regation are mentioned, rather than dramatized in the way her
alcoholic unhappiness is repeatedly dramatized. Even the poems
recited in these clips portray Parker as a victim of love, rather than as
the cool-hearted victimizer found in the second half of her first book
of poems, *Enough Rope* (1926), or the reviser of myth and legend
found in several of the poems in *Death and Taxes* (1931). The fact
that these scenes are excerpts constituting a small part of the film as
a whole, and that they are filmed in black and white in contrast to
the rich colors of the Roaring Twenties film scenes, visually reinforces the suggestion that Parker's political concerns and her po-

etry are of less importance than her alcoholism and her depression.

Why does Rudolph, whom Grimes describes as "a fan of the group," take such a narrow approach to Parker, aside from the fact that it was an easy approach to take, and that it could most likely be sold to and by Hollywood? The argument that the film's main focus is on the decade of the twenties fails to explain why her political work of that era, such as her march and arrest during the Sacco-Vanzetti protest in 1927, is ignored. The argument that the film is about the heyday of the Algonquin Round Table, not Parker's entire life, is lame because the title privileges her name, and with the exception of the opening scene, the film flashes forward to her life only. Anthony Lane, in a negative review of the film and of Parker for *New Yorker* magazine, provides another motivation: "The movie is more about drinking than about writing, which allows Rudolph to practice his fluid, dreamlike technique; there are plenty of smoky closeups and smooth flashbacks [*sic*], and . . . overlapping dialogue."[4] What Lane accurately describes is the technique of one artist distorting the technique (and life) of another. We also have yet another Hollywood movie in which a woman fares badly, in which a woman of substance is reduced to a woman of substance abuse.

These depictions of Parker's life and work recreate the limited literary landscape by which we know her, and which this study tries to correct by examining the context in which she wrote and lived. This may at first sound redundant, since Rudolph and the other commentators above seem to be trapped in a contextual web where Parker is concerned. The problem, however, is not context per se, but a context too narrowly defined by Parker's alcoholism, depression, suicide attempts, and disappointing love life. What the commentators above illustrate is that if these elements constitute the only context by which we know Parker and her work, she becomes a pathetic figure, her work an avenue for self-pity and excessive suffering.

Biographers have done relatively little to correct this tendency. Marion Meade, for example, too often uses lines from Parker's poetry and fiction as evidence for claims about Parker's mental state or actions. Alan Rudolph uses many of these same lines as dialogue in his film, a "mannerism," wrote Janet Maslin in the *New York Times*, that "becomes useful as it incorporates so much droll dialogue and lively biographical information."[5] This "mannerism," however, entangles the life and work in ways that obscure both, and that deny legitimacy and agency to the writer's imagination. It is particularly relevant that a woman's imagination is being denigrated. Would anyone dare claim that T. S. Eliot muttered in conversation, "In the room the women come and go, talking of Michelangelo," or that Ezra Pound spoke in an Old English meter? In addition to gender, Parker's accessibility and popularity make it easy for critics to grossly conflate her life and art, because for many, popular art is not art at all. Contextual emphasis produces a vicious backlash if it is used too narrowly or too selectively. This study will consider Parker in a much broader intellectual and literary context, one characterized by the collision between nineteenth-century sentimentalism and twentieth-century modernism.

* * *

A few words need to be said about the sources for Parker's work cited in this study. No complete edition of Parker's fiction, poetry, essays, or reviews exists. Individual volumes of Parker's fiction that are now out of print—*Laments for the Living* (1930) and *After Such Pleasures* (1933)—contain stories that are not included in the 1944 or 1973 editions of *The Portable Dorothy Parker*. A more recent volume edited by Colleen Breese, *Complete Stories* (1995), includes these stories but is not technically a complete edition, since it does not include "Who Might Be Interested," as well as other early fiction pieces that reveal elements of her technique. It does, however, contain a selection of Parker's longer, early sketches, and provides publishing data for each story so readers can get a sense of her development. *Here Lies: The Collected Stories of Dorothy Parker* (1939) contains a limited selection based on Parker's preferences.

The same condition exists for Parker's poetry. Out of print volumes—*Enough Rope* (1926), *Sunset Gun* (1928), *Death and Taxes* (1931)—contain poems that are not included in either edition of *The Portable Dorothy Parker* or in Stuart Y. Silverstein's compilation, *Not Much Fun: The Lost Poems of Dorothy Parker* (1996), which collects her previously uncollected poems. This is a useful anthology, although his treatment of Parker in the introduction seems at times unnecessarily harsh. Parker's selection of her poems, *Not So Deep as a Well* (1931), does not include a number of poems from her three individual volumes as well as those written after 1931.

Parker's critical writing is harder to come by. An incomplete selection of Parker's book reviews for the *New Yorker* can be found in *Constant Reader*, published in 1970. Although the 1973 *Portable Dorothy Parker* contains a selection of Parker's book and theater reviews as well as some uncollected articles, as this book goes to press most of her essays and early prose must be found in their original form of magazine publication—*Life, Vogue, Vanity Fair, Ainslee's, Saturday Evening Post, New Yorker, Harper's,* to name a few. Randall Calhoun's *Dorothy Parker: A Bio-Bibliography* (1993) provides an indispensable guide for this material, as well as for review citations regarding Parker's work in all genres.

Despite its shortcomings, I use the 1973 edition of *The Portable Dorothy Parker* as a first source whenever possible because of its publishing longevity; it thus offers the reader an easily available reference. I then refer to other sources—the Breese and Silverstein compilations when possible, and the original volumes of poetry and magazine issues as needed.

Acknowledgments

As my interest in this subject began during my years as a graduate student, a number of individuals and institutions deserve recognition for their assistance, patience, and insights. I take this opportunity to thank the graduate faculty of the Department of English at the University of Kentucky, in particular Dr. Ellen Rosenman, my thesis advisor, and the poet James Baker Hall who, while not directly involved with this project, offered insights and lessons about literature that aided my work and that continue to teach me. I also thank the Reference and Interlibrary Loan staff of the M. I. King (now William T. Young) Library for helping me locate some of the (at that time) uncollected stories by Dorothy Parker. Several individuals at the University of Cincinnati provided valuable assistance as my work continued there. Dr. Alison Rieke, my dissertation director, as well as the members of my dissertation committee, Dr. Lisa Marie Hogeland and Dr. Beth Ash, provided much guidance for this project. The staff of the Interlibrary Loan Office of Langsam Library worked diligently to retrieve reviews of Parker's work as well as uncollected prose by Parker. I am grateful to the Langsam Library for their collection of the *Vanity Fair* issues dating back to the teens and twenties, and to the Cincinnati Public Library for their collection of the old *Life* magazine issues, also dating back to the twenties.

Two forms of financial support also aided this project. I was able to complete a large portion of this study while on a Taft Memorial Fund Dissertation Fellowship awarded by the University of Cincinnati. Also, a Travel-to-Collections Grant, provided by *Tulsa Studies in Women's Literature* (Holly Laird, editor), of the University of Tulsa, enabled me to examine manuscripts at the McFarlin Library and consider Parker's work from the point of view of a British writer (Stevie Smith) she influenced.

A portion of this manuscript was revised and expanded while I was an instructor in the Department of Literature and Language at Northern Kentucky University. My employment in this department acquainted me with the Kentucky Philological Association, which provided a forum in which to present and "test" one of my revisions. I thank both the department and the KPA for providing not only that forum but other kinds of encouragement as well. Debbie Pope of NKU's Computing Services provided much needed technical assistance in converting this manuscript from one word processing software to another. In addition, I thank the students at NKU; our lively classroom discussions of Parker's stories added greatly to my analysis of her work.

More recently, technical, financial, and professional assistance has been provided by the Department of English at the Raymond Walters College campus of the University of Cincinnati. In particular, I thank Philip Luther, chair of the English department, and Dr. Barbara Bardes, dean of the college. The English department also provided a forum in which I could present and "test" another portion of this manuscript.

I also want to thank friends and colleagues who discussed portions of this manuscript with me, and who provided emotional support and encouragement: Debbie Barrett-Graves, Allison Russell, Antoinette Mastin, Mimi Pipino, Barbara Wenner, and Tami Phenix.

Special thanks go to all members of my family for their patience and understanding. In particular, my brother, Jay Pettit, kept me grounded with humor and much needed "bull" sessions over lunch. Last but certainly not least, my husband, Michael Lee Horn, endured the late nights and weekends I spent working, and never failed to offer encouragement, perspective, and love. His presence in particular reminds me that no writer works alone.

* * *

1924–1929, 1931–34, 1937–39, 1941, 1943, 1945, 1955, 1958, 1995 by The National Association for the Advancement of Colored People. Used by permission of Penguin, a division of Penguin Putnam Inc.

The author wishes to thank Gerald Duckworth and Company Ltd., London, England, for granting English Language rights for various excerpts throughout the British Commonwealth, for this edition.

The author wishes to thank Liveright Publishing Co. for permission to quote from *Gentlemen Prefer Blondes*, by Anita Loos.

"To a Tragic Poetess" from *88 Poems* by Ernest Hemingway, copyright © 1979 by The Ernest Hemingway Foundation and Nicholas Gerogiannis, reprinted by permission of Harcourt, Inc.

"He Bade Me Be Happy," "Forgive and Forget," and "Ah! Woman Still," by Francis Osgood; "Dorothy's Dower" by Phoebe Cary; and "Getting Along" and "Fern Life" by Lucy Larcom, from Walker, Cheryl, ed., *American Women Poets of the Nineteenth Century: An Anthology*, copyright © 1992 by Rutgers, The State University. Reprinted by permission of Rutgers University Press.

Lines from "Sanctuary" by Elinor Wylie from *Collected Poems* by Elinor Wylie, copyright 1932 by Alfred A. Knopf Inc., and renewed 1960 by Edwina C. Rubenstein. Reprinted by permission of the publisher.

"Oread" by H. D. from *H. D. Collected Poems—1912–1944*. Copyright © 1982 by The Estate of Hilda Doolittle. Reprinted by permission of New Directions Publishing Corp.

Portions of chapter 4 first appeared in "Material Girls in the Jazz Age: Dorothy Parker's 'Big Blonde' as an Answer to Anita Loos's *Gentlemen Prefer Blondes*," published in *Kentucky Philological Review*, vol. 12 (1998). Department of Literature and Language, Northern Kentucky University.

A Gendered Collision

Introduction

> Oh, both my shoes are shiny new,
>   And pristine is my hat;
> My dress is 1922. . . .
>   My life is all like that.
> —Dorothy Parker (1926)

Conventional wisdom holds that Dorothy Parker is a modern writer who is not quite modernist. While the content of her work typically includes a Roaring Twenties howl at modern life, her poems adhere to formal standards, and her fiction is linear. In other words, Parker's work as we know it lacks radical experimentation with form. At times her howl could be more of a whine. Consider these lines from "Paths," a poem first published in a 1926 issue of *Vanity Fair* and later that year included in her first volume of poetry, *Enough Rope*:

> I shall tread, another year,
>   Ways I walked with Grief,
> Past the dry, ungarnered ear
>   And the brittle leaf.
>
> I shall stand, a year apart,
>   Wondering, and shy,
> Thinking, "Here she broke her heart;
>   Here she pled to die."[1]

A woman mourning over lost love is one of Parker's familiar themes. This poem uses rhymed, trochaic lines in hymnal or common measure—a familiar form—and language that can be described as sentimental to discuss that theme. We are easily drawn to the pain the speaker suffers. Unlike many of her poems, this one refuses to undercut its sentiment with a biting, humorous reversal that would set it apart from lyric poetry by, for example, Sara Teasdale and Elinor Wylie.

21

Instead, the woman's grief, like the poem itself, seems too easy, too accessible to be considered modernist.

Parker achieves a very different effect in "'Sorry, the Line Is Busy,'" a prose piece that I prefer to call a modernist experimental short story, appearing in a 1921 issue of *Life*.[2] The story's title, a standard line used by telephone operators, is presented within quotation marks, suggesting that the otherwise silent operator is speaking, and that the title itself is technically the first line of the story. As such, the story has dropped us into the middle of an ongoing situation. The body of the story consists of four sequences of fragmented conversation by four disembodied voices who ironically experience breakdowns in communication. The breakdowns are ironic because the understated symbol and subject of the story—the telephone—conventionally represents increased and more rapid communication in the modern age. Parker opens and closes the body of the story with a first speaker who, through the story's silent telephone operator, is unable to complete his call. The second speaker refuses to finish her conversation about a man she met because she fears "someone on the wire" other than her intended receiver will hear her. The third speaker, a woman whose speech is choked with clichés, has made a surprise phone call to "Wallie" who cuts her off. A suspiciously apologetic husband telling his wife he is "tied up down-town" and will be home late rounds out the group. The four speakers remain isolated and alienated, albeit in varying degrees, from the people whom they have called (or in the case of the first speaker, attempted to call), and of course from each other. The operator, a human conduit through which connections are to be made, provides no solution.

Additionally, the form of the story both reinforces and complicates the story's content. The message delivered by the title, as well as the caesura that slows it down, communicate delay. The lack of a narrative voice to tie the speakers together intensifies their isolation and alienation. But without a narrator, certain questions remain unanswered. Why can't the first speaker complete his call? Is the technology flawed? Is the silent operator incompetent or merely busy listening to the other conversations? The operator's role becomes important here: Are we hearing these voices through the ears of the operator, or as passersby? And what are we to make of the poor quality of communication by those who manage to complete their calls? With regard to these questions, readers are left in a kind of communication limbo approaching that of the story's speakers. The final line in the story spoken by the first speaker—"Operator, let me speak to the manager."—can be read as a plea for order in the dysfunctional world of modern communication technology.

Fragmented conversation, disembodied voices, irony, isolation, alienation, frustration with modernity—why hasn't "'Sorry, the Line Is Busy'" been associated with the high modernist mode of James Joyce, T. S. Eliot, and Ezra Pound? One reason may be its publishing history. *Life*, at the time the story was published, was a popular magazine of humorous prose, light verse, jokes, and cartoons. The story's appearance in such a magazine guaranteed it would not be considered serious art. Furthermore, "'Sorry, the Line Is Busy'" was an illustrated story; five people—four in telephone booths in the background, and an operator in the foreground—appear above the story, prompting us to wonder if the illustration was drawn for the story or the story written for the illustration. In fact, with its numbered individuals and pertly smiling operator who looks away from the switchboard, the illustration grossly simplifies Parker's text, implying answers to questions about the operator's role in the communication breakdown, and increasing accessibility to the story's supposed meaning. Parker's story needs no illustration; "'Sorry, the Line Is Busy'" is strictly stand-alone prose.

Unfortunately, Parker and her subsequent editors did not think so. The story was never included in any of her volumes, and one Parker scholar described it as a "prose squib."[3] Parker wrote several catalogs of disembodied voices for *Life* in the early 1920s. Some of these offer humorous, generalized examples of what liars, mothers, or the elderly would say, rather than closely adhere in both form and content to a modernist theme, and may therefore deserve the label "prose squib." Yet given its complexity, "'Sorry, the Line Is Busy'" raises several points of contention with our traditional history of modernist literature: that experimental work could be found in a mass circulation magazine instead of a relatively obscure "little magazine;" that experimental work could be produced by a woman better known for working in more popular and conventional forms; and that such work could appear before such mainstream modernist productions as James Joyce's *Ulysses* (1922), T. S. Eliot's *The Waste Land*, (1922), or Ernest Hemingway's *In Our Time* (1925).

A later but uncollected story by Parker, also published in *Life*, joins "'Sorry, the Line Is Busy'" in challenging the traditional concept of modernism as well as the notion that developments in literary form flow from the top down. "A Piece about Christmas" appeared in the 1 December 1927 issue of *Life*. The date is important because the story, an internal monologue, was written before Parker's better known monologues—"A Telephone Call" (1928) and "The Waltz" (1933), among others. Like "The Waltz" this story has a complaining speaker and a circular form, and thus appears to be a warm-up for the later story. But "A Piece about Christmas" performs a literary act not seen in "The Waltz"; it functions as a form of metafiction, prefiguring postmodernist prose as did Parker's contemporary Gertrude Stein. As the speaker writes her piece about Christmas, she complains about the fact that she cannot write it: "What can you say about Christmas, anyway? It's all been said. Dickens said it all in *A Christmas Carol.* Marley was dead. There's all Christmas, right there." Her concern is the unspoken but assumed definition of what is an appropriate Christmas piece, something "cheerful," something that could have been written by "James Branch Cabell or H. C. Witwer or Mary Roberts Rinehart or Peter B. Kyne."[4] In short, the speaker is trying to avoid the sentimental, and does so by focusing on her problems with the assignment rather than the season. The irony, of course, is that the speaker does write her Christmas piece, but it is a piece about writing, or not-writing, rather than about Christmas in the traditional sense.

If setting the poem "Paths" alongside the stories "'Sorry, the Line Is Busy'" and "A Piece about Christmas" offers a striking contrast, consider an earlier poem by Parker: "Any Porch," her first published poem, appeared in a 1915 issue of *Vanity Fair,* two years before the fragmented voices of Eliot's "Prufrock" were published. "Any Porch" contains eighteen fragments of conversation by disembodied voices in a rhymed, nine-stanza ballad. The form of the poem gives us a sense of enclosure, yet it begins and ends nowhere. "Any Porch" continually picks up snippets of conversation, only to drop them and move on to another one, leaving us with a fragmented sense of experience. In terms of content, the poem seems to satirize the clichéd thinking and language of women of leisure (though the gender of all speakers is not absolute) without relying on rhetorical content; the language speaks for itself. But the poem's modernist aspects may be overlooked by readers schooled in New Critical values because of its traditional form and its apparent content: the frivolous conversation of women as suggested by the first stanza:

> "I'm reading that new thing of Locke's —
> So whimsical, isn't he? Yes —
> "My dear, have you seen those new smocks?
> They're nightgowns—no more, no less."[5]

Yet another reading of this poem is possible. The speakers in "Any Porch" tell a story they are literally not telling to each other, a story of American preoccupation with fashion, gossip, and other trivial pursuits against a backdrop of weightier issues—philosophy, morality, sexuality, feminist politics, and war in Europe. The poem offers an implied judgment against such preoccupations.

The irony in "Any Porch" resides not merely in the content, but in the interface between an older, familiar form and contemporary content. In contrast, the familiar form of "Paths" contains familiar content; the speaker appears lost in a familiarly rendered sentimental reflection. In yet another variation, the speakers in "'Sorry, the Line Is Busy'" tell us their story by *not* telling their story to the receivers of their calls, that is, they tell the story of not-telling as does the speaker in "A Piece about Christmas." Such a radical confluence of techniques by one writer deserves our attention. Where and how do we locate Parker on a map of literary modernism? "Paths" would presumably keep her off the map, whereas "'Sorry, the Line Is Busy,'" "A Piece about Christmas," and "Any Porch," if read outside of their publishing venues, might not. The latter three pieces, however, have been considered practice runs for Parker's later, greater work in fiction. Yet these four pieces, considered together, illustrate the collision of sentimental reserve and modernist verve found in Parker's work overall, and represents the real Parker Persona.

Referring to her personality and its effect on her work, Alexander Woollcott, in his famous portrait of Parker, referred to her as a combination of "Little Nell and Lady Macbeth."[6] Two points need to be made about this often quoted summation of Parker. First, the dual nature Parker seems to possess is not unique to her, but rather symptomatic of the times in which she lived. Babe Ruth comes to mind as another popular figure from the twenties who could alternate between congeniality and nastiness. A similar pattern occurs in literary figures and works as well. Masking and the use of personae, holdovers from decadent posturing, were popular techniques among poets as diverse as Pound, Eliot, Wylie, and Louise Bogan. Nella Larsen wrote of passing for white in her novels *Passing* and *Quicksand*. Langston Hughes wrote in standard English and in Black dialect, and a number of Harlem Renaissance writers wrote from both African and American identities. Colette, H. D., Djuna Barnes, and Virginia Woolf lived bisexual lives; Gertrude Stein and others wrote in a lesbian code. In *Terrible Honesty*, Ann Douglas points to the "manic depressive pattern in modern American culture" and characterizes New

York in the 1920s as "Mongrel Manhattan." This was a generation, Douglas observes, profoundly influenced by the theories of Sigmund Freud, convinced of at least two selves at work.[7] This leads to a second observation regarding Woollcott's remark: Like all dualities, "Little Nell and Lady Macbeth" no doubt contains some truth, but remains a bit simplistic. There is more at work in Parker's life and work than two moods or personalities. Rather, a complex array of competing interests and tensions falling under the categories of sentimentalism and modernism characterize Parker's career. As the epigraph titled "Autobiography" to this introduction illustrates, Parker sensed the complexity of her own life and times. She used the metaphor of fashion to describe a self composed of old and new values. The fashion or clothing metaphor is significant, for it reflects not only the mass production of clothing seen for the first time in the twenties, but the anxiety of shifting identities, of masking, posing, and personae. We can usefully see her as a writer responding to several traditions, caught in the collision of nineteenth-century sentimentalism and twentieth-century modernism.

This is not the first study to look at the conjunction of sentimentalism and modernism, nor the first book-length study of Parker, but it is the first to combine these two realms. As such, it draws on the work of feminist scholars who have redefined our concepts of nineteenth-century sentimentalism and twentieth-century modernism, and offers close readings of Parker's poetry and fiction in light of this scholarship. Modernism is an important designation for Parker's work because she wrote and published within the years—1890–1930 by one conservative dating—in which modernist works were conceived.[8] Sentimentalism becomes an important issue for Parker studies not only because a sentimental tradition borders modernism, but because Parker's work and life have been repeatedly criticized for being sentimental. At issue in this study is not whether Parker had moments of sentimentality in her life and work; she did, as do we all from time to time. The necessary question is, "How has critical attention to these moments distorted the value of her work overall?" Therefore, I examine this criticism, which I term the sentimental infection, for its flawed assumptions and its effect on Parker's literary reputation, and then offer alternative readings of her poetry and fiction. While this study presupposes that Parker's work is too often read within a narrow frame of autobiography, I nevertheless examine pertinent aspects of her life—those considered sentimental by friends and biographers—even as I expand the context in which her work should be understood. Her work tells us more than that she drank and was at times unhappy and vitriolic. In effect, I propose to complicate rather than simplify our reading of Parker's work in order to counter the simplistic assumptions that autobiographical readings can produce.

Feminist critics have been divided as to the nature and value of sentimental works by women writers in the nineteenth century, but one point has become clear: A literary tradition, consisting of both male and female writers, and responding in form and content to social, cultural, and political events in nineteenth-century America, has emerged.[9] Characterized by linear narrative or conventional poetic forms, didacticism, moral piety, stereotypes, domestic scenes, and emotional tripwires, this tradition, though highly popular in its day, was denigrated by the school of New Criticism arising out of modernism. Jane Tompkins offers the best defense for the sentimental tradition in *Sensational Designs* in which she evaluates novels from this period in light of the "cultural 'work' they were designed to do."[10] Thus, in a novel seeking to communicate social injustice to a broad community, such as Harriet Beecher Stowe's *Uncle Tom's Cabin*, stereotypes become an asset rather than a weakness. As we will see, a number of Parker's poems and stories applied the techniques of sentimental literature and had "cultural 'work'" to perform, as well as a receptive audience for that performance.

Significantly, Parker is not alone in her use of those techniques. Cheryl Walker and Suzanne Clark have traced aspects of nineteenth-century sentimentalism in the works of modernist writers such as Amy Lowell, Sara Teasdale, Elinor Wylie, Louise Bogan, Edna St. Vincent Millay, H. D., Emma Goldman, and Kay Boyle.[11] It would be wrong, however, to interpret this tendency as strictly a female phenomenon. In the most general sense, we can see that William Butler Yeats's manor houses, T. S. Eliot's metaphysical poets, and Ezra Pound's classicism are underlain by a sentimental longing for an idealized past. Specific studies point to the same tendency. E. E. Cummings, as Norman Friedman argues, provides the most extreme example of a modernist operating within two traditions. The form of his verse—language explosions ranging from sentences and syntax to individual words and punctuation—is highly experimental, but his content—praising spring, childhood, love, and satirizing visions of wastelands—has ties to the sentimental privileging of feeling. Carol T. Christ and Howard W. Fulweiler also have examined the relationship between nineteenth-century sentimentalism and the formal qualities of D. H. Lawrence, Eliot, Pound, and Yeats.[12] Yet whatever tint of sentimentalism occurred in the works of male modernists, it was not enough to exclude them from the canon.

If our appreciation of sentimental literature has been broadened, our concept of modernism and of the modernist canon has been reconstituted by feminist recovery projects. Until recently, modernism defined as the narrow set of aesthetic principles discussed above excluded the women writers who helped develop or abided by these principles. Yet even within this expanded version of modernism, Parker remains in a marginal position. The gender bias in canon formation is only one aspect of modernism's exclusionary politics; the privileging of experimental form is another. Writers using traditional forms, accessible language, and realism have not been considered modernist even though their works may deal with modernist themes of alienation and disenchantment with history and contemporary culture. At best, such works, often produced by women and minority writers, were tagged with such insulting labels as "low" or "minor" modernist works.

Closely related to accessibility and realism is the issue of popularity. Modernism based on the obscurities of experimental form could not possibly include works that had a mass audience, and yet a mass audience with its demands for entertainment and cultural products had been expanding, according to Andreas Huyssen, since the nineteenth century. Social and cultural changes in the twentieth century— urbanization and economic growth; the invention of the telephone, electricity, film, radio, record players; and an increase in mass circulation magazines and newspapers with their attendant advertising— intensified the growth of a consuming middle class. The "masculinist mystique of much of modernism," Huyssen argues, results from a fear of being consumed by a mass culture that, like sentimentalism, was gendered feminine and critically degraded.[13] Thus the gendered split between popular and serious art became one between sentimentalism and modernism, and would ultimately distort our understanding of early twentieth-century literature. Evidently, Parker was aware of the high-low split, though she may not have connected it with gender in all cases. In a negative review of the Russian vaudevillian show, *The Chauve Souris*, Parker writes, "if I say what I think about it I must forever roam the earth bearing the brand of the lowbrow."[14] The self-deprecating or "lowbrow" critic is a persona Parker repeatedly used in her theater and book reviews throughout her career.

Clearly, issues of inclusion and exclusion arise when we conceptualize modernism as a collection of aesthetic principles rather than as a literary period, that is, a period of production that has links both to the past and to the evolving culture in which literary production takes place. I make this claim with Cary Nelson's warning in mind, that the ideological biases behind literary histories give us limited views of the past, and that any given historical narrative is too narrow to encompass the whole of modern poetry, let alone a literature as large as modernism.[15] His observations are well founded, and yet when aesthetic principles constitute the "narrative" of modernism, we see similar distortions and limitations. In *The Concept of Modernism*, Astradur Eysteinsson reveals how scholars of modernism have created metonymical versions of modernism by identifying it with only one of its elements. When these concepts of modernism are considered collectively, we see modernism as a movement that reflects modernity and critiques it; is outside of history and shocks us into it; subverts order and rationality and imposes aesthetic order on chaos; promotes gender separation and deconstructs gender boundaries; and involves impersonality and extreme subjectivity. Unfortunately, Eysteinsson reveals his aesthetic bias when he argues that these concepts are linked by modernism's break from tradition, but his point remains clear: Modernism is more than its singular or composite aesthetics, and more, as others have shown, than a simple break from the past.[16]

In this study of Parker's work, literary decadence, a British import spawned by Oscar Wilde's American lecture tour in 1882 and 1883, provides a contact zone for nineteenth-century sentimentalism and twentieth-century modernism. The decadents and aesthetes of the 1880s and 1890s were developing a number of conventions, some of them paralleling those found in the poetry of American women, that also would continue into early twentieth-century literature. Emphasis on form, the primacy of art, an occupation with death, a world-weary attitude, and the language of flowers and gems permeated this work. And, as Thomas Reed Whissen points out, decadents and aesthetes rejected the positivist view of literature that had been dominant in the nineteenth century.[17] Several of Parker's female contemporaries—Katherine Mansfield, H. D., Djuna Barnes, Elinor Wylie, and Edna St. Vincent Millay—made use of decadent techniques.[18] In the complex matrix of Parker's poetry and fiction we see her use decadent techniques in a rejection of domestic values associated with nineteenth-century sentimentalism; she also mocks and rejects these techniques and the attitudes behind them.

A close examination of Parker's poetry and fiction supports what Cheryl Walker, Suzanne Clark, Andreas Huyssen, and others have observed: Just as modernism did not begin with the twentieth century but had its roots in the mid- to late-nineteenth century, sentimentalism did not end with the close of the nineteenth; it extended through the decadence and aestheticism of the 1890s and into the twentieth century. As seen in the examples that opened this introduction, Parker's work ranges from the purely sentimental to the highly modernist, though most of her work contains elements of both. Collectively her work represents a gendered collision of literary values. I characterize the collision as gendered because, in terms of literary debate and canon formation, values associated with sentimental and popular literature have been considered feminine, while values associated with modernist literature have been considered masculine. I characterize the event as a collision because parts of both sets of values remain behind; there is no complete blasting away of nineteenth-century values in accordance with the vision of Wyndham Lewis and Ezra Pound. The emergence of Parker as an innovative and highly popular author and the exclusion of her work from the mainstream modernist canon are functions of this gendered collision.[19]

Other critical frames, in addition to those cited above, make such a reading possible. Elaine Showalter's concept of a woman writer's "double-voiced discourse," where a woman simultaneously uses the dominant discourse of male literary tradition and the muted discourse of one outside of the mainstream, seems to apply to Parker, although, given the popularity of sentimental discourse, we have to wonder how truly "muted" it is. The concept of a modernist literary battle between the sexes, as described by Sandra Gilbert and Susan Gubar in *No Man's Land*, certainly supports the idea of a collision of values, as well as describes a theme Parker often employs.[20] It may be useful, however, to think of the collision as fruitful in terms of the literature produced rather than as a script for winners and losers. Finally, Parker has always been appreciated as a humorist, though that designation has not served her well in terms of the traditional modernist canon. Studies by Suzanne Bunkers and Emily Toth recast her humor as a feminist project, and Nancy Walker links that feminist humor to an ongoing American women's tradition.[21] These studies are valuable, yet the category of humor remains a limitation if it is the only one applied to Parker.

If we are to accurately identify Parker's location on the literary landscape, we must move beyond conventional readings of Parker as primarily a humorist, as a "minor" modernist, or as a wasted talent dominated by men. To do this, we must read her lesser-known works and reconsider her more frequently anthologized pieces. And we must recognize that the appropriate context in which to read Parker's work is much broader than the Algonquin Round Table, broader even than the whole of modernism regardless of how the period is dated. Parker's modernism, like that of many of her contemporaries, is deeply indebted to nineteenth-century sentimentalism. Taken as a whole, her poetry and fiction performs more than one type of "cultural 'work'" and reverberates with conflict and contradiction. At times it carries forward the formal elements of nineteenth-century tradition, at other times it struggles to break free from them; at times her work incorporates the given mythologies, at other times it rewrites them; at times her work cries or laughs at society in order to critique it, at other times it seems designed to make a buck. Her work is often informed by a feminist sensibility, but feminism ultimately could not save her from the psychic torment created by modern male–female relationships, which exploited sexual love outside of marriage and created large-scale physical and emotional consequences for which few were prepared. These conflicts can only result from a collision of values.

This study will consider Parker's creative, critical, and political engagements—activities that spanned almost six decades—in its examination of her work, as well as the cultural and historical elements that inform it. Chapter 1 examines the context in which Parker began her career and first achieved success, a period of time in the late teens and twenties in which both sentimental and modernist values were evident in the magazines in which she published. But as Parker's career progresses, critical response to the sentimental turns sour; chapter 2 investigates this process, which I call the "sentimental infection" for its negative effect on Parker's literary reputation. Two issues intersect within the discussion of Parker's sentimental infection: the use of stereotypes and Parker's relationship to Black culture. These issues are also discussed, requiring an examination of her relevant critical and creative pieces within the frame of her political life. In order to examine the negative charge of sentimentality, and to offer alternative readings of her work, chapters 3 and 4 look at Parker's sentimental connection, the ties to her literary predecessors in the nineteenth century as seen in her poetry and her fiction. These connections are not always pure, for at times Parker's poems and stories work simultaneously with and against the sentimental tradition. Finally, chapter 5 examines how the strangest of literary bedfellows, decadence and feminism, facilitate Parker's move away from the sentimental tradition and against literary and social conventions, such as excessive rhetoric and domesticity. Both poetry and fiction are discussed in this chapter. Also included are Parker's re-visions of traditional myths and legends in which women have been silenced. Parker gave voice to a number of social concerns and silenced female characters. This study will present alternative readings in which that voice can be heard.

1

Sex and Context:
The Production and Popularity of
Dorothy Parker's Work

Three book-length biographies and a number of biographical sketches and articles have been written about Dorothy Parker, all of which adequately document the succession of phases that constitute the Parker Persona: the orphan who wrote for a living; the hard-drinking poet and wit of the Algonquin Round Table; the communist Hollywood screenwriter; the lonely, nonproductive divorcée found dead in a New York hotel. These "stories," although often told with a sense of nostalgic appreciation or sympathy, nevertheless conclude that Parker was the gifted writer who drank and politicked herself away from literary greatness.[1] This conclusion presumes two points: that literary greatness is a singular concept based on indisputable standards, and that literary greatness was Parker's goal. Given what we know about the politics of literary reputations and literary history, this conclusion seems less than satisfactory. Using Nathaniel Hawthorne as an example, Jane Tompkins convincingly argues in *Sensational Designs* that literary reputations are contextual, based largely on a writer's circle of friends and contacts with the "machinery of publishing and reviewing." And as we saw in the example of Parker's "'Sorry, the Line Is Busy,'" our interpretation of a text is "mediated" by the circumstances in which we read it; a story read in a mass market magazine may fall prey to the assumption that it is entertainment rather than "serious" literature. Finally, as Cary Nelson tells us in *Repression and Recovery*, writers often have motivations other than competing for a place in the canon. These motivations, when political, can lead to a writer's exclusion from serious critical consideration. Conventional literary history, argues Nelson, has "told a selective

33

story substantially constituted by its cultural presuppositions and restricted by its ideological filters."[2] Both of these observations apply to Parker because she has yet to be read in the appropriate context, and her literary production is a function of that context.

A brief example illustrates this point. Biographers, in fact Parker herself, point to the fact that Parker wrote to earn a living. "After my father died," Parker told Marion Capron in a *Paris Review* interview, "there wasn't any money. I had to work."[3] In terms of context, this fact is significant, yet how this contextual information and Parker's work get interpreted is problematic. In *Wit's End: Days and Nights of the Algonquin Round Table,* James R. Gaines uses Parker as evidence for his claim that

> [h]owever diverse the Algonquinites were in personality, they were unanimous in writing mainly for money. None of them took up the solitary life of the exiles, subsisting on small remittances from home. They came to writing as a business from the beginning, and so it remained for all but a few of them.[4]

Gaines, who argues overall that Algonquin writers failed to live up to their potential, simply regurgitates the romantic and well-known assumption that impoverished exiles, rather than writers with commercial success, produce important literary works. Marion Meade also emphasizes economics as a factor in the quality of Parker's poetry: "Much of what she wrote was mediocre. Nearly everything she wrote found a buyer, in itself a comment on the quality of her work."[5] Meade thus assumes that if a literary work is purchased, it has no value as serious literature. The bias in these comments of Gaines and Meade illustrates that they have read Parker's work by its publication venue or context alone. Certainly such a reading is too narrowly contextual.

If we read Parker like Gaines and Meade do, we miss much that is significant about her work. The fact that Parker wrote and published several poems about money in the 1920s—a decade known for its economic boom—suggests the extent to which money was an issue for Parker, her editors, and her readers. The financial anxiety imbedded in these poems, often masked with humor, reveals that the boom has limited coverage, and that women remain reliant on men to gain economic security. In "Rhyme of an Involuntary Violet," the speaker is jealous of women who parlay sexual favors—"their 'Yes's'"—into expensive gifts from men that they then "advertis[e]," suggesting the concept, to be discussed in more detail in chapter 4, of conspicuous consumption. The speaker's implied wish in "One Perfect Rose" is to get "One perfect limousine" instead of the flower. Other poems link economic issues to literary pursuits. The speaker would take money over the fame of poets in "Ballade of Understandable Ambitions"; wouldn't write verse if she could seduce a rich man in "The Temptress"; and acknowledges that her poetry must conform to public and sentimental tastes if she is to "fetch the bacon home" in "The Far-Sighted Muse." These poems about money, written for money, humorously exhibit the money-grubbing ethos of the twenties, but they make other observations as well. The poems to some extent reveal Parker's initial lack of wealth (her big money will come from Hollywood in the 1930s and 1940s), and at the same time reify the romanticized image of the impoverished artist, the "poet in the garret." They draw attention to the gap between art and the commercial success needed by an author simply to exist. They also offer an implied critique of capitalism that echoes one made by Emma Goldman: it makes prostitutes out of women.[6] Parker will later extend this analysis using a more serious tone in her fiction.

Reading Parker in popular magazines, or reading her with the knowledge that she published in *Vanity Fair*, *Life*, and the *New Yorker* rather than in *Broom*, *Blast*, or the *Little Review*, not only reinforces the belief that she wrote only for money, but places her contextually outside the realm of "serious" literature as we have come to define it through canonical works. One of the issues this kind of reading overlooks is the careful attention Parker paid to poetic form, itself an indicator that she took her art seriously. Forms of seriousness is another issue. As Nelson makes clear in *Repression and Recovery* with his examples of protest poetry and songs, there are other kinds of seriousness toward which writers aspire, yet the explicit political nature of these works—their seriousness—keeps them from being considered serious candidates for inclusion in the canon. The implied political nature of Parker's poems is missed altogether by critics who place too much emphasis on the fact that she "wrote for money" and published in popular magazines.

It also is important to examine how biographies of Parker, and how biographical readings of Parker's work, have influenced her literary reputation. Most biographical works, with the exception of Gaines's *Wit's End*, tend to emphasize a "modern," twentieth-century context without drawing adequate connections to nineteenth-century values and influences present in early twentieth-century literary culture. Presumably, this blind spot occurs because these scholars

worked within the conventional literary history that reads modernism as a break from nineteenth-century literary values, rather than as
a merging of, collision with, or even a continuation of those values.
Their failure to recognize this continuity as a condition of early twentieth-century literature obscures an important dimension of Parker's
work, and invites us to accept her reputation as it was constructed
under the influence of modernist criticism, rather than consider it in
its full context.

The sweetly acidic nature of Parker's personality baffled those who
tried to assess the value of her work. Wyatt Cooper, who conducted a
series of interviews with Parker during the latter part of her life, has
suggested that we may never fully understand Parker because of her
paradoxical nature.[7] This perceived paradox of Parker's life certainly
echoes the conflicts present in her work: poems that mourn for lost
love and callously reject it, stories with sympathetic and cruelly satiric
character portrayals, essays that often use the language of qualification
to express strongly negative opinions about books or plays. We can
begin to understand the complex nature of Parker's work by recog-
nizing the complicated nature of early twentieth-century literature
overall. While modernist criticism would ultimately remove the sentimental from the canon of twentieth-century works, it could not remove it from the scene of literary production. Thus, Parker wrote
from within the wreckage of colliding literary values, a collision of
nineteenth-century sentimentalism and twentieth-century modernism. Not only her life, but her literary work reflects this collision.

Given the hard-boiled cynicism for which Parker is justifiably famous, it might seem strange to link her work with anything resem-
bling nineteenth-century sentimentalism. Yet she lived in a time when
a nineteenth-century sensibility remained prevalent. As a theater critic
in the teens and twenties, she reviewed several plays set in the nineteenth century: *The Tavern* by George M. Cohan, *Not So Long Ago* by
Arthur Richman, *Little Old New York* by Rida Johnson Young, *The Fair
Circassian* by Gladys Unger, and *Abraham Lincoln* by John Drinkwater,
among others. If we can assume she read the authors alluded to in
her writing, the list is wide-ranging, though most are from the nineteenth century: Scott, Wordsworth, Coleridge, Shelley, Keats, Byron,
Landor, Lamb, Tennyson, Carlyle, Dickens, Thackeray, Procter, Reade,
Rossetti, Kipling, Gissing, Henley, Wilde, Poe, Stowe, and Freeman.[8]
Parker's nineteenth-century reading, based on this list alone, includes
British and American writers, the canonized and the lesser known,
and ranges from Romantic, to sentimental, to the decadent. It would

certainly be difficult to escape these influences altogether. Parker criticized plays and books for sentimentality, but she also rejected and mocked modernist verse in "Oh, Look—I Can Do It, Too," and in "Verses in the Night."[9] As this study will show, a number of other works by Parker display this tension between the sentimental and the modern. It exists in her work because it surrounded her working life.

While Parker's work maintained a large readership and received its share of positive reviews, she was ultimately condemned for being sentimental in both her life and her work. Both sentimentalist and modernist traits occur in Parker's poetry and fiction, but to understand them as traits with historical relevance or necessity rather than as flaws or strengths, we must examine the context in which her work was produced and received. This chapter focuses first on three areas of that context that produced a distinctive influence on Parker and/ or revealed a collision of nineteenth-century and modern values: Parker's years with *Vanity Fair* magazine as an aspect of her relationship to mass culture; Parker's relationship to the *Smart Set* magazine as an aspect of her relationship to avant-garde or "serious" art; and her friendships with other Algonquin Round Table members— Robert Benchley, Franklin Pierce Adams, Heywood Hale Broun, George S. Kaufman, Ruth Hale, Jane Grant, and Alexander Woollcott—which constituted the milieu in which Parker's literary values were formed. I then provide an overview of the positive reviews of Parker's work to show how she parlayed her values into a successful literary career.

ART VERSUS BACON

Ezra Pound and other modernist critics developed and retained a discourse about literature that would ultimately negotiate assignments of literary value—what Andreas Huyssen calls "the great divide," the discourse that insists on a separation between "serious" art and mass culture.[10] Literary historians of the modernist period also have relied on this discourse. In "An Introductory Reminiscence" to Carl Dolmetsch's *The Smart Set: A History and Anthology*, S. N. Behrman says of the late teens and early 1920s, "In those days, ambitious literati could be divided, roughly, into two classes: those with a greater grip on reality, who wanted to write for the *Saturday Evening Post* or *Cosmopolitan* and those more vaporous, who wanted to write for the *Smart Set*."[11] While this account highlights separation, the "serious" and "commercial" exist side by side in the works of many early twentieth-century publications and authors. Dorothy Parker published in both kinds of publications, but the machinery of publishing and reviewing for which she is best known is largely that of the mainstream press. Left penniless after her father died in 1913, Parker sold a poem to *Vanity Fair* managing editor Frank Crowninshield in 1914, a transaction that vaulted her into mass circulation magazine publishing, first with *Vogue,* then *Vanity Fair, Life,* the *Saturday Evening Post,* and the *New Yorker,* among other magazines and newspapers.

Mass circulation magazines traditionally have been accused of lowering literary standards. David Perkins suggests they "contributed to the decline of the quality of verse"; Frederick Hoffman attributes the rise of the little magazine to the narrow view of popular-magazine editors. In *Wit's End,* James R. Gaines argues that the commercial magazines limited a writer's literary innovation; payment-per-word resulted in padded style, serious topics were avoided, and editors catered to advertisers and formula.[12] While none of these assertions is completely false, as generalizations about the magazine trade applied to literary production they are somewhat misleading. With respect to padding, we need to keep in mind that more people read in the early part of the century, and there were more newspapers and magazines to read. Between 1885 and 1905 there were 11,000 periodicals in the United States, some of which discontinued or merged with others as the decade progressed; in New York City alone in 1920 there were fourteen daily newspapers in circulation.[13] What reads like padding to late-twentieth-century readers schooled in imagist brevity would not have been perceived as such by Parker's audience. Furthermore, much of Parker's poetry and fiction, especially the pieces for *Life,* are anything but padded; their brevity gives them a modernist effect.

It is important to note as well that modernist brevity was not purely a "high culture" phenomenon. It existed in popular light verse, in song lyrics by, for example, Ira Gershwin, and in all forms of magazine writing.[14] It was a by-product of popular culture developments in advertising and the slang of the flapper generation. Modernist brevity reflected the quickening pace of life brought on by technological developments in communication, entertainment, and transportation. Writers and publications on both sides of "the great divide" used modernist brevity and helped perpetuate it as a legitimate literary technique.

The accusation that popular magazines emphasize light or humorous subjects and are thus outside the serious literary mode associated with modernist writing also requires examination. *Life* was at that time a magazine of humor along the lines of *Punch*, *Puck*, and *Judge*, but other magazines also reflected the post–World War I atmosphere of frivolity. Frank Crowninshield's editorial statement in the first issue of *Vanity Fair* expresses this preference for the light touch:

> We as a nation have come to realize the need for more cheerfulness, for hiding a solemn face, for a fair measure of pluck, and for great good humor. *Vanity Fair* means to be as cheerful as anybody. It will print humor, it will look at the stage, at the arts, at the world of letters, at sport, and at the highly vitalized, electric, and diversified life of our day from the frankly cheerful angle of the optimist, or, which is much the same thing, from the mock-cheerful angle of the satirist.[15]

Vanity Fair's light humor, however, did not keep it from presenting more serious arts and topics. Its satire required a sophisticated readership not too far removed from the type of highbrow audience sought by Pound, Eliot, and the little magazines. *Vanity Fair* cartoons by Fish, with captions often supplied by Parker, satirized men, women, and all aspects of artistic and social life. If the magazine devoted a number of pages in each issue to fashion, travel, and home life, issues pulled at random reveal the rest of the magazine's character. In December 1916 the magazine satirized the female "Vorticiste" and "Vers Librist" with "Any girl can be a Gertrude Stein. . . . Close your eyes and open your dictionary, write down a word—any word. Repeat the process until your page is full and then leave the rest to your loving readers." In March 1919 it published a series of legitimate poems by Stein. In July 1923, amid full-page advertisements for Fisk tires, Dodge Brothers touring cars, Gorham Trophies in sterling silver, Whitman's Chocolates, Campbell Soup, and Dobbs Hats, as well as quarter- and half-page advertisements for knickers, pipes, and luggage, the following works appear: installments of Edgar Lee Masters' the *Spoon River Anthology*; an essay on contemporary English prose by T. S. Eliot; "Miss Furr and Miss Skeene" by Gertrude Stein; *Water-Ice,* a short play by Djuna Barnes; poems by Louise Bogan and Leonie Adams; and a theater review by Alexander Woollcott. A November 1916 issue includes articles on the Vorticists and Constantine Brancusi's sculpture, as well as an essay on Oscar Wilde by Arthur Symons.[16]

Yet if *Vanity Fair* desired sophisticated readers, it at the same time did not separate the arts into serious and popular modes, nor reject voices originating in the nineteenth century the way modernist critics would. In fact, in October 1916 the magazine honored a group later castigated by John Crowe Ransom—those "Distinguished American

Women Poets Who Have Made the Lyric Verse Written by Women in America More Interesting Than That of the Men"—a group that included Elinor Wylie, Genevieve Taggard, Edna Millay, Sara Teasdale, Lizette Woodworth Reese, Aline Kilmer, Louise Bogan, and Amy Lowell. Crowninshield's *Vanity Fair* was a mixed bag of entertainment and art, light humor and satiric critique, creating an aura of avant-garde gentility. "It was said of Crowninshield," writes James Gaines, "that he would let his writers say anything as long as they said it in evening clothes."[17]

Starting her career as she did in such an atmosphere, Parker's *Vanity Fair* work not surprisingly reflects a mixture of conservative and radical styles. We have already seen how Parker's "Any Porch" offers a pastiche of fragmented, disembodied voices written in ballad form. Her popular "Hate Songs," published in *Vanity Fair* in 1916–1919, and in *Life* in 1920–1923, were written in free verse, and were the antithesis of genteel, feminine poetry in their repeated satiric declarations of hatred for everything from bohemians to relatives. Despite this modernist leaning, Parker would rely on conventional rhyme and meter for her poetry and, as noted earlier, even went so far as to mock "modernist verse" in a series of four poems under the title "Oh, Look—I Can Do It, Too" in a December 1915 issue of *Vanity Fair*. Her distaste for modernist verse forms may reflect her editors' preferences as much as her own.

In her early *Vanity Fair* essays (1916–1919), Parker typically launches a modern critique by mocking conspicuously genteel behavior ("Are You a Glossy?" and "How to Know the Glossies"), self-righteous do-gooders ("Good Souls"), and simplistic movie scripts that trade on these conventional pieties ("Is Your Little Girl Safe?"). But in "The Christmas Magazines" she castigates the Christmas sentimentality prevalent in magazines, only to close with the admission that she buys them every year and will continue to do so.[18] In Parker's theater reviews we find a critic who is clearly looking for quality productions, only to be saddled with clichés, patriotic melodrama, and misplaced sentiment. Her negative criticism is often sarcastic and direct, as in her 1918 review of *Toot-Toot!*: "There are frequent stretches in the evening's entertainment when one is glad to have something to read." At other times, her reviews are characterized by self-consciousness and self-qualification. She opens her July 1918 "Mortality in the Drama" with an anecdote of her difficulties as a critic. Other reviews contain phrases such as "I do hate to be boastful," "I do hate to be a gloom," "I may be unwomanly," "I may be hypercritical," and "So I must again conclude that I am all wrong."[19] Parker's self-qualification continues in her later career as a book critic for the *New Yorker* and *Esquire*, and functions on three levels: the voice of the world-weary, perpetually disappointed critic; women's rhetorical timidity as analyzed by Robin Lakoff in *Language and Woman's Place;* and the parodic voice of feminine timidity.[20] Even if used as a comic device, Parker's qualification suggests that she was responding to an expectation of feminine decorum, a remnant of nineteenth-century assumptions about appropriate female behavior.

Parker's Victorian sensibilities did not stop with verbal qualification. Born in 1893, Parker was too young to be an original New Woman, too old to be a flapper. Despite poems and stories with a modern focus on drinking and nonmarital relationships, Parker lampooned the younger generation glorified by F. Scott Fitzgerald's *This Side of Paradise* (1920) in pieces like "Hymn of Hate: The Younger Set," "Professional Youth," and "Ballade of a Not Insupportable Loss," a stanza of which reads:

> Think not, reader, that I'd complain.
> Squander on me no sympathy.
> Though they've vanished, I feel no pain,—
> I get on—rather swimmingly.
> I'd not cavil at Fate's decree;
> Rather, give it a rousing cheer,
> Still, there's something I cannot see—
> Where did the flappers disappear?[21]

Similar attitudes were shared by Parker's friends. James R. Gaines convincingly argues in *Wit's End* that many of the Algonquin Round Table members were plagued by "remnants of Victorianism." Theirs was a generation that could remember life before World War I and continued to maintain some of its values. George S. Kaufman, Franklin Pierce Adams, Alexander Woollcott, and for a time, Robert Benchley "held almost to a Temperance Union attitude toward drinking." Frank Case, owner of the Algonquin Hotel where the group met daily for lunch, would not allow women to smoke in his lobby; no one joined Ruth Hale in her subsequent boycott. The plight of women held little interest for the Round Table men, and when Jane Grant and Ruth Hale formed the Lucy Stone League—an organization encouraging women to keep their maiden names—they received little support from the men. Parker refused to join the league, claiming, "I married to change my name." If what passed for a feminist movement in those

days, as Ann Douglas argues, was associated with Victorian notions of
sexual propriety, white racial superiority, and temperance, it would
have had little or at most a mixed appeal for Parker. And all of the
Algonquin men, argues Gaines, "suffered from the sexual repressions
commonly ascribed to the Victorian era," seeing their wives as "good
women" to keep at home while they visited prostitutes.[22] During the
1920s, Parker was writing the bulk of her poetry and fiction while
daily immersing herself in this collision of values.

Parker's verbal qualification did not prevent her from experiencing a gendered collision of her own; she was fired as *Vanity Fair*'s theater critic for comparing actress Billie Burke, wife of the influential
Florenz Ziegfeld, with burlesque performer Eva Tanguay. By the time
this comment appeared in a January 1920 review of Somerset
Maugham's *Caesar's Wife*, Parker had been reviewing plays for *Vanity
Fair* for two years, and had been with Condé Nast publications for six
years. The play closed, as did two other plays—one produced by
Charles Dillingham, the other by David Belasco—that Parker had
panned.[23] Evidently her influence as a critic was substantial and threat-
ening to the male-dominated world of theater production and magazine advertising. After leaving *Vanity Fair*, she found work with *Life*
and *Ainslee's* where she felt free to lampoon Ziegfeld and his Follies,
yet she remained aware of her vulnerability as an author writing for
money, of the need to write what would please editors and readers.
She describes that vulnerability in "The Far-Sighted Muse," an important poem in terms of how a female poet perceived her work and
her audience, published in a 9 March 1922 issue of *Life*. The last
stanza continues the theme of the first two:

> Everything's great, in this good old world;
>   (This is the stuff they can always use.)
> God's in His heaven, and the hill's dew-pearled;
>   (This will provide for the baby's shoes.)
> Hunger and War, do not mean a thing;—
>   Everything's rosy, where'er we roam;
> Hark, how the little birds gaily sing!
>   (This is what fetches the bacon home.)[24]

"The Far-Sighted Muse" says much about Parker's position amid
conflicting literary values. On the one hand, it acknowledges the pressure to conform to the tastes of magazine editors, who had a history
of encouraging women poets in the nineteenth century to write about

genteel, domestic subjects.[25] Writing for a living meant circumscrib-
ing the amount of literary risk Parker could afford to take. On the
other hand, her clichéd images of dew-pearled hills and little singing
birds satirize the genteel mode. Very little of Parker's poetry follows
the Pollyanna formula she describes, suggesting we can read "The
Far-Sighted Muse" as a protest against an old tradition that to some
extent remains current.

Whereas many of her poems, particularly those published in *Life*,
are humorous, others deal with the dark side of life and love. One
reason these dark poems fetched the bacon home was that the forms
of her verse—ballads, sonnets, rhymed couplets, and the popular
French forms (ballade, triolet, rondeau)—were the ones in demand
by commercial magazines. Parker's first literary mentor, Franklin
Pierce Adams, had helped make these forms popular in his Conning
Tower column, and had encouraged Parker to use them. "Franklin P.
Adams once gave me a book of French forms and told me to copy
their design, that by copying them I would get precision in prose,"
she told Marion Capron.[26] Thus, Parker may have used these forms
not because of their economic potential, but because they might serve
as a kind of apprenticeship to what she hoped would be more accomplished work. Parker's comment also suggests she didn't take her
poetry writing seriously, further playing into the hands of later de-
tractors who would dismiss her as a light verse poet. In any case, we
see here a confluence of causes—the need for money, Adams's
influence, the pressure of editors and tradition, and the desire for
accomplished work—affecting Parker's literary production.

Parker published two stories in the *Smart Set,* a magazine which by
1911 was seeking an avant-garde audience. Like *Vanity Fair*, its editorial orientation and contents reveal a mixture of nineteenth- and twentieth-century tastes. In a February 1913 editorial, editor Willard
Huntington Wright rejects the effeminacy and piety associated with
nineteenth-century literature:

> I believe that this is a day of enlightenment on the part of magazine
> readers. Men and women have grown tired of effeminacy and the falsi-
> ties of current fiction, essays and poetry. A widespread critical awaken-
> ing has come, and with it a demand for better literary material. The
> demand for pious uplift, for stultification, and for the fictional avoid-
> ance of the facts of life has diminished. The reader of today demands
> truth.[27]

"Truth" for Wright meant unhappy or disillusioned endings to fiction and poetry. H. L. Mencken and George Jean Nathan, who as co-editors replaced Wright in 1914, attempted to maintain his policy. Like Wright, Mencken and Nathan embraced an aesthetic point of view along the lines of A. C. Swinburne, Walter Pater, and Oscar Wilde. They continued their previously created Owen Hatteras, a collaborative literary persona who, in a *Smart Set* column, "jeered at marriage, romantic love, sentimentalism in all forms. He scoffed at reformism, conventional piety, and all types of supernaturalism."[28] It comes as no surprise, then, that the stories Parker published in the *Smart Set*, "Such a Pretty Little Picture" (1922) and "Too Bad" (1923), are both about failed marriages and are humorous in only a sardonic way.

Mencken and Nathan may have been sporadic visitors to the Round Table luncheons, but they were not regular members. They nevertheless shared certain values with some of the Round Table members. Like Parker, Nathan, whose specialty was theater criticism, detested the sentimental melodrama that dominated the theater in the teens and early twenties. He allowed, however, for "intelligent emotion" derived from broad and amoral experience and refined taste. In other words, emotion became sentiment and therefore feminine when it involved ideology or morality, what Nathan called the "'pious piffle of the Uplift.'" Mencken's philosophy of criticism, published in the March 1916 issue of the *Smart Set*, was that "readers and connoisseurs of criticism delight in brutality and esteem a critic in proportion as he is lethal."[29] Parker's critique of Katharine Hepburn's acting, that she "ran the whole gamut of emotions from A to B," is one of many examples in keeping with Mencken's philosophy.[30] Mencken also believed that humor was a most effective tool against the sentimentality and Puritanism of mass culture, what he called the "booboisie," and he distrusted ideologies that promoted the masses. Like his nineteenth-century predecessors, Mencken conflated mass culture with the sentimental, a move that would continue through the 1930s and 1940s when Parker was aggressively embracing leftist causes. Mencken's Nietzschean-derived version of Huyssen's "great divide," shared by Nathan, not only preceded that of the Algonquin Round Table, but was more extreme and more vocal. It is possible, of course, that Parker's use of humor and distaste for sentimental theater developed on its own. Yet as an established cultural force and the powerful publisher of two of her earliest pieces of fiction, Mencken and Nathan must have influenced Parker in a conflicting way, for her concern about issues related to the masses would become increasingly apparent. Meade reports that Parker admired Mencken, but left during a dinner with him when he began to make derogatory remarks about Blacks.[31]

To complicate the matter, the contents of the *Smart Set* often contradicted its purported orientation. Works by future canonized modernists—Joseph Conrad, James Joyce, Ezra Pound, D. H. Lawrence, Eugene O'Neill, W. B. Yeats—appear, as well as works by those who would later be perceived, at best, as on the modernist fringe: Elinor Wylie, Sara Teasdale, Amy Lowell, and Babette Deutsch. But Mencken also published verse rooted in nineteenth-century sentimentalism by Abigail Cresson, Grace Hazard Conkling, Amanda Benjamin Hall, Joyce Kilmer, Ella Wheeler Wilcox, and Lizette Woodworth Reese whom he particularly liked. These were not poets selected because "better" poetry was not available, as David Perkins has argued in his first volume of *A History of Modern Poetry*, but because poetry springing from emotion was the type of poetry Mencken preferred. The *Smart Set*, Carl Dolmetsch tells us, "scorned the 'free verse' movement and all experiments more radical than the milder forms of imagism," giving its avant-garde ideals a rather conservative edge. Finally, for editors inclined against sentimental ideologies of the masses, they published a number of leftist ideologues: John Reed, Floyd Dell, and Maxwell Anderson.[32] Although the *Smart Set* packaged itself as an avant-garde publication in contrast to the mass-marketed *Vanity Fair*, it too, offered a mixture of the sentimental and the modern.

The issue of art versus bacon, to which the juxtaposition of *Vanity Fair* and the *Smart Set* draws attention, was not unique to Parker; it concerned many of her cohorts at the Algonquin Round Table, and resulted in self- and group-denigration. Adams, Broun, and Woollcott came to believe their work was commercially successful but otherwise unimportant. George S. Kaufman and Moss Hart focused on the conflict between serious playwriting and commercial success in *Merrily We Roll Along*, a play with a character based on Parker who encourages her friends to produce intellectual work but refuses to do it herself.[33] The portrait of Parker as a lovelorn, self-pitying alcoholic is not flattering, but it suggests the extent to which she and her circle of friends were aware of the bifurcation between serious and commercial art. Kaufman and other Round Table members perpetuated Andreas Huyssen's "great divide," and in doing so paradoxically played into the arguments of modern criticism that would devalue their work.

In the mid-twenties, long before the Algonquin Round Table disbanded, Parker became disenchanted with the group, though there is evidence to suggest her feelings had been swayed by Dr. Alvan Barach, Parker's (and Heywood Broun's) psychotherapist in 1925–26. Barach, who read literature and wrote poetry and fiction as a hobby, occasionally attended Round Table gatherings. He was surprised when his pontifications about serious literature were met with jokes and derision by Round Table members. The Round Table, he then concluded, spent too much time on trivial pursuits, a point he made to Parker during her sessions with him for depression and alcoholism. She became notably critical of the Round Table during and after this period, though Barach failed to help her with her drinking problem. In the end, Parker suspected her work fell into the commercial or mass market category. She rejected light verse in the 1930s because it was politically useless, and later claimed that her verse was dated and her prose limited to its precision.[34]

Parker started her literary career among publications and individuals located within "the great divide," but could maintain no consistent position about it. Significantly, Parker's closest friends and literary influences were men: Frank Crowninshield, a guardian of the genteel avant-garde; George Jean Nathan, arbiter of antisentimental but emotionally intelligent theater; H. L. Mencken, purveyor of humorously abusive criticism with a taste for sentimental poetry; Franklin Pierce Adams, advocate for form and precision; and other Algonquin Round Table members who celebrated serious art and denigrated their own work. Within this context, Parker, when she could have any confidence about her work at all, might easily have seen her rhymed and metered verse and her stories, both of which appealed to female experience and emotion, as "modern" as anything being published. Certainly her growing readership did.

THE "HARD DARK CRYSTALS" OF PARKER'S POETRY

Parker's critical reception begins with her books of poetry, which were collections of poems previously published in magazines. All three of Parker's books—*Enough Rope* (1926), *Sunset Gun* (1928), and *Death and Taxes* (1931)—went into multiple printings, a rare event in poetry book publishing today. The books were reviewed by other poets as well as critics in major magazines and newspapers; the reviews were by and large positive, or a mixture of positive and negative comments. Reviewers and critics compared Parker's poetry with a broad range of writers: Roman (Horace, Martial, Catullus), British (Thomas Campion, Richard Lovelace, Robert Herrick, Jonathan Swift, Matthew Prior, Alexander Pope, William Wordsworth, Thomas Hood, Robert Browning, A. E. Housman, Rupert Brooke, Alice Meynell) and American (Edna Millay, Elinor Wylie, Sara Teasdale, Franklin Adams, H. L. Mencken, Samuel Hoffenstein, Phyllis McGinley). Consistently located in the light verse tradition by reviewers, Parker's poetry went by several labels—light verse, flapper verse, vers de société, and versicles—terms suggesting insignificance that would carry little weight among creators and guardians of the traditional canon. An overview of these positive reviews, however, suggests that Parker was destined for a place there.

Dedicated to Elinor Wylie and a phenomenal success, *Enough Rope* went through twenty-four printings by Boni and Liveright from 1926–1933, nine printings by Pocketbooks, Inc., from 1939–1941, and another printing by Sundial Press in 1940. Reviewers, for the most part, were as gracious with words as the reading public was generous with its dollars. For at least one reviewer, the poems accumulate power when published as a collection. J. F., a reviewer for *Bookman*, claims their effect as a collection is "devastating. Singly, they are lovely. As a volume they are terrifying, but only as they reflect what seems to be a fiery, discontented personality, a lovely personality withal." Both Edmund Wilson and Marie Luhrs appreciate Parker's frankness; Wilson and poet Genevieve Taggard note her epigrammatic quality, which for Taggard helped make Parker's poetry "excellent . . . light verse." An anonymous reviewer for the *Saturday Review of Literature* also applauds Parker's skill with light verse and agrees with Wilson that her irony is another strength. Not surprisingly, four reviewers compare Parker with another highly popular poet, Edna St. Vincent Millay. At issue is Parker's use of the Millay influence. Taggard, Luhrs, and an anonymous reviewer for the *Nation* claim that Parker's imitations of Millay failed to yield her best poetry, Taggard adding that Parker discarded that influence in the second half of the book and "worked into something quite her own . . . . whisky straight, not champagne." Wilson writes that Parker, though influenced by Millay, maintained her individuality, in part because she "invented a new kind of epigram: she has made the comic anti-climax tragic. . . . We have nothing like the hard dark crystals of Dorothy Parker's irony."[35]

Sunset Gun (1928), a slimmer volume, also went into multiple printings: thirteen by Boni and Liveright, with one reprint each by Sun Dial Press (1939) and Pocket Books (1940). This time, although Garetta Busey of the *New York Herald Tribune* makes reference to

Parker's "Millaysian rhythms," the most frequent comparison made is with *Enough Rope*. Busey, William Rose Benét, and Herschel Brickell claim that Parker's first two books are comparable; Edith Walton, while praising *Sunset Gun* for its "gallant bravado," "sly and jaunty irony," and its lyricism, argues without explication in the *New Republic* that *Enough Rope* is better: "*Sunset Gun* is hardly so brave a salute as *Enough Rope*." Nevertheless, readers like Parker's poetry, claims Busey, because she does what we were taught as children not to do: "She sasses back at Life, or the Universe, or God, or What Have You in nimble and absurd rhyme. . . . And besides, we like her because she laughs at herself. We always like people to laugh at themselves. It takes their attention away from us." Writing for *Bookman*, H. M. Robinson notes that Parker's poetry may be repetitive, but never dull, while R. A. Simon of the *New York Evening Post* claims Parker is the best at vers de société. Benét in the *Saturday Review of Literature* sees her power as being able to elicit several responses—distress, admiration, tenderness, and laughter—within one or a very few poems. Edwin Clark of the *New York Times* admires her "tinctured mixture of the sad and gay," as well as the fact that her poems stand on more than the cleverness of their ironic concluding quatrains or couplets: "She does not have to depend on the last line reverse twist for effectiveness. Happily, this is being acquired without losing the gem-like sparkle of her verse."[36]

When it came out in 1931, *Death and Taxes* met with mixed reviews, yet this last volume of Parker's original verse also went through multiple printings: nine by Viking Press and two editions by Sun Dial Press in 1939 and 1940. Some of those who praise the book notice a difference in tone. Franklin Pierce Adams claims *Death and Taxes* is Parker's "saddest and her best book;" Horace Gregory agrees, stating in the *New York Evening Post* that its "verse is a trifle less gay than the earlier two volumes." Fanny Butcher of the *Chicago Daily Tribune* praises it as a continuation of the "flippant, and always amusing" poetry of *Enough Rope*. An anonymous reviewer for the *Nation* calls Parker a "master of ironical humor," adding that "Mrs. Parker as a light verse writer is actually a better poet than many of our very serious composers in meter." Percy Hutchison, in the *New York Times Book Review*, also links Parker with the light verse tradition, a line of "English minor poets" that includes Richard Lovelace and Robert Herrick. Another anonymous reviewer for the *Springfield Republican* (Massachusetts) describes Parker's diction as an "unmannered . . . compound of hard wit and surprise, lightly fashioned and concise" through which she achieves "individual expression."[37]

Not So Deep as a Well: Collected Poems (1936), dedicated to Franklin Pierce Adams, went through six printings with Viking Press, was published in Toronto (1936) and London (1937), and was reissued by the Modern Library in New York (1944). Most of the positive reviews claim Parker's poems endure over time. Louis Kronenberger, again placing Parker in the light verse tradition, writes in the *New York Times Book Review*: "One comes back to Mrs. Parker's light verse with the greatest pleasure; with its sharp wit, its clean bite, its perfectly conscious—and hence delightful—archness, it stands re-reading amply." William Rose Benét, writing in the *Saturday Review of Literature*, agrees, claiming Parker's poetry contains "an exquisitely distilled bitterness that improves with age." The *Collected Poems* illustrate, claims Benét, that Parker's poetry improved as her career progressed: "As I reread poems I have already read a great many times, it seems to me that this notable talent has become clearer and finer through the progress of three books," moving from ballads to French forms, from stereotypes to epigrammatic wit.[38]

The popularity of Parker's poetry raises a significant issue regarding her later reputation. Her work appealed to a mass audience in part because its initial outlet was through mass circulation magazines, but also because she tapped a cultural nerve. Parker's poetry can be described, by borrowing the military title of Volume 3 of Sandra Gilbert and Susan Gubar's *No Man's Land*, as a "letter from the front." The practice of women's social independence and equality was in its infancy in the late teens and twenties, and Parker captured the experience with sass, self-deprecating humor, and implied critique. Yet this ability to connect with a situation during a particular historical moment—that is, the late teens, 1920s, and early 1930s—has led male critics such as Brendan Gill to label her a period writer.[39] With its implication that Parker has limited scope and range, this designation worked against her inclusion in the traditional canon. Clearly, such a reading ignores the fact that gender inequities are not limited to any one historical moment. Gender issues would infiltrate reviews of Parker's fiction in a more direct fashion.

A FEMALE HEMINGWAY?

Parker published two books of short fiction, *Laments for the Living* in 1930 and *After Such Pleasures* in 1933, as well as a collected volume, *Here Lies* (1939), which contains most but not all of the first two volumes, two stories published in magazines, and one previously unpublished story. Like her poetry, the public read Parker's fiction in magazines before seeing it in book form, where, for Fanny Butcher of the *Chicago Tribune*, the stories seem "more impressive in a book than they did in the various magazines." Parker's volumes of fiction also met with popular and critical approval, with each volume going through multiple printings. Ten Viking Press editions of *Laments for the Living* were published between 1930 and 1936, as well as editions published in London (Longman) and on the Continent (Crosby Continental Editions) and a 1947 reissue by World Publishing Company in Cleveland, Ohio. Five Viking Press editions of *After Such Pleasures* came out between 1933 and 1935, as well as editions by Longman and Sun Dial Press in New York. *Here Lies* was published simultaneously by Viking, Longman, and the Literary Guild of America, and later reissued as *The Collected Stories of Dorothy Parker*.[40]

Reviewers praise Parker's satire, wit, economy, ear for dialogue, and sharp observation. They debate the relative value of her longer and shorter stories, described as short, slight, vignettes, sketches, minor tales, talk sketches, and monologues—problematic labels in a culture that measures success in terms of accumulation and size. Several reviewers agree that Parker's stories gather power as a collection. Reviewers make fewer comparisons between Parker's fiction and that of other writers than they made with her poetry. Passing references are made to A. E. Housman, Katherine Mansfield, and Jane Austen; more detailed comparisons are made with John P. Marquand, Ring Lardner, and Ernest Hemingway. The latter two prompt the most interest, for they entail an important critical discussion of Parker's fiction: the relationship between Parker's writing and Parker's gender, an issue that was not raised with her poetry.

Bonnie Kime Scott and others have noted the ways in which some early twentieth-century women writers, such as Djuna Barnes, Mina Loy, and Marianne Moore, have been admitted to the "male category" of modernism based on comparisons of their works with that of Pound, Eliot, or Joyce.[41] Parker's comparison with Lardner and Hemingway did not result in such an outcome, in part because Lardner is now perhaps more of a marginal figure than Parker. In the minds of reviewers at the time of Parker's publication, however, the sparse narrative and focused dialogue of Lardner and Hemingway represented the model of modern linear fiction. They became the test against which Parker's narrative economy and ear for dialogue had to stand. At times the comparisons are framed around the question, "Is Parker as good as . . . ?"; in effect assigning masculine gender to brevity and dialogue. At other times the discussion is more specifically framed around the effects of gender on writing.

Morrie Ryskind, an anonymous reviewer for *Forum*, Ogden Nash, and T. S. Matthews, in his review of *Laments for the Living*, judge Parker to be as good as Lardner in terms of dialogue, economy, and impact, though in his review of *After Such Pleasures*, Matthews claims Parker's "seriously intended stories are not on a par with the best of" Lardner's. An anonymous reviewer for the *Nation* agrees, stating flatly, "She is not as good as Ring Lardner." Edgar Johnson's *Kenyon Review* critique of *Here Lies*, which compares Parker with John P. Marquand, is also negative, but his position differs from that of the majority of critics. Where most reviewers praise, at least to some degree, Parker's technique, Johnson claims "she has substance and significant theme and vital emotion," but she lacks "deftness and detachment. . . . [S]he has produced satire without art." Parker fares better in comparisons with Hemingway. Gladys Graham in the *Saturday Review of Literature* writes: "Mrs. Parker can cut away detail with a ruthlessness not to be equaled elsewhere in this Hemmingway-Held, brevity-or-burst generation" [*sic*]. Matthews, as well as Herschel Brickell and Fanny Butcher, find her comparable. Butcher observes that Hemingway and Parker, using different techniques, achieve the same end:

> He works from the outside, with thought and emotion implied by the action. She works from the inside, with thought set down and action and outside pressure inferred. But they both reach the highly emotional reaction of reality in their readers.[42]

Butcher's observation that Hemingway's fiction is motivated by external action while Parker's is motivated by internal thought is debatable; more important, it reflects the active-male/passive-female dichotomy so prevalent in nineteenth-century assumptions about the sexes.

Some of Parker's reviewers more directly address the issue of authorial sex and gender. Because of the logistical limitations imposed by the book review format, these gender-oriented discussions are not developed at length. Their presence, however, indicates the extent to which early twentieth-century reviewers are preoccupied with the gender of authorship, specifically the difference between male and female writers. Parker's fiction elicits from some reviewers the conviction that she fits into both categories, but the ways in which reviewers assign gender to various writing techniques is, if not surprising, somewhat problematic for Parker's long-term reputation.

Three reviewers consider Parker's blurring of gender boundaries a great asset. An anonymous reviewer for the *Springfield* (Massachusetts) *Sunday Union and Republican* praises *After Such Pleasures* by claiming Parker's "characters are fashioned with a neat telling irony and polished with a keen feminine wit and even sympathy." Although this reviewer does not explicitly define his or her terms, the juxtaposition of "feminine wit" and "irony" suggests the latter trait is considered a masculine one by the reviewer. John Mair offers another version of the feminine in his review, in *New Statesman and Nation*, of *Here Lies*. Comparing Parker's "humorous detachment" with that of Jane Austen, Mair praises Parker for having it both ways:

> Although she has what is usually termed a "masculine" intelligence, Miss Parker writes from a pleasingly feminine point of view. She is far harder on female than on male stupidities, and is the surest guide I know through the inferno of the feminine middle class. . . . She stands in a class by herself, both as a master of the satirical short story and as a woman writer who is not self-conscious about her sex. She is one of the first literary fruits of female emancipation.[43]

Mair's appreciation of Parker's fiction raises some problematic questions. If Parker has a "feminine point of view" by virtue of her focus on and criticism of female characters, what exactly is "masculine intelligence"? A willingness to be harder on "female . . . stupidities"? A reference to irony? When Mair places Parker in two distinct categories, as a "master of the satirical short story" and as a "woman writer," he assigns masculine gender to satire as well as success. Parker, "in a class by herself," appears to be an anomaly by virtue of her success. Critically cut from a woman's tradition and the feminist assessments of culture occurring in journalism, fiction, and poetry in the teens, twenties, and thirties, the inherent feminism of Parker's critique is lost—to readers and to Parker herself.

Issues concerning sex and gender become the focus in other reviews. In his *New York Herald Tribune* review of *After Such Pleasures*, Morrie Ryskind calls Parker "a feminine Housman and a female Lardner." Parker's writing is "feminine" by virtue of her focus on female characters, and "female" by virtue of being less "Puritanical" than Lardner, an interesting reversal of a value often associated with women into the twentieth century. In "Here We Are," argues Ryskind, "Mrs. Parker, being a woman, takes sex right in her stride and portrays a delicate situation deftly, without any leering." But the masculinity of her work is tied to her diction, nourished no doubt by her association with the Algonquin Round Table.

> Dorothy Parker has the sort of mind that we males, for want of a better word, have labeled "masculine," just as we label the movie hero who fights his way through fire and flood a "manly" fellow. When the wits of the town are mentioned in print or gathered in fun, she is sure to be included in the otherwise male group. She speaks the language of the boys, she knows all the words, but she speaks, nevertheless, in a woman's voice. Just as she sees with a woman's eyes.[44]

"Wit," with its attendant forms of irony and satire, and the language used to deliver it, can be read as masculine attributes in Ryskind's analysis.

How might Parker have interpreted herself and her success as a result of reading these gender-oriented reviews? In many cases, to succeed as a woman writer means to write better than a man, to write like a man, or to temper feminine sympathy with the male attributes of wit, economy, irony, and intelligence. To be a successful woman writer is to be one of the quirky exceptions to literary success and tradition, a respected outsider like Jane Austen, an isolated, "token woman" in the words of Adrienne Rich.[45] Detailed comparisons with female contemporaries—Virginia Woolf, Djuna Barnes, Katherine Mansfield—are unnecessary because they, by virtue of their sex, do not set the standard. It is highly possible—and ironic—that Parker, who would later reject her work and her association with the Algonquin Round Table as frivolous, might have been plagued by the question, How seriously can one take an exception to the rule?

A Portable Reputation

During the 1920s and early 1930s when Parker was the most productive in terms of her poetry and fiction, she moved within a circle of publishers and critics who gave her the public and critical exposure upon which literary reputations are made. Within the Algonquin Round Table alone, Adams published her poems in his widely read Conning Tower column and reviewed her work; Harold Ross published her in the *New Yorker;* and Woollcott, Broun, and Robert Benchley reviewed her work, including her 1929 play *Close Harmony*

(with Elmer Rice). Other friends on the margins of the Round Table—
not only Crowninshield, Mencken, and Nathan, but Edmund Wilson, Stephen Vincent Benét, and E. B. White—also promoted her
work. The Round Table, Gaines reminds us, had been criticized for
logrolling.[46] Yet the popularity of the work itself in terms of sales suggests that Parker's poetry and fiction—with its poetic conventions
and narrative innovations, its decadent preoccupation with death, its
modern cynicism toward relationships, and its sentimental longing
for love—appealed to an audience characterized by a mixture of tastes.

Parker's works were collected again in the Viking Press Portable
series. The 1944 edition includes an introduction by W. Somerset
Maugham, previously published stories and poems selected and arranged by Parker, one new poem,"War Song," and five new stories:
"The Lovely Leave," "The Standard of Living," "Song of the Shirt,
1941," "Mrs. Hofstadter on Josephine Street," and "Cousin Larry."
The 1973 edition includes the original *Portable* plus three later stories—"I Live on Your Visits," "Lolita," and "Bolt Behind the Blue"—
play reviews from *Vanity Fair* and the *New Yorker,* book reviews from
the *New Yorker* and *Esquire,* four uncollected articles, and an introduction by Brendan Gill. This edition is also notable for what it lacks: all
of her *Life* magazine prose; several of her accomplished monologues
and dialogues ("The Garter," "But the One on the Right," "The Mantle
of Whistler," "A Young Woman in Green Lace," among others); some
of her longer, more fully narrated stories ("Advice to the Little Peyton
Girl," "The Game,"); and several poems collected in previously published but now out-of-print volumes ("Verse Reporting Late Arrival at
a Conclusion," "Day Dreams," "Folk Tune," "Spring Song," "Finis,"
"Autobiography," "Ballade of Big Plans," "Biographies," and "Song in
a Minor Key" from *Enough Rope;* "Partial Comfort" and "For R. C. B."
from *Sunset Gun;* and "The Apple Tree" from *Death and Taxes*). None
of her uncollected early verse is included. These deletions could have
been due to a number of factors, such as space considerations, rep-
etition of form and content, or more importantly, Parker's sense of
what constituted her best work in an era dominated by New Critical
values.

With the publication of the two *Portable Dorothy Parker*'s, however,
we see both a simultaneous expansion and contraction of her reputation. Both books sold well; the 1973 edition is still in print today. At
the same time, the number of reviews drops off. Where her books
overall average twelve reviews per book, the 1944 *Portable* received
eight; the 1973 *Portable*, an expanded version, received four. Most of

the reviews are positive, citing the convenience of having a sizable chunk of Parker in compact form. But reviewers debate whether Parker's achievement lay in poetry or fiction, and begin to label Parker a "period writer" of the 1920s and early 1930s, further narrowing her accomplishments.[47]

These two critical positions say more about the limited ways in which Parker has been read than about Parker's work. Her accomplishments in two genres prompt a debate that diminishes both rather than praises her for her versatility. And to label her a "period writer" seems entirely myopic. Parker's speakeasies and bathtub gin may suggest the 1920s alone, but her thematic concerns—love, adultery, abortion, racism, war, and tension between generations and genders—are timeless issues to all but those who choose to ignore them. These readings of Parker were offered between the 1940s and 1973, when New Criticism had a stranglehold on the academic study of literature, and modernism became a narrowly defined concept. By this time, Parker's leftist politics were firmly and publicly established, a move that conveniently dovetailed with the New Critical charge against her of sentimentality.

2

The Sentimental Infection:
Critical Responses to Sentimentality
in Dorothy Parker's
Life, Politics, and Literary Production

The term *sentimental*, encoded by its historical locations and the politics of gender, requires a brief examination. Our understanding of what we refer to as "sentimental" has changed over time, ranging from deeply felt but reasonable feelings in the eighteenth century, to feminized idealism about humanity in the nineteenth century, to cheap emotional excess in the twentieth century. In his study of eighteenth-century sentimental novels, R. F. Brissenden examines the ambiguity of two words—sentimental and wit—often applied to Dorothy Parker. Both the "sense" family of words, which includes sentiment, sentimentality, and sentimental, and the word "wit" exhibit what Brissenden calls a "fundamental ambiguity"—both refer to either a physical or mental awareness, or a combination of the two. Both words, then, encompass feeling and intellect, elements that, as Suzanne Clark reminds us in *Sentimental Modernism*, modernist literary criticism sets against each other. In many ways, Parker's work is embroiled in this conflict, further complicated by the fact that throughout the nineteenth century sentimentality connotes feeling over intellect and is gendered feminine.[1]

In the twentieth century, "sentimental" becomes largely a pejorative term at a time when New Criticism and other conservative criticisms are developing. I. A. Richards' *Practical Criticism* (1929), a book that greatly influenced the development of New Criticism, states: "Among the politer terms of abuse, there are few so effective as 'sentimental.'" In a more recent assessment, John Frederick Nims claims "the sentimentalist is less concerned with the object of his emotion than with the fact that he himself is feeling it," and that the sentimental writer plays on our stock responses, delivers a literary sucker punch, so to speak.[2] I do not intend to argue that all uses of sentiment create a kind of literature that I enjoy; the biases embedded in modernist literary values, not enjoyment, are the issue here. When we evaluate judgments against sentimentality, important questions need to be considered: "Whose sentiment?" "For what purpose?" "Whose standards are behind the evaluation?" Nims uses John Crowe Ransom, who dismissed the female-as-poet in his famous New Critical assessment of Edna St. Vincent Millay, as an example of a nonsentimental poet. Charles Dickens and William Makepeace Thackeray are located within the sentimental genre, yet their works have remained canonized. The line of nineteenth-century American realistic novels by James Fenimore Cooper, Nathaniel Hawthorne, Herman Melville, Mark Twain, and Frank Norris remains canonized despite its melodramatic escape from society to a pastoralized wilderness.[3] Yet not until feminist scholars began to recover and reassess women's literature did works by Mary Gaskell, Susanna Rowson, Harriet Beecher Stowe, Rose Terry Cook, Elizabeth Warner, and others approach legitimate status. Clearly, one aspect of discrediting the sentimental has been along gender lines; women's feelings are less important than the feelings or intellectual pursuits of men. Another aspect of critical disdain for the sentimental, and one that has impact on Parker's literary reputation from the 1930s onward, comes from Lionel Trilling. In his rejection of Theodore Dreiser, Trilling argues that literature sympathetic to victims of capitalism is a sentimental manipulation toward totalitarianism. Literary liberalism, to Trilling's way of thinking, runs dangerously close to Stalinism.[4] Thus, the sentimental in twentieth-century literary discussion becomes a depository for negative associations: an outdated convention, excessive emotion, feminine weakness and tradition, and leftist politics. Such a conflation of values would have dire consequences for Parker's long-term literary reputation.

Nevertheless, in two positive reviews of Parker's *Laments for the Living*, the sentimental is seen as a legitimate technique of early-twentieth-century literature. Mary Ross, writing for the *New York Herald Tribune Books* (1930), claims: "A recurrent surprise of modern realism is that when one shucks off its hard-boiled exterior there is a gush of sentiment beneath that would have stirred a mid-Victorian maiden."[5] Writing in the *Chicago Tribune* (1930), Fanny Butcher makes a distinction between two kinds of sentiment: the "false heart break" used by some writers, and Parker's "authentic satires, coated with laughter, with a tear slipping off the old heart." Butcher argues that Parker's stories carry forward the essence of her poetry and of modern life as well:

> Completely characteristic of her—our—day, her poems are apparently hard boiled criticisms of life and love and living and underneath as sentiment-inducing as the Sweet Alices of another day. "Laugh, Clown, Laugh" is the sentimental war cry of our generation.[6]

Ross and Butcher suggest that there is a legitimate use of the sentimental in modern literature, but in terms of Parker criticism, their arguments are the exception to the rule.

This chapter examines the charge of sentimentality launched against Parker's personal life, politics, and literary production made by friends, biographers, and critics. It is a charge that increases as Parker's career continues, and is a somewhat surprising charge, given her reputation as a caustic wit. I will argue that Parker has been misread as a sentimentalist, insofar as the sentimental has been identified with excessive, unwarranted emotion and subsequently devalued. Part of Parker's politics and writing concern racial issues in some admirable and problematic ways. Racial stereotypes become a relevant factor here because of their origins in nineteenth-century sentimental literature. Therefore, an extensive discussion of Parker's use of racial stereotypes, and of her relationship to Black culture in general, is included. While the pejorative charge of sentimentality—or "the sentimental infection," as I call it—may have kept Parker in the margins of the modernist canon, a reevaluation of this charge also opens up the possibility of more complex readings of her work.

THE SENTIMENTAL INFECTION IN PARKER'S PERSONAL LIFE

Friends and biographers of Parker have pointed out that Parker's personal life and choices were marked by sentimentality. In the preface to his largely sympathetic study of Parker, Arthur F. Kinney claims she was "foolishly sentimental." He goes on to note that in a letter to Noel Coward, Alexander Woollcott commented that the character of Daisy Lester in Charles Brackett's 1934 novel *Entirely Surrounded* is an accurate portrayal of Parker. Kinney adds that if the portrait of Parker "is as accurate as Woollcott claimed, then she was always unhappy, self-pitying, embarrassing, sentimental." Kinney reiterated the point in a 1986 *Massachusetts Review* article, saying both Parker and Woollcott "revealed streaks of sentimentality."[7] While these observations may be in some way accurate, we do well to recognize the subjective nature of such observations. In a cultural climate where the intellect is a man's domain and feelings are a woman's domain—a dichotomy held over from nineteenth-century attitudes—any strong expression of feeling by a woman is open to the charge of sentimentality.

Parker's sentimentality reportedly encompassed animals, domesticity, and politics. John Keats reports that some of Parker's friends "thought her love of animals was somewhat misdirected when it was not overflowingly sentimental." Such an assumption may say more about Parker's friends than about Parker. At any rate, Parker's work illustrates she was capable of applying her feelings for animals to satiric purposes. A dog owner from childhood and throughout her life, Parker wrote two poems about dogs: "Verse for a Certain Dog," in which the dog's endearing qualities are countered by parenthetical commands and threats, and "To My Dog" (*Life*, 28 July 1921) in which the dog becomes a metaphor for the type of charming but flirtatious and troublesome man "that women always fall for."[8] The ousted female dog in Parker's short story, "Mr. Durant," not only becomes the pointer to the protagonist's misogyny, but provides the symbolic linking of misogyny and adultery. In "Big Blonde," Hazel Morse's sympathy for an abused horse stands in contrast to the lack of sympathy and understanding she receives. And the home nurse in "Horsie" is ridiculed by her employers for having a horselike face. In these stories, Parker seems to be suggesting that our mistreatment of animals runs parallel to our treatment of humans. If the sentiment they contain seems heavy to some readers, Parker nevertheless bonds it to satiric force.

Parker's response to domesticity is a bit more complex. More will be said about this in chapter 5, but here again the perceptions of Parker's life often fail to include the appropriate contextual issues, and at times are at odds with her work. Early friends of Parker knew her as a resident of New York City hotels who let restaurants provide food and maids handle laundry and housekeeping, and who had an abortion after the man who impregnated her left the relationship. Not surprisingly, some of Parker's works use the theme of antidomesticity. "Wives" and "Husbands," two "Hymns of Hate" published in *Life* magazine in 1923, delineate the types she finds objectionable, ranging from "Splendid Housekeepers" and "Home Bodies" to "Veteran Sirens" and "He-Men." Parker also criticizes "Domestic" women in a "Hate Song" published under the pseudonym Henriette Rousseau in a 1916 issue of *Vanity Fair*. The poem "Day-Dreams" mocks and rejects domestic married life, while the poem "The Story of Mrs. W___" and the short story "Such a Pretty Little Picture," published in the *Smart Set* in 1922, associate domesticity with death and entrapment.[9] The antidomestic theme of these works is understandable, since they were written in the 1920s, during a period when Parker was estranged from and divorcing her husband, and going through a number of unsuccessful relationships. Parker's friends and biographers, however, could not imagine that a different context—a marriage where the husband wanted to have children with her—would produce different values in Parker.

During her marriage to Alan Campbell in the 1930s and 1940s, while both were writing for Hollywood film studios, Parker wrote in a letter to Alexander Woollcott, "I love having a house, I love its being pretty wherever you look, I love a big yard full of dogs." Parker later purchased a farm in Bucks County, Pennsylvania, took up knitting, and tried to conceive a child. In *The Algonquin Wits*, Robert Drennan records that "Leonard Lyons once asked Dorothy Parker to describe her Bucks County farm in two words, to which she replied, 'Want it?'" In another letter to Woollcott, however, Parker said of her Bucks County home: "I do love this place." But "her tearful desire to have a family and a house in the country," Kinney writes, "was laughed off as alcoholic sentimentality."[10] These simplistic readings of Parker's personal life as reported by biographers are visually reinforced in Alan Rudolph's *Mrs. Parker and the Vicious Circle* (1994). This film offers a portrait of a crying Parker, dog in arms, staggering down a New York City street rather than one of a portrait of a productive writer at work. We never see the Bucks County farm. Even more problematic is the effect these interpretations of her life have on interpretations of her work. As we will see, "Clothe the Naked" becomes a sentimental portrait of poor African Americans rather than an examination of the intersection of racism and class politics. Parker's emotional responses to the events in her life likely influenced her work—as would any writer's, male or female—but her responses represent a complexity of character that the pejorative use of "sentimental" dismisses out-of-hand.

THE SENTIMENTAL INFECTION IN PARKER'S POLITICS

Parker's political consciousness has its roots in her childhood. According to Marion Meade, Parker was aware that the economic comfort her family enjoyed was at the expense of low-paid workers in her father's garment manufacturing business; she developed a penchant for the underdog.[11] It might at first seem surprising, then, that she turns her early invective against radicals in three "Hate Songs" published in *Vanity Fair:* "Men" (Feb. 1917), "Slackers" (Dec. 1917), and "Bohemians" (Oct. 1918). In "Men" she hates "Serious Thinkers" who

> . . . talk about Humanity
> As if they had just invented it;
> They have to keep helping it along.
> They revel in strikes
> And they are eternally getting up petitions.
> They are doing a wonderful thing for the Great
> Unwashed,—
> They are living right down among them.
> They can hardly wait
> For "The Masses" to appear on the newsstands, . . .[12]

Parker, who saw both world wars as battles on behalf of the underdog, and who had husbands in both of them, attacked, among the "Slackers," the "Socialists" who "will prove—with a street corner and a soap box— / That the whole darned war was Morgan's fault." She criticized "Radicals" in "Bohemians" because "They are always in revolt about something. // Their one ambition is to get themselves arrested, / So that they can come out and be Heroes." It would be a mistake, however, to assume from these poems that Parker did not have leftist sympathies. Aside from the context in which these pieces were produced, what Parker exploited in her "Hate Songs" were pretentious individuals whose behavior represented shallowness, self-importance, and insincerity. She disliked them for their facade of political activity that contributed nothing to the cause. Parker was equally hard on glib patriotism. She chides the New York theater for relying on patriotic themes during World War I, and later claims attachment to E. M. Forster's famous declaration, "It has never happened to me that I've had to choose between betraying a friend and betraying my country, but if it ever does so happen I hope to have the guts to betray my country."[13]

Parker's first brush with leftist politics was the Actor's Equity strike in 1919, which virtually shut down Broadway. Her descriptions of it in three *Vanity Fair* pieces—"The New Plays—If Any" (Oct. 1919), "The Actor's Demands" (under the pseudonym Helen Wells, Oct. 1919), and "The Union Forever" (Nov. 1919)—clearly reveal her sympathy for the striking actors. In 1922 Parker published "Poem in the American Manner" in *Life* magazine, which is as much a statement of Parker's sympathy for the downtrodden as it is a parody of rural American dialect and political insensitivity:

> I dunno yer highfalutin' words, but here's the way it seems
> When I'm peekin' out th' winder o' my little House o' Dreams;
> I've ben lookin' 'roun' this big ol' world, as bizzy as a hive,
> An' I want t' tell ye, neighbor mine, it's good t' be alive.
> I've ben settin' here, a-thinkin' hard, an' say, it seems t' me
> That this big ol' world is jest about as good as it kin be,
> With its starvin' little babies, an' its battles, an' its strikes,
> An' its profiteers, an' hold-up men—th' dawggone little tykes!—
> An' its hungry men that fought fer us, that nobody employs.
> An' I t'ink, "Why, shucks, we're jest a lot o' grown-up little boys!"
> An' I settle back, an' light my pipe, an' reach fer Mother's hand,
> An' I wouldn't swap my peace o' mind fer nothin' in the land;
> Fer this world uv ours, that jest was made fer folks like me an' you
> Is a purty good ol' place t' live—say, neighbor, ain't it true?[14]

This poem carries in it a certain class tension, the urban sophisticate mocking the uneducated, perhaps lower-income individual. But also implicit in this satire is Parker's irritation with those who remain complacent about status quo politics as long as they have their own "peace o' mind." The poem more strongly states the same concern we saw in her much earlier poem, published in 1915, "Any Porch." Her politics took a more radical turn in 1927 when she was arrested for marching in protest of the Sacco-Vanzetti executions in Boston. After her arrest, she turned her wrath on then-lover Seward Collins for being one of the shallow types she criticizes in "Bohemians." Meade reports that Collins "said that he felt terrible because he had arrived late and missed the glory of being arrested. The sight of him angered Dorothy. There was still time, she told him." No one, according to Keats and Meade, doubted the sincerity of her actions or the depth of her political commitment then.[15] At a time when *Enough Rope* was breaking sales records and establishing Parker as an important poet of light verse, she was revealing her concern for serious political causes.

Parker's political activities in the 1930s, however, have been the target of much criticism. When she became involved in anti-fascist and pro-communist activities in Hollywood, friends and colleagues cast doubt on the depth of her political acumen, particularly where communism was concerned. She gave speeches, helped organize committees such as the Anti-Nazi League, served on the Motion Picture Artists committee and the board of directors of the Screen Writers Guild, lent her name to more than thirty fund-raising activities, and helped raise money for Loyalist Spain, China, and the Scottsboro defendants. She wrote stories ("Soldiers of the Republic," "Who Might Be Interested") and articles for *New Masses* ("Incredible, Fantastic . . . and True," "Not Enough," and "Sophisticated Poetry—And the Hell with It") about the Spanish Civil War. Parker also helped Ernest Hemingway and Lillian Hellman finance the film *The Spanish Earth*, and helped stage a demonstration to support striking waiters in New York. As Diane Johnson reports in her biography of Dashiell Hammett, Parker was on the editorial council of *Equality*, "a monthly journal to defend democratic rights and combat anti-Semitism and racism," and wanted to be a World War II correspondent but was denied a passport due to her pro-communist activities. Meade reports that the FBI kept a file on Parker.[16]

Keats, however, reports that "bona fide Communists" as well as Parker's other friends "thought she was politically naive in calling herself a Communist," and none of them "could imagine her plowing through the dense thickets of dialectical materialism as set forth by Marx and Engels." Her friends concluded that Parker "could never look critically at the Communist Party, once she decided that the Party really wanted to help suffering humanity," and that she "entertained a somewhat romantic notion of what Communism was all about." A more problematic assessment comes from Stuart Y. Silverstein, who, in his introduction to *Not Much Fun*, accuses her of being a Stalinist who failed to speak out against the Great Purge of 1936–38 or Stalin's nonaggression pact with Hitler. "Emotional sentimentality," among other things, writes Silverstein, characterizes Parker's "flirtation with the revolutionary struggle." In other words, sentimentality led to sloppy politics. Suspicions that Parker's position regarding Spain was sentimental may in part be grounded in media accounts of her crying about it, as in Dixie Tighe's article in the *New York Post:* "There were tears in the shining eyes of Miss Parker when she disclosed . . . that the tragedy of Spain had tempered her wit and urged her into a desire to raise funds for the American hospitals in Spain." A certain amount of intellectual elitism exists behind these statements regarding the role of emotion in Parker's politics. Doesn't an emotional response to a situation often precede—in fact, necessarily precede—political action? It is also important to remember that Parker, however sophisticated and worldly she appeared in print, had relatively little formal education, particularly where economics, political philosophy, and world history were concerned, subjects that would help one analyze a volatile political situation in-process.[17] Her lack of formal education in these areas may not excuse her errors in judgment, but it helps us understand why they may have occurred. Even if Parker, like many in her day, did not have the clarity of insight regarding communism that historians now claim to possess, she nevertheless contributed materially to causes she believed were for the good of humanity.

Accusations of political sentimentality continue through the second half of her life and after her death. Edmund Wilson, in a 1944 *New Yorker* review of the Viking *Portable Dorothy Parker*, remarks that Parker's political work during her Hollywood years was a waste of time. In her memoir, *An Unfinished Woman*, Parker's close friend Lillian Hellman writes that Parker "believed in socialism but seldom, except in the sticky sentimental minutes, could stand the sight of a working radical." Kinney quotes and agrees with Harold Clurman who, in his *Los Angeles Times* article, claims Parker's "'radicalism was not insincere [but] it was sentimental.'" As recently as 1986 Kinney attributes Parker's radicalism in the 1930s to creative frustration: "She submerged her own failing energies to write the way Hollywood wanted her to write into an activity of a more political sort."[18] This interpretation discredits Parker's political sincerity by failing to recognize that her political activities in the 1930s were part of a lifelong commitment to equality and justice as evidenced by her early reviews, poems, and political work, as well as her later actions. Also, it must be remembered that from the 1930s through the Cold War period, it was much safer to negate Parker's leftist position than to risk being blacklisted with her.

Parker's concern with racial equality, seen in both her actions and her writing, also was subject to charges of sentimentality. As Meade points out, Parker was no doubt sensitized to racial issues by virtue of the fact that she was half-Jewish, as her stepmother and Catholic teachers repeatedly reminded her. While racism was not Parker's major theme, a number of her works address the issue. The conditions of her last will and testament, then, do not seem out of character. In admiration for Dr. Martin Luther King, Jr., Parker left her literary estate to him, to be passed on to the National Association for the Advancement of Colored People in the event of his death. Lillian Hellman, Parker's friend and executrix, vehemently criticized Parker's decision. Hellman told Nora Ephron in 1973, "It's one thing to have real feeling for Black people, but to have the kind of blind sentimentality about the N. A. A. C. P., a group so conservative that even many Blacks don't have respect for, is something else."[19] Hellman's response, if placed in the context of the Black Panther Party politics acutely critical of the N. A. A. C. P. in the late 1960s and early 1970s, says more about the politics of the day than it does about Parker's alleged sentimentality. In fact, Parker's handling of racial issues is much more complex, and worthy of a chronological examination.

Over the course of her career and personal life, Parker both criticized the use of racial stereotypes and used them. An early example of her flirtation with stereotypes occurs in a 1917 *Vanity Fair* "Hate Song" titled "Relatives" (and published under her maiden name, Rothschild). Parker opens the final stanza with: "And then there are Husbands; / The White Woman's Burden."[20] By alluding to the "White man's burden," the approving euphemism coined by Rudyard Kipling for late nineteenth- and early twentieth-century British imperialism, Parker draws an analogy between the racism of imperialism and the sexism of marriage. But the image of the "White Woman's Burden" with its singling out of woman by a White racial identity also leads to some problematic assumptions: (1) that husbands are not a burden for Black women, or (2) that Black women do not have husbands. Parker may not have intended either of these readings, and indeed it is possible to read "White Woman's Burden" as a satirical comment on the imperialistic attitude behind the original euphemism. It seems clear, however, that she knew she was addressing a White audience. Significantly, at the time the poem was published, magazines such as *Life* included cartoons and jokes that occasionally used Black racial stereotypes.[21]

A few years later, Parker examines the handling of race in New York theater productions. As Ann Douglas notes, the use of blackface performers declined during the 1920s, and Parker's theater reviews reflect this trend. Although she praises a blackface performance in one review, she criticizes two others, as well as a "Mammy" type of song by Al Jolson.[22] Her 1920 *Ainslee's* review of *Come Seven*, a comedy by Octavus Roy Cohen based on his *Saturday Evening Post* stories of Negro life, calls the play "amusing" and "entertaining," but criticizes it for using White actors in blackface to portray Negro characters: "The actors' portrayal of the negro [sic] race goes only as deep as a layer of burnt cork, and so, one cannot help but feel, does the author's." The result, explains Parker, is the portrayal of stereotypes:

> The comedy, while adroit and amusing, is less a picture of the negro than a picture postcard. The characters who appear in it are not of the colored race, but of the blackface race—the typical stage negroes, lazy, luridly dressed, addicted to crap shooting, and infallibly mispronouncing every word of more than three syllables [sic].[23]

Parker makes it clear that the story of the Negro would be better portrayed by Negro writers and actors. She ends her review highly critical of Cohen: "Mr. Cohen has been called the Montague Glass of the colored race, and the comparison is a happy one, save that he is far less flattering in his portrayal of the negro [sic] than is Mr. Glass in his delineation of the Jew."[24]

In her 1921 *Ainslee's* review of Eugene O'Neill's *The Emperor Jones*, Parker commends "the superb performance of Charles Gilpin, a negro [sic] actor, in the title role." She laments the length of time it took Gilpin to be given this opportunity, and speaks of the neglect of Negro actors in general:

> In no way are our producers more wasteful of genius than in their regard of negro actors. What has become of Opal Cooper, who some seasons ago appeared with the Negro Players? Since that time, his opportunities have probably consisted of an offer to play one-fourth of a quartet in an uptown cabaret, and a chance to don a white cotton wig and say "Gord bress you, Marse Robert," as an old family retainer in a heart-interest drama with its scene laid below the Thomas Dixon line [sic].[25]

Parker's pun on the Mason-Dixon Line, the "Thomas Dixon line," alludes to Thomas Dixon, whose racist novel, *The Clansman* (1905), became the basis for D. W. Griffith's film, *Birth of a Nation* in 1915. Parker might also have had in mind Augustus Thomas, a popular playwright in the early 1900s whose vacuous plays were often set in the South, and whose politics leaned toward the conservative. With this single, simple allusion, Parker creates a devastating analysis: Any play set "below the Thomas Dixon line" is racist and lacks even the substance found in Thomas's vacuous plays. A further implication is that the content overall of plays using offensive racial stereotypes offers nothing of value.[26] Like racial stereotypes, type-casting of African American actors becomes a target of Parker's critical pen.

Two other works, the poem "The Dark Girl's Rhyme" and the story "Arrangement in Black and White," provide another glimpse of Parker's interaction with racial issues. Published in 1926, "The Dark Girl's Rhyme" uses a female speaker and a short measure, a variant of the ballad stanza, to recount how racial difference prevents a love affair between a White man and "a dark girl." Parker's poem might be usefully compared with Ralph Waldo Emerson's "The Rommany Girl," a ballad that addresses racial and cultural differences, and interracial love from the point of view of the female gypsy speaker. The similarities suggest that Emerson's poem might have served as a model for Parker, but differences regarding racial identity exist. Although the actual races in Parker's poem are not named, they are alluded to in ways that are revealing and at times disturbing. I read the male figure as White by implication; he stands in contrast to the dark girl as the object of her forbidden love. He was "Of a pious race," whereas the dark girl describes her ancestors as "folk of flood and flame," "them without a name," "silly stock," and:

> Devil-gotten sinners,
>   Throwing back their heads,
> Fiddling for their dinners,
>   Kissing for their beds.[27]

A moral lapse is associated with the dark girl's family echoing the nineteenth-century association of sexual promiscuity with dark-skinned people.[28] The poem makes economic differences a factor as well. While the dark girl's family travels aimlessly "Up and down a mountain," suggesting a kind of gypsy existence and casting further doubt as to the precise identification of the girl's race, the man is found "in a marketplace" and harvesting crops. This brings up the issue of the poem's setting overall. Unlike most of Parker's poems, the setting here is rural, not urban; premodern, not contemporary. "Sires" and "hags," along with "a-springing" and "a-swinging," add relatively archaic sounds and images to the setting. Perhaps these strategies were intended to mask or soften the poem's modern and volatile subject of interracial love. The poem's closing stanzas —

> Not a one had seen us
>   Wouldn't help him flee,

Angry ran between us
Blood of him and me.

How shall I be mating
Who have looked above —
Living for a hating,
Dying of a love?[29]

— both validate interracial love, and record its impossibility due to the prejudice of others. It is not anger that exists between the two would-be lovers, but the adjective "Angry," referring to the attitudes of others who would observe such a love match. The poem implies a moral lesson rather than states one—an issue I discuss further in upcoming chapters—through its use of blurred racial identity and possible stereotyping.

"Arrangement in Black and White," published in 1927, offers a pointedly different approach to stereotypes. The story uses dramatic irony to expose a woman's racism, and her own blindness to it, during a party where she hopes to meet a famous African American singer named Walter Williams. The woman's conversation with the party hostess consists of a series of gaffs—"Well, I think you're simply marvelous, giving this perfectly marvelous party for him, and having him meet all these white people, and all. Isn't he terribly grateful?"[sic]; "Isn't it marvelous, the way they all have music in them? It just seems to be right in them"; "You know, so many colored people, you give them an inch, and they walk all over you. But he doesn't try any of that"; and "Oh, wait till I tell Burton I called him 'Mister'!"—which intensify when she finally speaks with Walter Williams. She almost uses the epithet "nigger" when she learns from Williams that an actress she believed to be White is actually Black. The nameless female guest and her absent husband, Burton—who she says "is really awfully fond of colored people. Well, he says to himself, he wouldn't have white servants"[sic]—typify racist attitudes and hypocrisy. The story also mocks the voyeurism associated with White interest in primitivism during the 1920s. Arthur F. Kinney reports that the story was based on an incident with Paul Robeson, but given the reference to light skin color and the name Walter Williams, Parker also may have had in mind Bert Williams, the Black performer forced to perform in blackface.[30]

Both the epithet and primitivism become issues in Parker's subsequent work. Early in 1928 Parker published her story "A Terrible Day

Tomorrow" in the *New Yorker*.[31] This dialogue uses dramatic irony to provide a profile of a nameless alcoholic in denial; he vows to go on the wagon as he orders drink after drink for himself and his female companion. As his intoxication increases, he becomes impatient with the service at the speakeasy: "'What's the matter, can't I get a drink here? Am I a nigger or something?'" The use of the offensive epithet by this protagonist associates racism with his deteriorating condition, but Parker must have been uncomfortable about its use after the fact; she left this story out of her collections. Given her reputation for drinking, perhaps she feared readers would link the story's use of the epithet with her personal beliefs. Later that year, Parker used the occasion of a book review to criticize the voyeurism perpetuated by Carl Van Vechten. Her review of Claude McKay's *Home to Harlem* speaks to her sensitivity about racial issues. "We needed, and we needed badly," she writes in "The Compleat Bungler," "a book about Harlem Negroes by a Negro. . . . Mr. McKay's novel seems to me a vitally important addition to American letters. And for his easily achieved feat of putting even further into their place the writings of Mr. Carl Van Vechten, I shall be grateful to him from now on."[32] Parker's call for authenticity echoes that of Black intellectuals of the period such as Alain Locke, though it is not known if the two ever met.

Biographers of Parker have told us much about her White Algonquin friends, but very little about her contact with Black culture. As the above discussion suggests, her earliest exposure to Black culture, outside of hotel and family maids, may have been through Black drama, though initially that drama was written by White playwrights. Cohen and O'Neill were not the only Whites to depict Negro life on stage; Ridgley Torrence, Ernest H. Culbertson, Paul Green, and Lucy White did so as well. With the exception of Cohen, their plays, using Black dialect and at times containing Mammy figures we might now read as problematic stereotypes, were celebrated by Black intellectuals of the twenties for their realism and contribution to Negro drama. Alain Locke and Montgomery Gregory included them in their 1927 anthology *Plays of Negro Life*, but it is not known if Parker read this anthology or Locke's other important collection published in 1925, *The New Negro*. She likely read, however, articles by her editors and her Algonquin cohorts—H. L. Mencken, Haywood Hale Broun, and Alexander Woollcott—that praised Negro theater or promoted Negro causes. And as Ann Douglas and Sascha Feinstein have shown, Black cultural productions in theater, music, poetry, and prose were permeating the culture at large.[33] Even without evidence to the contrary, it would be difficult if not impossible for Parker not to be influenced by these events.

How, then, do we understand Parker's use of stereotypes in "Mrs. Hofstadter on Josephine Street" and "Clothe the Naked"? Both of these stories were written in the 1930s when Parker's politics and literary interests were geared to the left, when she believed literature should be in service to humanity. Taken together, they provide an interesting study of how Parker attempted to negotiate political issues concerning race, class, and gender on artistic grounds, and how her negotiations became linked with the sentimental infection.

"Mrs. Hofstadter on Josephine Street," published in the *New Yorker* in 1934 and added to *The Portable Dorothy Parker* ten years later, brings together White, Black, and Jewish characters. A White couple trying to hire quiet, domestic help end up with a happy but overly talkative and inept Black male house servant named Horace Wrenn. One reading of Horace is that he is a step-'n'-fetch-it stereotype; several elements in the story also link him to the South. The fact that Horace is employed by a man from the "Old South," whom the narrator-wife refers to as "the Colonel" aligns Horace's paid-for service with slavery. He claims to make the traditional Southern drink, a mint julep, though he uses neither bourbon nor mint. Horace also wears white, a conventional color for house servant clothing, but also indicative of Horace's efforts to whiten himself, since he claims, "I don't hold nothing against the colored race, but Horace just doesn't mix with them, that's all." He proudly announces that his daughter is "taken for white every day of the week" [*sic*] and that his sister, a hairdresser, "never touches a colored head." This prompts the narrator to recall a Jewish man who anglicized his name: "Nothing ever became of him," she tells herself, suggesting that the price for denying one's cultural identity is obliteration. Horace also appears to be rejecting his own race, but he doesn't fit into the White world either. The story's title becomes Horace's refrain of self-justification: Mrs. Hofstadter on Josephine Street was his former employer who, according to Horace, didn't know how she was "going to get along without Horace."[34] His poor performance and constant chatter leads to his firing by the Colonel, however, discrediting that point of view.

What were Parker's intentions in creating this contact zone between White, Black, and Jewish identities? She certainly implies an analogy between Black and Jewish assimilation into White culture. Kinney suggests, however, that Parker was uncomfortable with the racial implications of this story; she revised it several times. The original *New Yorker* version of the story contained direct statements of the narrator's hatred toward Horace, countered with a defense that race was not the issue: "Horace's design and status were no matter; black, white, or polka-dotted, cook or ambassador to the court of St. James's, I should have hated him" [*sic*]. She also passes judgment on hatred in general; it "stuns you, dumbs you, renders you sick and silent."[35] These statements and others, as Kinney points out, were removed when the story was included in the 1944 and 1973 editions of *The Portable Dorothy Parker*. Perhaps she feared her direct statements of hatred would be considered racially offensive, or, as in the case of "A Terrible Day Tomorrow," perhaps she thought readers would associate her remarks with her personal beliefs. Or perhaps she deleted them for aesthetic reasons; she wanted to reduce the story's didacticism.

The protagonist's name itself, however, may shed some light on the story's purpose. Many of Parker's character names contain puns or allusions to historical, contemporary, or literary figures, and Horace Wrenn is no exception. "Horace," of course, alludes to the Latin satiric poet whose realism and irony—the persona of the satirist is mocked as well as his victims—became, as Kinney tells us, an important model for Parker.[36] "Wrenn" likely alludes to the English architect Sir Christopher Wren, whose life spanned the late seventeenth and early eighteenth centuries, a period in which Horace's work greatly influenced British culture. Rather than influential, however, the "work" of Parker's Horace Wrenn, with its pretentious mannerisms and unappealing food, becomes the focus of mockery. The Colonel and his wife are also victims of Parker's satire, for they are domestically inept without a servant, and incapable of hiring a competent one. In a world where Horace Wrenn's employment options are limited to service work, he becomes a symbol of cultural degeneration. John O'Hara, in a review of the 1944 *Portable*, praises the story, writing in the *New York Times Book Review* that "Miss Parker and Miss Parker alone, could have reported (and I'm quite sure it's reporting) on a Horace Wrenn without infuriating Negroes and whites" [*sic*][37] O'Hara's comment prompts two observations. First, we can't be certain how O'Hara, a White critic, would know that African American readers might not be offended by Horace Wrenn's portrayal, regardless of Parker's satiric models. Second, if we accept at face value O'Hara's autobiographical reading of the story, we may simplify or miss its complicated nature. Parker presents an unflattering portrait of one race serving another, and touches on the importance of cul-

tural identity in a way that prefigures late twentieth-century attention
to multicultural issues. Yet by using a stereotype, she teeters uncomfortably in her efforts to explore racial issues. How could she write
about African American characters without relying on stereotypes or
falling prey to the Van Vechten voyeurism she detested? Despite her
good intentions, the answer seems to allude her in cases such as these.

Published in 1938, "Clothe the Naked" explores the intersection
of gender, race, and capitalist economics, but does so through the
use of Aunt Jemima and Sambo stereotypes. The story's protagonist,
"Big Lannie," is an obese, impoverished, African-American laundress
who depends on Mrs. Delabarre Ewing and other upper-class, racist
White women for employment. She raises her blind grandson
Raymond who, despite life's difficulties, is always smiling and content. Chapter 4 offers more detailed analysis of this story and an alternative reading of its use of stereotypes; here it is the story's reception
and its connection to the charge of sentimentality that is of interest.
Neither the *New Yorker*, one of Parker's more frequent publishing venues, nor *Harper's* would publish it; Meade reports that *Scribner's* finally
took it in 1938. As Keats notes, "magazine editors did not want her to
speak to the condition of man. They wanted the wry, witty, and sophisticated Dorothy Parker to amuse them, and this enraged her."
When the story appeared in the collected volume *Here Lies* in 1939,
Florence Haxton Britten singled it out for criticism: "This story of a
blind colored child whose heart is broken by the ridicule of other
children when he steps out all innocently bedecked in Mr. Ewing's
discarded full-dress coat is sixteen pages of saturate sentimentality
unmitigated by any hard reserves of common sense save for a sardonic portrait of the complacently charitable Mrs. Ewing, who gave
the offending coat to the black boy's gran" [*sic*]. Kinney later seems
to refute that argument when he writes, "The story is not so much
sentimental as it is angry," a description nevertheless suggesting runaway emotion. Both Keats and Kinney appreciate the story, though
Kinney argues that "the case of race is unnecessary." Accusing Parker
of a lack of imagination, Meade claims, "Dorothy had no conflicts
over artistic integrity. Without prompting, she was inspired to produce dutifully proletarian stories. . . . [It] is a dull, heavy-handed mani-
festo."[38] Considered collectively, these responses to "Clothe the Naked"
link sentimentality with Parker's political interests, a critical move
that undercuts the seriousness of her work overall. Are the commentators above reading Parker's stereotypes as a sentimental fallacy? They
do not specifically define them as such, but they correctly recognize

Parker's project as one in sympathy with the African-American characters in the story. Thus, the stereotypes are not intended to be offensive, even if in reality they are.

Parker is also aware of and disturbed by her ability to use racial epithets in her personal life. In 1942 she wrote a long letter to Alexander Woollcott describing the Philadelphia enlistment office where her husband, Alan Campbell, was being inducted into the army. She includes a series of comments concerning race, ranging from sympathy to aggression. In what could potentially be described as a "sentimental" moment by friends or biographers, Parker recounts her tears at seeing one of the men volunteering to join the army, "a tall, thin young Negro . . . carrying a six-inch square of muslin in which were his personal effects. It looked so exactly like a bean bag. . . . That, of course has nothing to do with war. Except, also of course, that a man who had no more than that was going to fight for it." Later she notes how, on that particular day, the recruits are largely White Anglo-Saxon. Finally, Parker describes her anger at a Jewish woman there who referred to the new recruits as "'poor suckers caught in the draft.'" Parker, who supported the war and was proud of Campbell's volunteering, responded by calling the woman a "Sheeny bitch," and was then repulsed by her action and its implications: "The horror lies in the ease with which it came to me—And worse horror lies in the knowledge that if she had been black, I would have said 'You nigger bitch'—Dear God. The things I have fought against all my life. And that's what I did." [*sic*][39]

We can admire Parker's honesty here even as we acknowledge that at times her writing about racial issues was clumsy or inconsistent. Were writers less sensitive, less aware of the problems of racial stereotyping in the twenties, thirties, and forties than we are in the nineties? If White writers were, Black writers and intellectuals were not. Montgomery Gregory, whose article "The Drama of Negro Life" appeared in Alain Locke's *The New Negro*, notes the "tremendous sentimental interest in the black population of the south," and goes on to chart the "descent from sentimentalism to grotesque comedy," a move that leads to the use of caricatures and stereotypes of Blacks[*sic*].[40] This link between the sentimental and the use of racial stereotypes represents the sentimental infection at its worst. Both Locke and Gregory called for realism to counter this tendency. Perhaps Parker thought she was offering realism, though it is worthwhile to recall the tendency to generalize in much of her work. Her popular "Hate Songs" were invectives against types of people—actresses, husbands, bohemians, etc.—not individuals. And the nameless characters in many of her stories also are intended to represent types: insincere lovers, alcoholics, upper-class snobs, or hypocrites. The line between generalization and racial stereotype is, in the words of W. E. B. Du Bois, the "color line." Parker may not have been aware that she crossed it.

Clearly, Parker was a writer positioned in and reflecting a racist culture. A comment made by Sandra A. Zagarell about Harriet Beecher Stowe in her review of Joan D. Hedrick's *Harriet Beecher Stowe: A Life* may apply to Parker. Both Stowe and Parker wrote for race reform, yet had Black servants. Perhaps Parker, like Stowe, was to some degree invested in her era's ideologies about race.[41] Or perhaps it is fair to say that Parker's good intentions could not always counter the pervasive racism around her. Perhaps at times there was a certain amount of thoughtlessness in her selections, of insensitivity in the expediency of humor, shadowing her genuine concern for the unfortunate plight of others. As for Parker's politics as a whole, for them to be based in sentimentality she would have to be more concerned with her own emotional state over the issues than with the issues themselves. Her course of action over the years, all at the risk of losing her reputation and livelihood, suggests this is not the case.

THE SENTIMENTAL INFECTION IN PARKER'S WORK

With all the suspicion cast on Parker's personal feelings and politics, it comes as no surprise that she would be accused of parlaying her sentiments into art, to the detriment of the latter. Kinney claims Parker's inability to keep emotion in check came at a cost, that "her price in her own work was to move toward sentimentality." Parker's "personal struggle with runaway emotion," argues Ross Labrie, "is uncomfortably apparent in some of her work, as it was even more uncomfortably apparent in her life. The slope toward sentimentality was always to be reckoned with." Excessive sentiment, then, seemed to be the link between Parker's self-dramatization and her literary work. Meade argues that Parker's "largely false" claim of a deprived childhood, and her version of herself as an unloved orphan, were based on Dickensian melodrama, and provided self-justification for the rude cleverness that became Parker's literary hallmark. Autobiography, sentiment, and art again intersect in Meade's biography, when she recounts Donald Stewart's impression that in any relationship, Parker was more concerned with "'her emotion; she was not worrying about your emotion.'" Meade thus interprets the significance of this passage in terms of literary production: "While striking fancy poses and whipping herself into an emotional frenzy got her adrenaline moving, that white-hot heat also served a serious purpose; it generated salable verse and enabled her to deposit checks into her bank account."[42]

The cruelest attack against Parker, which entwined personal, political, and poetical aspects, came from a writer and colleague she greatly admired: Ernest Hemingway. The critique came in the form of a satirical poem, "To a Tragic Poetess," written in Paris in 1926 during Parker's first trip to Europe. It was read aloud to a gathering of friends that did not include Parker, but according to Keats, Parker found out about the poem and was hurt by it. Anyone familiar with the life of Hemingway, with his 1964 memoir, *Moveable Feast*, or with Sandra Gilbert and Susan Gubar's discussion of him in Volume 1 of *No Man's Land*, will recall Hemingway's tendency to direct venom against those who had helped and admired him, and one could argue that Parker, like Gertrude Stein and many others, was simply "fair game." Since Hemingway is known as a fiction writer rather than as a poet, it might be questionable how much influence his poetic invective has had. Given, however, the amount of scholarship, anthologizing, and classroom time Hemingway's work has received in contrast to Parker's, it would be impossible to discount his influence altogether.

As Gilbert and Gubar point out, "To a Tragic Poetess" mocks Parker's suicide attempts by comparing them to the "successful suicides of men who seemed destroyed by female indifference."[43] But Hemingway attacks as well Parker's sentiment and her validity as a writer in such a way that the two become inseparable. The poem opens with Parker's suicide attempts, and the implication that these attempts were meant to fail is clear:

> Oh thou who with a safety razor blade
> a new one to avoid infection
> Slit both thy wrists
> the scars defy detection
> Who over-veronaled to try and peek
> into the shade
> Of that undistant country from whose bourne
> no traveller returns who hasn't been there.

But always vomited in time
and bound your wrists up[44]

Indeed, Meade provides evidence that Parker's suicide attempts were
intended to be discovered in time; in 1922 she ordered a meal to be
delivered to her room right before she cut her wrists; in 1926 she
hurled a glass through a window shortly after taking an overdose of
veronal. She adds that one of Parker's Round Table friends, Marc
Connelly, dismissed at least one of the suicide attempts as sentimentality, calling it "'a little bit of theater, a young lady's concept of Victorian melodrama. Coffins and all that, you know.'"[45]

Both Keats and Meade have linked Parker's first suicide attempt
with her depression over her abortion in 1922, so Hemingway's poem
appears to be biographically accurate.[46] But by juxtaposing the abortion and his perception of Parker's sentiments, Hemingway negates
not only the real trauma felt by Parker, but the inherent politics of
her act—reproductive rights for women, an issue politicized in the
first decades of this century by such women as Emma Goldman and
Margaret Sanger. Furthermore, the poem links the act of abortion
with sentiment:

To tell how you could see his little hands
already formed
You'd waited months too long
That was the trouble.
But you loved dogs and other people's children
and hated Spain where they are cruel to donkeys.
Hoping the bulls would kill the matadors.[47]

Certainly one reading of this passage is that Hemingway views Parker's
love for "other people's children" as sentimental since she is not having one of her own. He further attacks her sensibility, and betrays his
own ignorance of how humor functions in the face of death, by criti-
cizing her for making "a joke about a funeral passing in the rain / It
gave no pain / because you did not know the people." The poem
then connects the abortion with Parker's work. After stating that
Parker returns to Paris from Spain "to write more poems for the *New
Yorker,*" Hemingway returns, in a taunting, malicious tone, to the abortion:

To celebrate in borrowed cadence
your former gnaw and itch for Charley

who went away and left you not so flat behind him
And it performed so late those little hands
those well formed little hands
And were there little feet and had
the testicles descended?[48]

Hemingway's assumption that the fetus was male (biographers have not confirmed this) fits snugly with the poem's theme of women's cruelty to men—a woman driving her grandfather to suicide and a boy exploding a stick of dynamite in his mouth "for love," both of which could easily pass for melodrama in "To a Tragic Poetess." Louis Kronenberger claims Hemingway "was hardboiled to conceal the fact that he was hopelessly sentimental."[49] Yet Hemingway accuses Parker of using her own pain to create an emotional, unoriginal, superficial art, an art that "celebrate[s] in borrowed cadence."

The poem further invalidates Parker's experience as material for art when, after cataloging successful male suicides in Spain, it closes with: "Thus tragic poetesses are made / by observation." Hemingway seems to be leveling a dual charge—that "tragic poetesses are made" either by dwelling in their own pain and emotion, essentially a charge of sentimentality similar to that made against Parker by Hemingway's friend Donald Stewart, or by the passive observation of the pain of others. It is a curious charge, coming from a writer whose novels often document personal and observed suffering. In Volume 1 of *No Man's Land*, Gilbert and Gubar link Hemingway's invective against women writers with that of male modernism in general, invoking a "battle of the sexes" paradigm for which they provide ample evidence. But Hemingway's poem as well as the other critiques of Parker's life and work also illustrate the difficulty with which modernists responded to the sentimental aesthetic.

Edmund Wilson offers another example of this difficulty. In his review of *Enough Rope* in the *New Republic*, Wilson appreciates Parker's vividness and distinct voice, but says few poems in the book were completely successful; he derogatorily links them with the sentimental tradition, saying many were "too deeply saturated with the jargon of ordinary feminine poetry . . . go in too much for plaintive Aprils, for red stains on velvet gowns and for 'pretty maids' and 'likely lads.'"[50] With the publication of *Sunset Gun* (1928) and *Death and Taxes* (1931), more direct charges of sentimentality would arise and would form, along with "To a Tragic Poetess" and anecdotes about Parker's sentimentality in life, a nexus of criticism that would eventually shadow her work as a whole. What empowers this critique is its connection to the broader critical context of American modernist literary criticism in which sentimentality is discredited. Thus, even a positive review offers limited affirmation if it acknowledges a sentimental quality in Parker's work.

Genevieve Taggard's generally positive review of *Enough Rope* in the *New York Herald Tribune* locates a period of sentimentality in the poems. Taggard concludes: "The tragic, the ironic, and the sentimental all seem to have been temporary disguises or successive phases" from which Parker moved beyond in the second section. Other critics, however, believe Parker's work continues to use elements of sentimentality. Henry Morton Robinson writes that *Sunset Gun* contains the best of her work so far, but he notes the repetitive "sentimental stage" she uses for her poems. When Edith Walton writes, in her review of *Sunset Gun,* that Parker is "willing, at times, to pluck a string of genuine emotion," she implies that at other times, Parker's emotion is less than genuine, or sentimental. Similarly, Lynn Z. Bloom seems at first to offer an antisentimental reading of Parker's poetry when she writes that Parker "undermines her sentiment with cynical punch lines, either one-liners or couplets," only to undercut this position later by stating that as a collection, "the cynical persona and comic tone suggest verbal ingenuity rather than authentic emotion or experience."[51] Inauthentic emotion, of course, is synonymous with sentimentality.

Critics also find Parker's mix of hard-hearted cleverness and sweetness paradoxical and disarming. Louis Kronenberger claims Parker's poetry is "a constant shuttling between sentimentality and cynicism" and that "the high technical polish of her sentimental poems makes them artificial; there is nothing more incongruous than studied heartbreak." Both Robinson and Walton note Parker's ability to reconcile pain and flippancy, but do not discuss it in detail. Critics who knew Parker often dealt with the paradox by drawing parallels between her life and her work. When Alexander Woollcott, in "Our Mrs. Parker," characterizes her "so odd a blend of Little Nell and Lady Macbeth," and her work "so potent a distillation of nectar and wormwood, of ambrosia and deadly nightshade," he is suggesting a Dickensian sentimentality in her personality that parallels the "nectar" and "ambrosia" of her work.[52] William Rose Benét, married to Parker's friend Elinor Wylie, loves Parker's work but suggests it is a critic's nightmare:

You cannot put it into a particular pigeonhole. It is a perfect represen-
tation of the author, who is a paradox. A moth-gray cloak of demure-
ness hiding spangled ribaldry, a razor-keen intellect mocking a heart
dark with desperation. . . . What the devil can you do with such a girl?[53]

By this time the "girl" was thirty-five years old; Benét's use of the term,
coupled with his critical indecisiveness, weakens an otherwise positive review in the face of a growing male literary establishment. Similarly, Henry Seidel Canby writes a positive review of *Death and Taxes*
but claims he is attempting no real criticism of Parker.[54]

A critical posture of "I like it but I don't know why" could hardly
stand against the more explicitly negative criticism being offered and
later perpetuated in the atmosphere of New Criticism. As mentioned
previously, Harold Rosenberg believes Parker's wit fails, and he links
that failure with sentiment, saying it typically "occurs when the last
line hangs a sophisticated conclusion on a hackneyed sentiment"
which, after a while, is no longer surprising. Like Hemingway in "To
a Tragic Poetess," Rosenberg denigrates Parker's feelings for having
served her popularity rather than the claims of serious poetry: "One
regrets her contentment with the easy rhythms, the banal feelings
and phrases, by means of which she has become a social personage
mentioned in the newspaper notes."[55] Clearly, Rosenberg's assessment
fails to consider the traditions from which Parker is working.

The charge of sentimentality continues as Parker's career progresses.
An anonymous reviewer for the *New Republic* claims *Death and Taxes*
inclined "more toward sentimentality gone sour than toward the sharp
mind hitting the center of an emotional situation with a sharp phrase."
Herbert M. McLuhan's 1945 indictment against Parker's poetry also
focuses on sentiment, and manages to insult both Parker and those
who read her. Both Parker and Edna St. Vincent Millay, argues
McLuhan, "exploit long-established poetic fashions, appealing to a
semi-alert audience which is glad to recognize hackneyed sentiment
in a chic . . . modern setting." Brendan Gill agrees in part; in his
introduction to the 1973 edition of the Viking *Portable Dorothy Parker*,
Gill claims that A. E. Housman was Parker's "true literary mentor,"
and that his irreverence about life "often moved Mrs. Parker to strike
just the wrong note of lofty, sentimental not-caring."[56]

Parker's fiction also is accused of sentimentality. In his review of
After Such Pleasures, T. S. Matthews remarks, "Specializing as she does
in the humor of heartbreak she is sometimes led astray into sentimental byways."[57] Writing for the *Nation*, Mina Curtiss condemns as

sentimental both Parker's fiction and her politics as seen in *Here Lies*. Curtiss opens her review with:

> "I think with all my heart," Mrs. Parker said last spring. . . . What Mrs. Parker thought with all her heart was that workers have a right to picket, a hardly radical view. . . . I am all for heart-thinking in any romantic field, but when it comes to social causes affecting the lives of millions of people, I feel that head-thinking is of more value. . . . Mrs. Parker writes with penetration, finality and compassion. But when she starts thinking with her heart about men and women in relation to social causes both her art and her logic desert her.[58]

Curtiss's focus on Parker's use of feeling implies a sentimental infection, but she later makes the connection clear. Finding both "Arrangement in Black and White" and "Clothe the Naked" flawed in their execution, Curtiss claims that "the confusion, the sentimentality arise from heart- rather than head-thinking, which defeats Mrs. Parker utterly when she writes about the idle rich."[59]

Another critic of Parker's from the 1930s—a highbrow critic publishing in a highbrow magazine—does more to damage Parker's literary reputation than perhaps all her reviewers combined. In an overview of Parker's work published in a 1934 issue of the *English Journal*, Mark Van Doren applies Aristotelian and New Critical standards of unity, wholeness, and close reading of only the text to assess Parker's accomplishments. Her poetry, Van Doren claims, has "its unity and its wholeness. . . . It is neat and clear, and it is mordant; it is also— and this may be the reason for its popularity—sentimental. The terrible Mrs. Parker turns out to have a heart after all, a heart dripping with tender tears and very conscious of itself." Since "the bulk of her poetry is thin and voiceless," Van Doren prefers Parker's fiction. For this category he assumes that bigger is better. His favorite monologue by Parker is "Sentiment," but he prefers her more fully narrated stories—"Horsie," "Glory in the Daytime," and "Big Blonde"—and hopes one day she will write a satiric novel. Her best fiction, however, still falls short in Van Doren's estimation: "She is not a master even here, since she does not deal with any very great or significant area of life." Van Doren manages to belittle not only Parker's subject matter and technique, but those who read her work and like it.[60]

Two years later, Margaret Lawrence, in *The School of Femininity* (1936), offers a similarly damning assessment. Lawrence places under the rubric of sentimentality any emotion or desire for social change. Despite Parker's brevity and cleverness, observes Lawrence, her fiction

> is utterly sentimental. She is striving with her time. She hates a lot of what she sees. Only the sentimentalist ever strives with any time. Only the sentimentalist ever hates anything. The sentimentalist wants things to be different . . . [and] perfect. . . . The sentimentalist believes that things can be brought nearer perfection, and accordingly spends an amount of energy trying to bring it to pass.[61]

Lawrence is right about one thing—Parker did want "things to be different," as evidenced by both her political and creative work. But Lawrence's definition of the sentimentalist reflects a conservative, perhaps anticommunist bias directed toward writing by some critics in the 1930s. Her definition of sentimentality nevertheless conforms to an observation made by Suzanne Clark: "the term 'sentimental' makes a shorthand for everything modernism would exclude, the other of its literary/nonliterary dualism."[62] Works with feeling or political undertones did not belong in the canon.

Although he recommended *After Such Pleasures* to Louise Bogan, Edmund Wilson, in a *New Yorker* review of the 1944 *Portable Dorothy Parker*, states her short stories are "sometimes sentimental."[63] This criticism rises again in 1969 with the publication of Lillian Hellman's *An Unfinished Woman*. Hellman praises "Big Blonde," claims she's not an intelligent critic of her friends, and then comments on Parker's contempt for the behavior of the rich, a theme recurring in her fiction:

> But she wrote it too often in sentimental short stories about the little dressmaker or the servant as they are patronized by the people Dottie had dined with the night before. It was her way of paying back the rich and powerful, and if it is understandable in life it is too raw and unshaded in literature. . . . Her "put them in their place" stories are often undigested, the conclusions there on the first page.[64]

Despite its historical inaccuracies, *An Unfinished Woman* was a widely read, popular memoir, as the movie that sprang from it, *Julia*, would indicate. Thus, its negative response to Parker's sentiment would find a large audience.

Arthur F. Kinney's assessment of Parker's fiction mirrored his assessment of her life and poetry; it has its moments of success and moments of failure due to sentimentality. At times he emphasizes the latter, as in his preface to *Dorothy Parker*, where he mentions Parker's sentimentality twice in two pages: "Although her work is softer and more sentimental than, say, the stories of Bernard Malamud, there is still present some of the hardness and pity Irving Howe finds in *The Magic Barrel*'; and, "She could be sentimental in her fiction and conversational in her essays." Later in his study he states, "When Dorothy Parker is careless, her work goes flat, words function unequally, and her attitude can collapse into sentimentality," and agrees with Ann Springer of the *Boston Evening Transcript* who "alluded to Dorothy Parker's sentimentality . . . and it is a proper charge against 'The Custard Heart,' a story reminiscent of 'A Certain Lady.'"[65] Kinney confirms the critical label previously conferred on Parker by reviewers and other critics. It is a damaging indictment, given the fact that Kinney's was the first book-length study of Parker's work.

CONCLUSION

The pattern of response to Parker's work, from celebration to an increasing concern with sentimentality, suggests evolving critical priorities rather than a drastic change in Parker's work. These evolving priorities, of course, resulted from the increasing influence of a modernist criticism largely initiated by I. A. Richards, Ezra Pound, and T. S. Eliot, and later perpetuated by Allen Tate, Cleanth Brooks, John Crowe Ransom, and Robert Penn Warren, which not only privileged the literary work as an object of art stripped of context, but simplified and negated the sentimental tradition.

While "close readings" of texts have their place in literary studies (indeed, I use them here), modernist criticism ignored elements of the relationship between author, text, and reader. "No discourse," Suzanne Clark argues in *Sentimental Modernism*, "can escape appealing to the emotions of its audience . . . [or] escape some relationship with its readers' narcissism or its readers' nostalgia; no criticism can be so objective that it avoids calling up the issues of ideology and subjectivity in its appeal to its audience."[66] Yet this is the very condition that modernist criticism struggled to deny. It can be no coincidence that the charge of sentimentality against Parker increases as high modernist values gain a foothold among intellectuals in and out of the academy.

This chapter has presented two conduits of critical response: book reviews by Parker's contemporaries, and later assessments by biographers and critics who would—and frequently did—take into account contextual issues. Yet what their accounts have given us is an example of contextual emphasis gone astray. Where Parker's contemporary critics responded to the modernist rejection of the sentimental, her biographers drew upon those responses as well as their own unexamined rejection of the sentimental to create a narrow frame through which to read Parker's life and work. Her complicated response to racial issues illustrates what is lost by reading her through such a frame. To dismiss Parker's work as sentimental is no longer valid. As chapter 1 made clear, we now have the critical tools and insights to see her work in a much broader context—that of the nineteenth-century sentimental tradition.

3

The Sentimental Connection I:
Dorothy Parker's Poetry
and the Sentimental Tradition

Born in 1893, Dorothy Parker lived her first eight years during the Victorian era. She would come to poetry during the first decade of the twentieth century when women poets were going through what Louise Bogan in *Achievement in American Poetry* calls a "transition" from older to bolder poetic forms and content. Like any period of transition, rejected works and the values they represent would still be in circulation, and would become part of the discourse of literary debate in the early part of the twentieth century. Even if Parker read no nineteenth-century American women poets, a highly unlikely scenario for a young woman interested in poetry at the turn of the century, she may have absorbed elements of the American tradition via her known reading of its British counterpart. Despite cultural differences between Great Britain and the United States, their nineteenth-century sentimental literatures share certain basic characteristics: romance, moral imperative, cultural critique, and a simplistic duality of good and evil. Also, as David Perkins points out, American literary culture was still highly influenced by Great Britain at the turn of the century, so that a literary cross-fertilization of sorts was taking place.[1]

Parker did not keep a reading notebook, so we can only speculate which American women writers she might have read. Three anthologies of women poets had been published in 1848 and 1849; if these were not in circulation at the turn of the century, an influential collection that based its female selections on the earlier anthologies— E. C. Stedman's *An American Anthology, 1787–1900* (1900)—was available.[2] We do know, however, one of the nineteenth-century British women poets she read. Parker summarized for Marion Capron part of her reading at the Blessed Sacrament Academy in New York, where she attended school from 1900 to 1907: "At my convent we did have a textbook, one that devoted a page and a half to Adelaide Ann Proctor [*sic*]." Procter, who lived from 1825 to 1864, is described in the *Oxford Companion to English Literature* as the British author of "popular sentimental (and often morbid) verse."[3] It is impossible to know how much of Procter's poetry Parker read; "a page and a half" does not suggest much, but Procter's two-volume collection, *Legends and Lyrics*, had been available since 1858. Also, the fact that Parker recalled Procter late in her life suggests Procter left an impression.

Some of Procter's poems share formal and thematic characteristics with Parker's that are hard to ignore. Both poets often use the ballad form, frequently write about love and death, and at times offer instruction to their readers. Procter's "A Tryst with Death" describes a desire for death from the point of view of someone who is perhaps old or ill, as the first two stanzas indicate:

> I am footsore and very weary
> But I travel to meet a friend;
> The way is long and dreary,
> But I know that it soon must end.
>
> He is travelling fast like the whirlwind,
> And though I creep slowly on,
> We are drawing nearer, nearer,
> And the journey is almost done.[4]

Procter expresses little doubt that the desire for death will be met. Parker's death poems as a whole tend to be complicated by other factors. At times the poems express a desire for suicide due to the end of a love affair or a dissatisfaction with life in general, as in "Rhyme Against Living" and "Coda." In other poems, such as "The Trifler," death embodies a decadent eroticization, that is, death becomes the desired lover.[5] A sensibility informed by the decadent aestheticism of the 1890s separates Procter and Parker, but its preoccupation with death is nevertheless a focus that Procter and Parker share.

Procter's "A Love Token" suggests another possible comparison concerning the relative value of love. The poem opens with the question, "Do you grieve no costly offering / To the Lady you can make?" The speaker then instructs the lover to "Take a heart of virgin silver" and "Fashion it" with dreams, fancies, fears, daring, and tears, and then to "lay your offering / At the Lady's feet." The poem's last stanza, however, carries in it the rueful tone that ends many of Parker's "love" poems:

> Should her mood perchance be gracious —
> With disdainful smiling pride,
> She will place it with the trinkets
> Glittering at her side.[6]

One reading of Procter's poem is that it makes a moral judgment: the woman rejects the lover out of pride, and thus is unworthy of the love being offered. Yet the poem also casts suspicion on love itself since its value is relative; one lover's sincere love is another lover's emotional "trinket." Certainly this axiom operates in many of Parker's poems. The speaker in Parker's "Ballade at Thirty-Five," where every stanza ends with "I loved them until they loved me," expresses a similar note of nonchalance about love, as does "The Thin Edge":

> With you my heart is quiet here
> And all my thoughts are cool as rain.
> I sit and let the shifting year
> Go by before the window-pane,
> And reach my hand to yours, my dear . . .
> I wonder what it's like in Spain.[7]

An important difference is that "The Thin Edge," like many of Parker's poems, is in the first person, with the speaker relaying her own experience rather than trying to specifically instruct a second party, as is the case in "A Love Token." Exceptions can be found, however, in Parker's "To a Much Too Unfortunate Lady," "Chant for Dark Hours," "Unfortunate Coincidence," "Social Note," "For an Unknown Lady," "Prologue to a Saga," "For a Favorite Granddaughter," "Superfluous Advice," and "For a Lady Who Must Write Verse." These instructional poems are typically known for their wit, for their "tough-girl" attitude toward the disappointments of life and love, as in "Prologue to a Saga":

> Maidens, gather not the yew,
>   Leave the glossy myrtle sleeping;
> Any lad was born untrue,
>   Never a one is fit your weeping.
>
> Pretty dears, your tumult cease;
>   Love's a fardel, burthening double.

Clear your hearts, and have you peace—
Gangway, girls: I'll show you trouble.[8]

The irony in the poem—the speaker offers advice that she fails to follow herself—gives this poem a modern flavor, yet the desire to offer advice and instruction, even if by a bad example rather than by a morally superior position, echoes that of Procter. The language in the poem illustrates another area where the works of Procter and Parker intersect through the use of archaic words that would have been familiar to Procter's readers—"maidens," "lad," "fardel," "burthening." These words are in contrast to Parker's more modern diction—"Gangway, Girls: I'll show you trouble"—and assist Parker's satire on female romantic suffering. They nevertheless suggest a confluence of styles rather than a strictly twentieth-century or modern one. Parker's archaic diction also provides evidence that she was familiar with nineteenth-century poetry.

Thanks to the work of a number of feminist scholars, we can acknowledge the literary parallels between Parker and Procter as something other than a "negative influence." This chapter provides an overview of the characteristics of nineteenth-century women's poetry developed by feminist scholars that make such comparisons possible. An application of their observations to the relationship between Parker's poetry and that of her nineteenth-century American predecessors follow.

CHARACTERISTICS OF NINETEENTH-CENTURY WOMEN POETS

Feminist critics have approached nineteenth-century women's literature in one of two ways: a comprehensive survey that attempts to draw all women into a broad tradition, or a focus on writers who fit a particular, but perhaps not the only, tradition. Neither of these approaches is entirely satisfactory on its own, yet when combined they provide a range of useful characteristics that offer us a basis for comparing nineteenth- and twentieth-century poetry.

The comprehensive approach to a women's tradition is perhaps best represented by the criticism of Emily Stipes Watts and of Sandra Gilbert and Susan Gubar. Watts's 1977 study, *The Poetry of American Women from 1632 to 1945*, provides a comprehensive survey of American women poets that speaks to the variety of poems produced. Certain subjects dominate the poetry written prior to the twentieth century: children, death, and domestic and moral themes. Significant exceptions exist, however, that will be echoed by women poets in the twentieth century. A few women wrote nativist poems, poems that praise George Washington, recount regional legends, describe Native Americans, or address social issues such as slavery and feminism. Some poets wrote about dissatisfaction with husbands or marriage, or used mythological figures to circumvent the moral imperative expected of their work. At least two poets, Frances Osgood and Ella Wheeler Wilcox, wrote a nineteenth-century version of sophisticated poetry that anticipates the work of Edna St. Vincent Millay and Dorothy Parker. Watts also outlines the similarities between Emily Dickinson's poetry and that of other nineteenth-century women poets, such as domestic imagery, chrysalis and butterfly imagery, feminine realism, the nursery rhyme quality of verse, the desire to communicate, appreciation for women and concern about their narrow roles, and a preoccupation with death, particularly with respect to suicide.[9]

Watts's book was followed in 1979 by *The Madwoman in the Attic*, in which Sandra Gilbert and Susan Gubar define a poetics of renunciation which they link to their neo-Bloomian concept of "anxiety of authorship." Their tradition includes both the fiction and poetry of mostly British and a few American women. Two of their observations are of particular use where Parker's relationship to her poetry is concerned. Victorian restrictions on female behavior made self-assertion a difficult task. Yet because self-assertion is one of the demands of lyric poetry, the woman poet finds herself in what Suzanne Juhasz calls a "double bind." The theme of renunciation found in much of the poetry by nineteenth-century women is an end-product of this "double bind." The Victorian woman's concept of herself as poet was further complicated by the fact that "verse writing became a genteel accomplishment in the Victorian period, an elegant hobby like sketching, piano-playing, or needlepoint." Thus, even if the woman poet considered her poetry a vocation, her readers would approach it as an avocation, and respond to it critically as a category of writing outside of serious poetry.[10] As we will see, Parker would adopt a similar attitude toward her poetry.

In the 1980s and early 1990s, Cheryl Walker expands the field of study with two critical books, *The Nightingale's Burden* and *Masks Outrageous and Austere*, and an anthology, *American Women Poets of the Nineteenth Century*. Rather than approaching tradition through a broad survey, Walker defines a tradition and deals only with those poets who best serve it. Walker claims her "nightingale tradition"—poems that are "ambivalent, personal, passionate lyrics claiming some special wisdom derived from female experience"—is the dominant tradition through the nineteenth century, and carries over in a slightly modified form into the twentieth. "The nightingale's theme, or burden," writes Walker, "is contrapuntal, fraught with ambivalence. Though it is antique to the degree that it approves accommodation, it is modern in the sense in which it betrays a divided mind." In form, these poems are rhymed and metered. Thematically, as Walker points out in her introduction to *American Women Poets of the Nineteenth Century*, the types of poems associated with this tradition include the free-bird poem, in which "the speaker rejects the model of rebellion and flight she has invoked"; the sanctuary poem, which expresses a desire for a protective realm; the forbidden lover poem; the power fantasy; and the secret sorrow poem. Within these poetic types, Walker also acknowledges exotic and nativist poems, a preoccupation with death and suicide, and the use of the language of gems and flowers.[11] As is clear from these types, Walker's concept of this poetry closely matches that of Gilbert and Gubar in its identification of renunciation as the overriding theme. The nightingale poets sang of their pain, but were unable to transcend or transform it.

Early twentieth-century poets, argues Walker in *Masks Outrageous and Austere*, ignored the lessons of their nineteenth-century foremothers, and thus repeat their mistakes. Walker argues that a twentieth-century woman's desire to write out of her particular circumstances and the limitations imposed on her by patriarchal culture converge, resulting in literary productions characterized by masks: Amy Lowell's androgyne, Sara Teasdale's passionate virgin, Elinor Wylie's woman warrior, Edna Millay's bodily spirit, H. D.'s Greek persona, and Louise Bogan's stoic. Each mask enables the writer to explore issues relating to women and power, but these masks, like the culture out of which they in part arise, also limit the poet's ability to envision alternative scripts. Despite some brave posturing, their call tends to be one of anger or despair rather than transformation. Thus to Walker's way of thinking, all of them fail due to their refusal or inability to transcend patriarchal constrictions, except H. D., who moves beyond the nightingale tradition in *The Trilogy* and *Helen in Egypt*. Dorothy Parker also fits into this problematic category of failure, for Walker adds without explication, "Though far from cool herself, Dorothy Parker's mordant wit is consistent with the stoic persona" of Louise Bogan.[12]

Many of Walker's observations remain useful, but I disagree with her application of "success" and "failure" to the poets she studies. Overcoming the limitations imposed on early twentieth-century women by patriarchal culture is not a valid measure of success. Walker judges these works according to standards arising from feminist criticism, theory, and ideology developed in the late twentieth century, conceptual tools women poets at the century's beginning did not have. The mask became a popular convention with early twentieth-century poets such as Yeats and Pound; using it would indicate a certain level of accomplishment for a woman poet. At the very least, these poets are successful insofar as their work reveals the conflicts that American culture has presented to women's literary production.

By focusing on poems that fit into her concept of the nightingale tradition, Cheryl Walker also obscures two important aspects of nineteenth-century literature: women's humor and literary decadence. In *A Very Serious Thing: Women's Humor and American Culture*, Nancy Walker tells us, "From the work of the mid-nineteenth-century Fanny Fern to that of Deanne Stillman in the 1980s, female humorists have issued tongue-in-cheek advice to readers—most commonly on how to deal with men."[13] Cheryl Walker includes a few humorous poems in her anthology of nineteenth-century women poets, but fails to incorporate humor into her discussion of twentieth-century nightingale poets in *Masks Outrageous and Austere*. Her strategy overlooks an important aspect of women's literary protest against culturally imposed limitations. Humor, of course, is the category in which Parker is best known, and an important link Parker has with nineteenth-century women poets. As for literary decadence, Walker acknowledges certain changes in fin de siècle women's poetry, such as an eroticization of death. However, other types of influences from this important, proto-modernist decade, involving imagery, color, tone, subject, and formal qualities, remain unsatisfactorily shadowed beneath her "nightingale" umbrella.

Aside from these reservations, the characteristics of nineteenth-century women poets found in the studies of Emily Stipes Watts, Sandra Gilbert and Susan Gubar, Cheryl Walker, and Nancy Walker not only reconstruct American women's literary history, but prove valuable in assessing the connections between Parker's poetry and that of her predecessors. Yet restricting a discussion of Parker's poetry to Cheryl Walker's poetic types, for example, would only prove the ways in which Parker does or does not fit into Walker's classification. Therefore, I have grouped the observations made by these scholars into four categories to serve as a basis for examining Parker's poetry. These categories—Poetics of Shared Conventions, The Boundary of Gentility, Gender Rigidity, and Dangerous Retreats— provide an efficient method of applying the shared and different per- spectives of the critics discussed above. More important, they illustrate patterns of connection between Parker's work and that of her nine- teenth-century predecessors. These patterns of connection include not only formal or aesthetic considerations, but thematic concerns reflecting cultural pressures or codes of behavior from the nineteenth century that persist into the twentieth century.

POETICS OF SHARED CONVENTIONS

The Poetics of Shared Conventions concerns those aspects of a poem that make it appealing to a mass audience—accessible language, fa- miliar subjects, and conventional form. This category includes the observations of both Emily Stipes Watts and Cheryl Walker regarding the sentimental poet's use of rhyme and meter, and her desire to communicate with the public at large. Nineteenth-century women poets, Walker tells us, "operat[ed] within the fixed boundary of a shared discourse."[14] Thus, this poetic is grounded in shared experi- ence and language between author and reader, both of which are factors where Parker's use of humor is concerned. Parker's wit, how- ever, cannot be limited to any one category.

We have already seen that Parker, like Adelaide Ann Procter, fre- quently uses the ballad form in her poetry. Cheryl Walker points out the dominance of conventional forms, of regular rhyme and meter as well as shared discourse, what Watts would call the "nursery rhyme quality," within the sentimental tradition.[15] Parker uses the free verse form in her parodies of free verse, her "Hymns of Hate" for *Life*, and her "Hate Songs" for *Vanity Fair*. She also experiments with French forms popular at the turn of the century: the ballade, the triolet, the roundel, and the roundeau. But the ballad, sonnet, and rhymed cou- plets dominate her poetry, as does a familiar discourse. Parker rarely uses a French term or a Latin phrase; her diction may at times be poetic, but it is generally familiar and sometimes clichéd, as the first stanza of "The Veteran" demonstrates:

> When I was young and bold and strong,
> Oh, right was right, and wrong was wrong!

My plume on high, my flag unfurled,
I rode away to right the world.
"Come out, you dogs, and fight!" said I,
And wept there was but once to die.[16]

The poem closes with a tone of resignation, and acknowledges that
with age comes the wisdom to recognize that there is little difference
between battles lost and won. Parker, Arthur F. Kinney claims, "wanted
her verse to be simple, as colloquial as possible. . . . [S]he continually
crossed out words that were not simple enough."[17] But in addition to
simplicity, "The Veteran" contains two elements not typically expected
in Parker's poetry: a male speaker, and a subject having nothing to
do with love. It associates patriotism with youth, and doubt with age.
Published as it was in the mid-twenties, we might read it as a post-
euphoric response to the aftermath of World War I.

Parker's poetics of shared conventions has led to simplistic readings of her poetry. As we saw in chapter 2, Parker's diction has been
interpreted as a weakness by her critics, but what Edmund Wilson
calls "the jargon of ordinary feminine poetry" in Parker's poetry is
now open to other interpretations. Her poem "Recurrence" presents
another opportunity to re-evaluate her use of this language.

We shall have our little day.
Take my hand and travel still
Round and round the little way,
Up and down the little hill.

It is good to love again;
Scan the renovated skies,
Dip and drive the idling pen,
Sweetly tint the paling lies.

Trace the dripping, pierced heart,
Speak the fair, insistent verse,
Vow to God, and slip apart,
Little better, little worse.

Would we need not know before
How shall end this prettiness;
One of us must love the more,
One of us shall love the less.

Thus it is, and so it goes;
We shall have our day, my dear.

Where, unwilling, dies the rose
Buds the new, another year.[18]

"Recurrence" is not a difficult poem to understand; it describes the
temporary nature of love, its loss and eventual return. This is one of
Parker's most typical themes. For people who knew her and/or knew
of her numerous love affairs, a poem like "Recurrence" was to be
expected. Playwright and Algonquin Round Table member Marc
Connelly offers a typical impression of Parker in Aviva Slesin's film
for television, "The Ten-Year Lunch: The Wit and Legend of the
Algonquin Round Table": "Dottie was a 15-year-old girl romantically.
She was always falling in love . . . falling in love with some bum, somebody who was handsome and had the romantic responsibility of a
hoodlum."[19] Friends and critics of Parker, at times one and the same,
would thus read poems such as "Recurrence" as autobiographical
magazine verse filled with clichés, and stop the analysis there. The
poem is in fact richer than such a reading allows, and illustrates a
merging of sentimental and modern conventions.

"Recurrence" contains much that seems familiar. As a ballad, it
uses trochaic tetrameter with an ABAB rhyme scheme, although in a
recording of Parker reading the poem, she deviates from the
tetrameter in the fifth line by sounding light stresses on "It is" and
full stresses on "good," "love," and the second syllable of "again."[20]
The poem draws the clichéd parallel between new love and spring,
or the budding rose. Some of its lines sound trite, such as "Round
and round the little way, / Up and down the little hill" and "Thus it is,
and so it goes; / We shall have our day, my dear." There is a certain
preciousness in words like "little day" and "prettiness." A sense of the
melodramatic occurs in the line "trace the dripping, pierced heart,"
and if the tetrameter is to be maintained, we must give "pierced" a
two-syllable pronunciation. Stressing the *-ed* ending of a word to maintain the meter was a strategy used by many nineteenth-century poets,
most notably John Keats.

The sexual punning in the line "Dip and drive the idling pen" is
not only a counterpoint to the poem's delicacy; it is one of three
allusions to writing in the poem. The "renovated skies" are scanned,
and "fair, insistent verse" is spoken when love is underway. All of these
acts of writing are to be undertaken by both lovers, male and female.
If, as Gilbert and Gubar have argued, the pen is culturally configured
as the penis of literary creation, then Parker's conflation of love and
poetry seems to be an appropriation of male literary power.[21] Yet the

love she describes in such trite and familiar language does not possess the power of endurance.

The poem seems to end on a hopeful note—that love will return—
but is pervaded by a reality of love's impermanent nature. Whatever
returns will be lost once more. The metrical inconsistency in "It is
good to love again" reinforces the line's contention that, despite its
goodness, love is temporary, since it comes "again." The emotional
state of love, in its insubstantial repetitiveness, seems overused by
humans, trite. Thus, the use of trite language to describe it is appropriate, rather than simplistic or sentimental in the pejorative sense.
The trite travel metaphor for the conduct of a new relationship—
"Round and round the little way, / Up and down the little hill"—
echoes the repetitiveness, or cyclical nature of love. A relationship
based on lies and broken vows, which leaves its partners "Little better, little worse," is little more than "this prettiness" since it carries
appearance rather than substance. Parker's sentimental language in
"Recurrence" stands as a metaphorical equivalent for love without
commitment between men and women, since their triteness makes
them anything but romantic. Even their demise is no great tragedy.

In effect, Parker's sentimental conventions in "Recurrence" serve
a modernist project. The poem deromanticizes not only romance
but spring, just as Eliot's "The Waste Land" ("April is the cruelest
month") and Millay's "Spring" ("April / comes like an idiot") do.
"Recurrence" is one of several poems by Parker that moves in this
direction, although "Song of the Wilderness," "Wanderlust," "Song
of the Open Country," "Song for an April Dusk," "Monody," and
"Somewhat Delayed Spring Song" use humor to undercut romantic
notions of spring.[22] A more serious question, however, concerns what
the poem seems to imply about Parker's relationship to her poetry. If
the love she describes does not possess the power of endurance, can
the writing it seems to metaphorically represent endure? This question is discussed more fully later in the chapter in the section Dangerous Retreats. Here it reminds us of how trite and familiar language
can be linked to more complex issues.

"The Dramatists" provides another example. A failed, thus temporary, relationship is described with the trite lines, "A string of shiny
days we had, / A spotless sky, a yellow sun." The speaker predicts that
upon meeting new lovers, the two of them will melodramatically recall each other for purposes of effect, to show, perhaps, what sensitive lovers they are. The clichéd language and imagery of the final
stanza—

And each of us will sigh, and start
A-talking of a faded year
And lay a hand above a heart,
And dry a pretty tear.[23]

—make it clear that these actions are as shallow as the "string of shiny days" was, and in fact suggests a cycle of such relationships.

The general theme of "Recurrence" and "The Dramatists"—love—dominates Parker's poetry; its universal nature is another aspect of her poetics of shared discourse. Other poems, found in the 1973 edition of *The Portable,* use images and characters familiar to women: "The Satin Dress," "The Red Dress," "One Perfect Rose," "Godmother," and "For a Favorite Grand-daughter." Parker also uses familiar conventions, personifying love, joy, sorrow, pride, death, and beauty in poems like "The Trifler," "Convalescent," "Light of Love," "Anecdote," "A Dream Lies Dead," and "Sonnet on an Alpine Night."

A poetics of shared conventions intersects nicely with an overriding tendency of nineteenth-century sentimental works—an emphasis on and desire for human connection and bonding. Whereas the nineteenth-century sentimental bond could occur between mother and daughter, sister and sister, or friend and friend, Parker's bonding typically occurs between men and women. More often than not, the human bonds in Parker's poems fail to hold, as "Recurrence" and "The Dramatists" illustrate. Nevertheless, the fact that so many of Parker's poems deal with the struggle to establish and maintain heterosexual relationships, and with the problem of miscommunication between the sexes, suggests that human connection, however temporary or flawed, is an important theme for Parker.

The familiarity of Parker's form and diction, like that of Edna St. Vincent Millay, Elinor Wylie, Sara Teasdale, and Harlem Renaissance women poets, is in part a function of another factor these women share with nineteenth-century women writers—an awareness of a middle-class, magazine-reading audience with whom they wanted to communicate. Conventional form and diction provided an acceptable mode in which women writers could complain about the often unpleasant news of women's reality. For nineteenth-century women poets, the reality was often the machinations of death which, as Alicia Ostriker points out in *Stealing the Language,* were located within the realm of women's responsibilities: "Before hospitals and funeral establishments professionalized these matters, it was women, not men, who tended sickbeds and laid out the dead; it is small wonder if their poems are morbid." For Harlem Renaissance women poets, as Maureen Honey argues in her introduction to *Shadowed Dreams,* the reality also included racism; mastering conventional forms like the sonnet was tantamount to intellectual equality and empowerment.[24]

For many early twentieth-century women poets, and for Parker in particular, the unpleasant reality often centered on women's unstable position in early twentieth-century romance, where women's expanded freedom, the shortage of reliable birth control, and what Steven Seidman calls the "sexualization of love" converged to leave women particularly vulnerable in their relationships with men. Parker spoke of these difficulties in forms and language immediately accessible to her readers. Applicable to Parker's poetry is what Suzanne Clark says of Edna St. Vincent Millay: "Her poetics are founded on commonality. She may shock her audience, but she does not separate herself from them."[25] Clark's observation implies that even for the so-called modern woman there were limits to be heeded, limits that hinted of Victorian propriety.

THE BOUNDARY OF GENTILITY

The Boundary of Gentility examines the region of permissible topics for women poets of the nineteenth century, the ways in which these poets try to extend this boundary, and the extent to which this sense of propriety continues into the twentieth century. This category includes a discussion of themes noted by Emily Stipes Watts, Cheryl Walker, and Sandra Gilbert and Susan Gubar: religion, domestic issues, forbidden love, and the tension between sexual reticence and sexual exuberance. Alicia Ostriker provides the title for this category when she notes, in *Stealing the Language,* that the sexual theme is one of the primary "strains" exercised by women poets against the "boundaries of gentility."[26] The ways in which Parker's poetry makes similar moves is discussed in this section.

We are so accustomed to thinking of Parker as a wisecracking, at times shocking wit that the concept of gentility seems inappropriate in a discussion of her poetry. However, Parker worked within a range of acceptable methods and topics having parallels to the kinds of restrictions imposed on nineteenth-century women poets. The type and diction of Parker's poems suggests the extent to which she was aware of or guided by such restrictions. A number of her poems are songs—"A Very Short Song," "Somebody's Song," "Spring Song," "Love Song," "Song of One of the Girls," and "Song in a Minor Key" are six examples from *Enough Rope* alone. *Not Much Fun* contains eighteen songs. The song poem has a rich and complicated role in the lyric tradition. The Elizabethan songs of Wyatt, Shakespeare, and Jonson, among others, expressed simple emotion in a direct and musical manner, thus offering an acceptable model for women poets to use. Blake's *Songs of Innocence and of Experience* lent a dark underside to the form, while Whitman's song poems added a mystical dimension. The free verse and irony in Eliot's "The Love Song of J. Alfred Prufrock" stripped the song of its simplicity and recurring musical pattern. Parker's songs retain the accessibility or familiarity of formal verse patterns, but often contain a dark undercurrent that negates the simple romance of Elizabethan songs, or the transcendent powers of nature described in many nineteenth-century poems. Thus, her use of "song" in the titles of her poems is as ironic as Eliot's, yet the poems' form and complaint echoes that of nineteenth-century women poets in Cheryl Walker's nightingale tradition.

In terms of diction, one of the notable characteristics of Parker's poetry is the frequency with which she uses the word "Lady." The term is not used merely to assign gender; in Parker's poems "Lady" connotes a different set of assumptions than that found in, for example, her use of "girl." In *Enough Rope*, her first collection of poetry, Parker includes fifteen poems that either have "Lady" in the title, or address or refer to a "Lady" in the poem. Five poems are titled with, or address or describe a "girl." Parker's ladies tend to be proper, delicate, passive victims of love; her girls are more inclined toward modern moral looseness, as seen previously in "The Dark Girl's Rhyme" and "Prologue to a Saga." At times the speaker in Parker's Lady poems may console or offer advice to the suffering lady, as in "To a Much Too Unfortunate Lady," thus bestowing a Victorian sense of fragility and sympathy to the figure. At other times, Parker seems to be satirizing this delicacy, as in "Epitaph for a Darling Lady." Her satires are suggestive of the eighteenth-century tradition of satirizing "ladies" seen in the poetry of Alexander Pope, John Gay, and Edward Young, among others.[27] In Parker's Lady and Girl poems we find two conflicting notions of feminine behavior, one suggesting the propriety of a nineteenth-century drawing room, the other suggesting the fast life in a speakeasy.

Some of Parker's poems deal with themes a nineteenth-century audience would find wholly acceptable. Other poems deal with male/

female relationships outside of marriage, and while these seem far from genteel, their reticent approach to sexuality and admissions of promiscuity suggest that Parker was conscious of a code of behavior or expectation, no doubt enforced, as in the nineteenth century, by magazine editors. Like some of her nineteenth-century predecessors, Parker at times pushed against the boundary of gentility without breaking through it.

One of the very acceptable topics for women poets of the nineteenth century was religion, a topic not normally considered one of Parker's concerns. One religious motif seen in sentimental women writers is anxiety about reunion or reconciliation in the afterlife.[28] Parker touches on this theme in "Garden-Spot," a poem originally published in *Death and Taxes.*

> God's acre was her garden-spot, she said;
> She sat there often, of the summer days,
> Little and slim and sweet, among the dead,
> Her hair a fable in the leveled rays.
>
> She turned the fading wreath, the rusted cross,
> And knelt to coax about the wiry stem.
> I saw her gentle fingers on the moss
> Now it is anguish to remember them.
>
> And once I saw her weeping, when she rose
> And walked a way and turned to look around—
> The quick and envious tears of one that knows
> She shall not lie in consecrated ground.[29]

"Garden-Spot" is markedly different in tone from the smarty-pants poetry for which Parker is famous. The poem's opening image— "God's acre"—may have been borrowed from Henry Wadsworth Longfellow's poem with that title, linking Parker's poem to a male sentimentalist.[30] No satiric or ironic phrases or final couplet undercut the sentiment of spiritual isolation. The "Garden-Spot" variety of spiritual isolation differs from that associated with modernist texts. The denial of burial in "consecrated ground" suggests the subject is being isolated by the rules of religious convention, in this case, the rules regarding burial after a suicide. In the texts of Eliot, Joyce, and Pound, isolation occurs when an individual finds the conventions no longer useful and chooses to reject them. Parker's poem is thus more closely tied to the sentimental tradition, but it presents an opportunity to examine how the sentimental and the modern intersect. If "Garden-Spot" had been one of her earlier poems, published, for example, in *Vanity Fair*, one could argue that its sentimental aspects were older influences yet to be discarded, that she had yet to "kill" her literary predecessor, as Harold Bloom argues in *The Anxiety of Influence*.[31] But "Garden-Spot" came late, appearing in Parker's last individual poetry book among other poems that both continue and reject the sentimental tradition. A Bloomian analysis of Parker might thus conclude that she was a weak writer, grounds for dismissing her from the canon of "great works." A more accurate interpretation is that poems like "Garden-Spot" suggest ways in which twentieth-century literature incorporates aspects of the sentimental tradition. Its presence in the work of a writer also known for modernist sensibilities and modernist form in fiction suggests that the theme of spiritual isolation is not purely a modernist characteristic, nor a radical break from the past, but rather a different manifestation of a nineteenth-century concern.

Parker also maintains this consistency of tone, and comes closest to extolling the domestic and Christian virtues associated with nineteenth-century sentimentalism, in three of her Christmas poems: "The Maid-Servant at the Inn," "The Gentlest Lady," and "Prayer for a New Mother." "The Maid-Servant at the Inn" differs from the other two poems in that it gives voice to a marginal figure, a female we might compare with one of William Wordsworth's "common" people. The poem presents a conventional retelling of the birth of Jesus from the point of view of the maid-servant who, according to one traditional version of the events leading up to the Nativity, worked at the inn that denied lodging to Mary and Joseph. There is nothing surprising, however, in the maid's sentiments. Mary is described as "such a gentle thing," and the maid recalls:

> I mind my eyes were full of tears,
> For I was young, and quick distressed,
> But she was less than me in years
> That held a son against her breast.[32]

The image of a mother and child, associated with "tears," can be found in numerous poems and stories by nineteenth-century women. Parker maintains this emotional force through the end of the poem, where it becomes clear that the maid is recalling the birth at the approximate time of Christ's crucifixion. Thus, two holidays, Christmas and

Easter, merge into one without a humorous punch line to counter the poem's serious intentions. Though it is steeped in sentimental language and imagery, this poem is part of a tradition of Christmas poetry, as outlined by Robert Pinsky, that "expresses the idea of despair underlying religious celebration." The "dark beauty of Christmas," the ambivalence associated with sources of transformation, conflicts with and complicates the feel-good impulse of the season and of many seasonal poems.[33] Parker's Christmas poem, read within the tradition Pinsky defines, takes on a more complicated matrix. On the one hand, the image of death is certainly associated with the sentimental tradition. On the other hand, the presence of death in Parker's poem—part of its sentimental language—undercuts to some degree the coziness of the poem's Christmas sentiment. In light of this reading, defining the sentimental in a pejorative sense becomes more of a challenge.

As the titles indicate, both "The Gentlest Lady" and "Prayer for a New Mother" also focus on the mother figure. Again, Parker presents the expected virtues of Mary as mother in terminology readers of nineteenth-century sentimental poetry would recognize in "The Gentlest Lady":

> They say upon His birthday eve
> She'd rock Him to His rest
> As if she could not have Him leave
> The shelter of her breast.
> . . . .
> They say she'd kiss the boy awake,
> And hail Him gay and clear,
> But oh, her heart was like to break
> To count another year.[34]

Parker uses the conventional, sentimental imagery of a mother and child, a sheltering breast, and a breaking heart, but she also invests Mary with knowledge of the future.

"Prayer for a New Mother" asks that Mary be allowed to boast and plan like any mother, and to forget what she knows of the past. Again we have sentimental language revising what is typically a sentimentally rendered scene. The sense of wonder, the pastoral shepherds, and the noble wise men are replaced with more negative images: "The voices in the sky, the fear, the cold, / The gaping shepherds, and the queer old men / Piling their clumsy gifts of foreign gold." This revision strategy can be usefully compared with that of T. S. Eliot in "The Journey of the Magi," where the hardships of the journey to the Nativity and its aftermath are emphasized. In contrast to "The Gentlest Lady," "Prayer for a New Mother" offers a prayer that Mary will have no vision of the troubled future her son faces:

> .... the rumble of a crowd,
> The smell of rough-cut wood, the trail of red,
> The thick and chilly whiteness of the shroud
> That wraps the strange new body of the dead.[35]

Within the realm of what is considered serious poetry, these poems could be dismissed as seasonal lyrics, occasional verse, or magazine verse. But if we set aside classification by poetic types for a moment, the critical biases against them become less important to our reading of the poems. Our attention can then focus on other characteristics the poems possess. Their form, imagery, and subject matter are well within the sentimental tradition, yet in each poem Parker explores a new way to present a familiar story—using a marginal voice, a prophetic Mary, and a deromanticized setting. These aren't the poems that come to mind if we think of Parker as primarily a sophisticated wit, or as a hard-living, precariously loving, magazine personality. As part of her poetic oeuvre, however, they forge significant links to an American woman's tradition even as they strain against some of its conventions. Some of Parker's love poetry also makes a connection to this tradition, but in a slightly different manner.

Vers de société, or sophisticated verse, a type of light verse popular with many early twentieth-century magazine editors, became the form of choice Parker used for her exploration of male/female relationships. Because of its association with magazine publication in the twentieth century, this poetic type has remained unappreciated in many respects. Yet like the song poem, it is a type rich in tradition, beginning with ancient Greek and Roman poets, and continuing through every literary period. Also like the song poem, examples of sophisticated verse by male poets appeared in anthologies whereas those by women did not. At the beginning of the twentieth century, we see a relative explosion of female sophisticated versifiers: Carolyn Wells, Alice Duer Miller, Edna St. Vincent Millay, and Phyllis McGinley, in addition to Parker. Why? Sophisticated verse offered these women an acceptable and far-reaching vehicle for voicing concerns about the plight of modern women. Yet this type of poem has its own values of propriety. One Victorian definition of sophisticated verse characterizes it as "smoothly written verse, where a boudoir decorum is, or ought always to be, preserved; where sentiment never surges into passion, and where humor never overflows into boisterous merriment."[36] Parker's sophisticated poems remain within these guidelines.

On the surface, twentieth-century sophisticated verse, with its flippant or skeptical view toward love and its admissions of sexual promiscuity, seems light-years away from most nineteenth-century poetry by women, but in Parker's case it stops short of being sexually explicit. Not that Parker's poems are genteel in the nineteenth- or turn-of-the-century sense of the word, but they observe and sometimes test a code of propriety that, while different from the nineteenth-century code, sets limits nonetheless. At times her poems metaphorically mask sexuality; at other times they push against the border of what is permissible. The position of the speaker in Parker's sophisticated verse ranges from victimizer to victim, and the often-used infusion of satire, irony, and humor keeps them palatable for middle-class readers in the teens and twenties. Yet the comic surface of the poems and their popular reception masked the seriousness of their content, even to Parker.

In her speech to the League of American Writers, "Sophisticated Poetry—and the Hell with It," published in *New Masses* in 1939, and partially republished in Donald Ogden Stewart's 1940 anthology, *Fighting Words*, Parker reveals her perceptions of her work. The speech, delivered during the height of Parker's leftist political activity, unfortunately disparages her own poetry because it does not fit the politics of the day. But the speech also reveals the tensions that modern sexuality presented for women's poetry. Light verse had been essentially harmless, Parker argued, before the influence of World War I and, perhaps, of Edna Millay.

> Then something happened to the light verse writers—especially to the ladies among us. . . . We came right out in rhyme and acknowledged that we hadn't been virgins for quite awhile—whether we had or not. We let it be known our hearts broke much oftener than the classic once. . . . We were gallant and hard-riding and careless of life. We sneered in numbers in loping rhythms at the straight and the sharp and the decent. We were little black elves that had gone astray; we were a sort of ladies auxiliary of the legion of the damned. And, boy, were we proud of our shame! When Gertrude Stein spoke of a "lost generation," we took it to ourselves and considered it the prettiest compliment we had.[37]

Parker's work, however, tends to be more sexually reticent than this speech suggests. To write too bluntly about the complications of nonmarital sex at a time when the Victorian moral code was no longer explicit, but still guided what "good" people did, had its risks, as evidenced by the disjunction between Parker the Celebrity and Parker the Poet. Her popular bons mots were more sexually explicit than her poems. She was famous for such quips as "You can lead a horticulture but you can't make her think," and "One more drink and I would have been under the host," and for wiring someone pressuring her for a manuscript that she was "too fucking busy and vice versa."[38] But in her poem "Rainy Night," she masks her "lovely sins" in metaphorical language:

> I am sister to the rain;
>   Fey and sudden and unholy,
> Petulant at the windowpane,
>   quickly lost, remembered slowly.[39]

Similarly, the sins of the speaker in "Interview," one of Parker's Lady poems, are inferred by their opposites—the qualities a lady should have if she hopes to attract a man. The version below comes from *Enough Rope*.

> The ladies men admire, I've heard,
> Would shudder at a wicked word.
> Their candle gives a single light;
> They'd rather stay at home at night.
> They do not keep awake till three,
> Nor read erotic poetry.
> They never sanction the impure,
> Nor recognize an overture.
> They shrink from powders and from paints.
> So far, I've had no complaints.[40]

This poem pits practice against theory to mock social convention. In contrast to the iambic tetrameter throughout the poem, the uneven trimeter of the closing line, as well as its content, point to the speaker's difference from the "ladies men admire" in theory. While the speaker's sexual promiscuity is clear, the allusion to Millay's candle that burns at both ends, as well as the strategy of negation in the poem, rhetorically soften its delivery. Parker's shock factor is reserved for either nonsexual or nonpoetic expressions.

The fact that many of Parker's poems imply multiple lovers might seem more at odds with sentimental reticence than perhaps it is. Alicia Ostriker reminds us, as do Cheryl Walker and Emily Stipes Watts, that nineteenth-century poets such as Francis Osgood and Lizette Woodworth Reese "strain . . . the boundaries of gentility" at times.[41] Reese implies a sexual passion when she instructs life to "Unpetal the flower of me, / And cast it to the gust"; rather than leave her "free / Of any hurt at all."[42] Parker echoes this sentiment in her sonnet "Fair Weather," where the speaker desires the storm of love— "I have need of wilder, crueler waves;"— closing with:

> So let a love beat over me again,
> Loosing its million desperate breakers wide;
> Sudden and terrible to rise and wane;
> Roaring the heavens apart; a reckless tide
> That casts upon the heart, as it recedes,
> Splinters and spars and dripping, salty weeds.[43]

Both Reese and Parker use nature imagery to claim that love is painful yet desirable, employing a Romantic complex of pleasure and pain. Parker's ocean and shoreline imagery, however, also recall the imagist lines of H. D.'s "Oread," a poem, argues Susan Stanford Friedman in *Psyche Reborn*, that implies rather than explicitly states a desire for sexual passion:

> Whirl up, sea—
> whirl your pointed pines,
> splash your great pines on our rocks,
> hurl your green over us,
> cover us with your pools of fir.[44]

The shoreline position—a position on the edge, on the border, and one for which H. D. is known—is analogous to Parker's literary position, not as a location on the margins of modernism, but as a location between and often merging nineteenth- and twentieth-century, or conventional and modern, literary values and techniques.

The desire for love and the denial of love often go hand in hand, as the forbidden love poem illustrates. Maria Brooks's "Song" and Helen Hunt Jackson's "Esther Wynn's Love Letters" are two of many examples from the nineteenth century; this topic, Walker tells us in *The Nightingale's Burden*, "is a conspicuous feature of women's poetry from Emily Dickinson to Edna St. Vincent Millay."[45] As discussed previously, Parker's version of the forbidden love poem "The Dark Girl's Rhyme" more aggressively pushes against the boundary of gentility because of its theme of interracial love. Others, such as "Landscape" and "Two-Volume Novel," offer more muted forms of forbidden love; the speaker loves another who doesn't return the sentiment.[46] This becomes a more poignant issue in Parker's fiction.

GENDER RIGIDITY

The duality dominating social interaction in the nineteenth century whereby the male sphere was public and active, while the female sphere was private, home-based, and passive, has been acknowledged by a number of scholars.[47] If literary texts are influenced by the culture in which they are produced, we can expect to see this duality reflected in nineteenth-century women's literature in the form of expected roles and codes of behavior based on gender. The surprise is that we see it in Parker's work as well.

In "The American Renaissance Reenvisioned," Joanne Dobson claims that "a preoccupation with codified gender roles [is] a central aspect of sentimentalism."[48] Although she refers to fiction, her observation is applicable to nineteenth-century women's poetry as well. Two of Phoebe Cary's poems use parodic dialogue to examine a woman's position relative to her husband's in the public sphere of voting and the private sphere of domestic finance. In "Was He Henpecked" the husband objects to his wife voting or taking any other public role for a range of reasons—she lacks intelligence, she would become unsexed by politics, she belongs in the home where she can be exalted and protected—before admitting he fears she would "roost above" him.[49] In "Dorothy's Dower" a husband tells his newlywed wife to spend her dower on herself because he will be the provider; he adds:

> I like your sweet dependent ways
> I love you when you tease me;
> The more you ask, the more you spend,
> The better you will please me.[50]

But when the dower is gone, and the husband turns out to be a poor provider because he spends too much money on "cigars and brandy," he accuses his wife of being a spendthrift. Lucy Larcom's "Getting Along" gives an older woman's wry perspective on her marriage to a man who is emotionally distant and preoccupied with business. The couple has little in common in their remaining years, but are "getting along."[51]

The focus on gender-determined roles in these poems, as well as their humor, realism, and implied critique of these roles, places them in a line of poetic development that leads to Parker. Although women experience new sexual, social, and political freedoms at the time Parker is writing, some of her poems reveal that the basic rules of courtship have changed surprisingly little, and remain under the influence of expectations based on gender. Men remain the active players in courtship, initiating affairs and judging women in terms of classic beauty, while women remain the passive respondents. Gender rigidity is perhaps more dominant in Parker's fiction, but some of her poems take up the issue with fervor.

Parker's sonnet "I Know I Have Been Happiest" describes the termination, by the male partner, of a love affair, and ends on a comic note of ghostly haunting: "My gift shall be my absence, while I live; / But after that, my dear, I cannot swear." The humor, however, does not undercut the observations the speaker makes about the sexes in these seven lines:

> I will not make you songs of hearts denied,
> And you, being man, would have no tears of me,
> And should I offer you fidelity,
> You'd be, I think, a little terrified.
>
> Yet this the need of woman, this her curse:
> To range her little gifts, and give, and give,
> Because the throb of giving's sweet to bear.[52]

The language in these lines—"you, being man" and "this the need of woman"—makes it clear that Parker is making generalizations about men and women, rather than speaking of a particular or idiosyncratic case. Men avoid excess emotion, like the husband in Lucy Larcom's "Getting Along." They also avoid monogamy, an argument Parker makes again in "To a Much Too Unfortunate Lady" and "General Review of the Sex Situation." Women, on the other hand, offer a kind of masochistic giving and fidelity. "Tears" also belong to the realm of women, but significantly, the speaker's agreement to repress her "songs" and "tears" is analogous to the sentimental heroine's effort to control her feelings and passions, as observed by Nina Baym and Jane Tompkins.[53] The poem's cool tone is another aspect of the speaker's emotional control.

Parker articulates the active male/passive female dichotomy in some of her poems. In the angry "Chant for the Dark Hours," the men arrive for dates late if at all because they are detained by book shops, crap games, bars, golf courses, hat shops or other women. Meanwhile the women wait, read, sew, or sleep, in passive contrast to their lovers. The poem ends with the parenthetical phrase, "All your life you wait around for some damn man!" A similar outburst of anger occurs in "Men," in which the speaker resents the fact that men try to remake their female partners: "They'd alter all that they admired. / They make me sick, they make me tired." In her famous epigram "News Item," Parker uses modernist brevity to convey information—"Men seldom make passes / At girls who wear glasses"—and implies instruction—females shouldn't wear glasses if they want to attract males—a rhetorical move that echoes her other instructional poems, as well as those of Adelaide Ann Procter and other nineteenth-century women poets.[54] The fact that it is the men who "make passes" suggests that men are the active initiators in a relationship. If Parker, who wore glasses but took them off in the presence of men, wrote this poem out of personal experience, then not all of the rules regarding heterosexual dating had changed in the early twentieth century.

DANGEROUS RETREATS

Emily Stipes Watts, Sandra Gilbert and Susan Gubar, and Cheryl Walker base their studies of nineteenth-century women poets on the premise that literary production is a fundamentally different experience for women than it is for men. Many nineteenth-century women wrote out of financial necessity rather than a desire to create art, and lacking "wives," did so while running a household and raising children. Despite the popularity of women's poetry in the nineteenth century, women poets feared their success would alienate them from the sphere of feminine nurturance, "the one group," Walker tells us, "into which the patriarchy has allowed them free entry."[55] Their anxiety about their position in both literary and nonliterary cultures manifests itself in poems of martyrdom, suicide, power fantasies, and sanctuary, poems in which victimhood and renunciation are the dominant themes. Modern women poets, including Parker, also wrote these types of poems, suggesting that twentieth-century female literary production was an area mined with nineteenth-century expectations and restrictions. The dangerous retreats found in Parker's poetry constitute her most disturbing connection to the sentimental tradition.

Parker's two-stanza poem "Renunciation" tells us much about how she handles this theme. The speaker first tells her lover that although she lacks the beauty of Chloe, Helen, and other classical figures, she had been "fair enough" for him.[56] In the second stanza she records his flirtations with women also bearing classical names—Penelope, Chloe, Zoe—and suggests they part, receiving no objection from her now ex-lover. There is a dual renunciation here—by the male lover who is turning his attention away from the speaker, and by the speaker's call to end the relationship. "Renunciation" typifies Parker's form of retreat, which most often stems from disappointment with love, and ranges from physical and emotional withdrawal to suicide. Her poems about being a poet, in which she criticizes what is expected of female poets and belittles her own work, serve as precursors for her literary retreat—she ceases to write poetry during the second half of her life.

A sense of martyrdom over lost love, not undercut by satire or irony, appears in "Landscape," a poem which uses a convention of late Romantic and Victorian poets described by David Perkins: "One favorite technique was to put landscape and human emotion side by side so that the landscape became the exponent of the emotion."[57] Perkins uses an example by Tennyson, but women poets used this technique as well, as this excerpt from Lucy Larcom's "Fern-Life" illustrates:

> Yes, life! though it seems half a death,
> When the flowers of the glen
> Bend over, with color and breath,
> Till we tremble again;
>
> Till we shudder with exquisite pain
> Their beauty to see,
> While our dumb hope, through fibre and vein,
> Climbs up to be free.[58]

An unfulfilled desire, not specifically named in the poem, is the landscape's emotional parallel; whether that emotion is a general human one or of particularly female origin remains debatable.[59] In either case, the sense of limitation persists. The same applies to Parker's "Landscape," although the emotional parallel is clearly love. An idyllic, pastoral scene is described as:

> . . . the sweetest place
>> From here to heaven's end;
> The field is white with flowering lace,
>> The birches leap and bend,
>
> The hills, beneath the roving sun,
>> From green to purple pass,
> And little, trifling breezes run
>> Their fingers through the grass.

Despite the fact that the landscape is "gay," "calm," "pure," and thus capable of making the beholder "happier," it has no value for the speaker, who concludes:

> But me—I see it flat and gray
>> And blurred with misery,
> Because a lad a mile away
>> Has little need of me.[60]

Unlike many of Parker's poems, "Landscape" offers no alleviation of suffering, no cavalier movement toward the next relationship. We see this again in the short poem "Midnight," which also uses the language of gems, another characteristic Walker associates with nineteenth-century women poets:

> The Stars are soft as flowers, and as near;
>> The hills are webs of shadow, slowly spun;
> No separate leaf or single blade is here—
>> All blend to one.
>
> No Moonbeam cuts the air; a sapphire light
>> Rolls lazily, and slips again to rest.
> There is no edged thing in all this night,
>> Save in my breast.[61]

We can assume from Parker's reference to her heart ("my breast") that love is the culprit in "Midnight." She is more forthright in her Petrarchan sonnet "A Portrait," in which the speaker is victimized by her inability to maintain a lasting relationship "Because my love is quick to come and go." Again using the language of gems, the speaker claims hers is a "heavy" heart "That hangs about my neck—a clumsy stone / Cut with a birth, a death, a bridal day"; she seeks "to give the wretched thing away" without success.[62]

Parker's sanctuary poems also represent an emotional retreat from love, or from the world at large because of a disappointing love affair. In a sanctuary poem, explains Cheryl Walker, poets "imagine safe, enclosed spaces as protection against incursions from a hostile reality outside the walls." Walker goes on to argue that the twentieth-century poets she studies create sanctuaries, but unlike their nineteenth-century predecessors, recognize them as "suffocating and self-destructive."[63] The best example is provided by Parker's close friend, Elinor Wylie, in her poem "Sanctuary." The poem's speaker wants the bricklayer to make her

> . . . marvelous wall so thick
> Dead nor living may shake its strength.
>
> Full as a crystal cup with drink
> Is my cell with dreams, and quiet, and cool. . . .
> Stop, old man! You must leave a chink;
> How can I breathe? *You can't, you fool!*[64]

Wylie's sense of danger is less apparent in Parker's poem by the same title. The retreat in Parker's "Sanctuary" not only lacks a sense of danger, but appears deviously self-satisfying: "And sweet's the air with curly smoke / From all my burning bridges."[65] The speaker in her sonnet "The Homebody," "afraid to dream, afraid to feel," wants to protect herself from love by remaining at home with

> This little chair of scrubbed and sturdy deal,
> This easy book, this fire, sedate and slow.
> And I shall stay with them, nor cry the woe
> Of wounds across my breast that do not heal.[66]

The speaker's goal is to reach the point where her "heart is dead," and the sonnet contains no ironic phrases to undercut the sentiment. While the "easy book" and "fire sedate and slow" suggest an element of self-defeat, "The Homebody" does not boldly recognize the limitations of sanctuary as does Wylie's "Sanctuary." "Hearthside," a poem of both sanctuary and renunciation, also presents a retreat to the home. The speaker desires to travel overseas, but refuses to because it could lead to unsuccessful love; "Best to sit and watch the snow, / Turn the lock, and poke the fire," she concludes.[67]

Parker's three-stanza poem "Interior," however, creates a much smaller, more confined sanctuary than "The Homebody" and "Hearthside." The retreat is another effort to prevent heartbreak, but this time the sanctuary is the mind itself: "Her mind lives in a quiet room, / A narrow room, and tall." Significantly, Parker appropriates a domestic space for the room of the mind; she furnishes the room with lamps, pictures, and flowers. But this is a room separated from the rest of the house, a mind divided from the body that feels:

> Her mind lives tidily, apart
>   From cold and noise and pain,
> And bolts the door against the heart,
>   Out wailing in the rain.[68]

"Interior" reminds us, with its domestic metaphor for a psychological state of mind and its hymnal meter, of the poetry of Emily Dickinson, who also alluded to sanctuary in her work and whose poems were being published in the 1890s, teens, and 1920s. A retreat to the mind, Cheryl Walker reminds us, also occurs in many of Louise Bogan's poems. Dickinson, however, at times explored her sanctuary in a more positive light, claiming the benefits of solitude.[69] When we consider, however, Parker's concern with sanctuary and her unwillingness to recognize it poetically as self-defeating, a new reading of her sophisticated verse becomes possible. Poems in which the speaker more or less light-heartedly, and often quickly, moves on to a new relationship can be read as a form of emotional sanctuary, a retreat from long-term intimacy, or a retreat from attempts at long-term intimacy which, though desirable, seems an unlikely prospect. This motif begins as early as 1921 with "Lyric," originally published in *Life*. The poem describes the interdependency of objects in the natural world, closing with:

> If the blossoms refused their pale honey, the bees
>   Must in idleness hunger and pine;
> While the moss cannot live, when it's torn from the trees,
>   Nor the waxen-globed mistletoe twine.
> Were it not for the sunshine, the birds wouldn't sing,
>   And the heavens would never be blue.
> But of all Nature's works, the most wonderful thing
>   Is how well I get on without you.[70]

Parker manages to throw three strikes with one poem. She mocks the Romantic convention of nature poetry, the lyric convention of suffering over love, and the concept of suffering itself. The poem offers a categorical rejection of the major nineteenth-century values, romantic and sentimental, except for its emotional sanctuary.

"Now at Liberty" follows, without mockery of form, a nineteenth-century style used by Thomas Hood in which conventional sentiment is countered by parenthetical phrases expressing an opposite feeling. The first stanza provides the model for the rest of the poem:

> Little white love, your way you've taken;
>   Now I am left alone, alone.
> Little white love, my heart's forsaken.
>   (Whom shall I get by telephone?)
> Well do I know there's no returning;
>   Once you go out, it's done, it's done.
> All of my days are gray with yearning.
>   (Nevertheless, a girl needs fun.)[71]

In "Pattern," "Nocturne," and "The Burned Child," the speaker quickly recovers from a broken heart with the next available man; in "Surprise" she is relieved to find that she is the first to leave a relationship. The refrain of "Ballade at Thirty-Five," "I loved them until they loved me," is referred to by the speaker as "my strength and my weakness." Frances Osgood's "Forgive and Forget" presents a nineteenth-century version of the same attitude:

> "Forgive—forget! I own the wrong!"
> You fondly sigh'd when last I met you;
> The task is neither hard nor long—
> I do forgive—I *will* forget you![72]

Clearly, the comic note that often accompanies Parker's cavalier attitude toward lost love is not without precedent in the nineteenth century. It provides for Parker an emotional distance that makes sanctuary from love possible. The departing lover in Parker's "They Part" is chided for being a violent, vulgar thief; in "The Danger of Writing Defiant Verse" the speaker mocks the chivalric attitudes of her last lover, calling him "silly." Stupidity is the charge in "Little Words," in which Parker writes of her broken heart in "little words—so you, my dear, / Can spell them out." Parker's humor is more direct than that of, for example, Frances Osgood, but Osgood's comic intent is still clear. In "He Bade Me Be Happy," Osgood chides an ex-lover who says he wants her to forget him, and then resents it when she does, saying, "'Is this my reward?' he cried; 'falsehood and scorning / From her who was ever my idol, my pride!'"[73]

Suicide represents the most obvious form of renunciation. Parker's suicide poems are often read as autobiographical, but they also need to be read as part of a women's literary tradition; the theme of suicide pervades nineteenth-century women's poetry. Emily Stipes Watts argues that an attraction to suicide begins with Maria Brooks's long poem "Zophiel, or The Bride of Seven" (1833), carries on throughout the nineteenth century, including several of Emily Dickinson's poems, and continues into the poetry of Sylvia Plath and Anne Sexton.[74] Unlike her predecessors, Parker's poems about suicide can be humorous, but the amount and kind of humor in them varies, depending on the extent to which the poem is focused on humor, or on suicide. Her famous poem "Résumé" provides a humorous catalog of problems associated with methods of suicide, ending with a sense of resignation in the line, "You might as well live."[75] Another humorous catalog, this one listing the problems with life, occurs in "Swan Song," but ends with a desire for suicide: "Where's the nearest river?"[76] Only a form of black humor, at best, is present in the one-stanza poem "Cherry White":

> I never see that prettiest thing—
> A cherry bough gone white with Spring—
> But what I think, "How gay t'would be
> To hang me from a flowering tree."[77]

The imagery and tetrameter of the poem suggest Parker is responding to A. E. Housman's "Loveliest of trees, the cherry now" found in *A Shropshire Lad* (1896), and its suicide theme links it to nineteenth-century women's poetry. But other elements give it a modernist flavor. Though lacking terse imagist brevity and experimental form, the poem's image of white petals against a dark bough, and its symbolic conflation of life and death, recalls that found in an earlier poem, Ezra Pound's "In a Station of the Metro." The image of purity and innocence suggested by "white" in Parker's poem is further countered by "cherry," a blood-red color evoking life and death. Thus, "Cherry White" as the poem's title embodies modernist concision and symbolic density. The poem also expresses modernist anti-spring sentiment found in the poems of Eliot and Millay. Parker's "Rhyme Against Living" is equally bleak; the speaker draws a morbid conclusion from either emotionally low or emotionally high states of mind:

> If wild my breast and sore my pride,
> I bask in dreams of suicide;

If cool my heart and high my head,
I think, "How lucky are the dead!"[78]

Sandra Gilbert and Susan Gubar, as well as Cheryl Walker, interpret
the nineteenth-century poetic impulse toward suicide in terms of an
illness metaphor that allowed women writers to vent their anger about
patriarchy and the divided states of mind that patriarchy fostered in
them.[79] Read in this context, Parker's poems about suicide are more
than autobiographical wailings or love-sick whinings; they speak to
the instability of a woman writer's position in the early twentieth century. The humor with which Parker tries to soften the suicidal blow
magnifies for us her sense of self-division, since annihilation is not
inherently funny. Furthermore, if the theme of love is a traditionally
acceptable means for women to discuss issues of power, as Alicia
Ostriker points out in *Stealing the Language*, then Parker's suicidal
retreat from or because of the failures of heterosexual love in which
men remained the active initiators of relationships, speaks to patriarchy in general.[80] An individual male/female relationship becomes a
microcosm for the larger realm of a male-dominated social system.
An unfortunate fact of literary history is that Parker could not recognize the inherent politics of her light verse.

If suicide represents the ultimate renunciation, readers of Parker
can console themselves with the knowledge that, despite several suicide attempts, Parker died at age seventy-four of natural causes. Her
more problematic act of renunciation, and one that she did carry
through to completion, was her retreat from poetry. Although Parker's
rejection of light verse in the 1930s has been considered an aspect of
her turn toward leftist politics, the disparaging comments in her poems about women's poetry in general and her own poetry in particular suggest that other forces were at work much earlier. We hear the
voice of a woman who values her poetry in "Fighting Words," which
closes with, "say my verses do not scan, / and I get me another man!"
but this is not her dominant attitude.[81] Instead, Parker more typically
expresses ambivalence about success in general and discusses her
poetry in ways that not only belittles it, but in one instance addresses
the paradoxical standards that early twentieth-century women poets
were expected to follow.

Cheryl Walker notes that two popular nineteenth-century women
poets, Lizette Woodworth Reese and Louise Imogen Guiney, maintained a sense of martyrdom about their profession.[82] Significantly,
Parker enjoyed popular success as a poet, yet wrote poems express-

ing indifference about success. *Enough Rope* contains two of them.
The speaker in "Philosophy" claims:

> If I should labor through daylight and dark
>   Consecrate, valorous, serious, true,
> Then on the world I may blazon my mark;
>   And what if I don't, and what if I do?[83]

In "Observation," the speaker argues that if she avoids her bad hab-
its, she may "make my mark" and "amount to much," and then concludes, "But I shall stay the way I am, / Because I do not give a damn."[84]
These poems reverberate with the sophisticated nonchalance of the
1920s, a period known for its surface glitter and frolic. But they also
can be read as defensive posturing: against success in general, suggesting that Parker was uncomfortable, at some level, with her reputation; or against the kind of popular success that Parker was achieving
in the light verse form, suggesting anxiety over not being taken seriously. The second posture is indeed possible because other poems
show that Parker was aware of nineteenth-century critical attitudes
toward women's poetry that remained in place at the time she was
writing, attitudes that defined appropriate subject matter.

Nineteenth-century readers and critics expected women's poetry
to contain the poet's feelings, yet there were limits to what this feeling could entail. Two influential anthologists of the day, Caroline May
and Rufus Griswold, define these limits in the introductions to their
anthologies of female poets. May writes, "Deep emotions make a good
foundation for lofty and pure thoughts"; these thoughts are "changeless," and they derive from domestic experience. Griswold tells his
readers: "We should deem her the truest poet, whose emotions are
most refined by reason, whose force of passion is most expanded and
controlled into lofty and impersonal forms of imagination."[85] Feelings caged into lofty, changeless, impersonal expressions controlled
by reason—these were the expectations that no doubt prompted
Frances Osgood to write:

> Ah! woman still
> Must veil the shrine,
> Where feeling feeds the fire divine,
> Nor sing at will,
> Untaught by art,
> The music prison'd in her heart![86]

Women poets were encouraged to keep unbridled feeling out of their poetry long before modernist poets such as Pound used imagist, vorticist, and classical dicta to blast sentiment from literature. What develops without being articulated, however, is a politics of feeling, for the question is not whether feeling has a place in poetry, but whose feeling and for what purpose. How is the line drawn between legitimate feeling and the pejorative notion of sentimentality? As noted earlier, some feminist critics suspect the line is drawn on the basis of gender, since a number of modern males use aspects of the sentimental in their works. Parker seems to have drawn a similar conclusion.

In her poetry about writing poetry, Parker associates the use of feeling with diminished success, and diminished success with poetry by minor poets and women. It is the "minor poet," in her poem "Tombstones in the Starlight," whose

> . . . little trills and chirpings were his best.
> No music like the nightingale's was born
> Within his throat; but he, too, laid his breast
> Upon a thorn.[87]

The minor poet writes of his pain in "little" productions that will characterize, for Parker, what readers paradoxically expect and dislike in women's poetry. The poem's imagery and sentiment associating pain with the nightingale's song were likely influenced by a nineteenth-century Romantic poet Parker read, Samuel Taylor Coleridge. His conversation poem "The Nightingale," describes the poet who first developed the conceit as a man "whose heart was pierced" by (among other things) "neglected love."[88]

Parker ties her criticism of "little" poetry to female poets in her poem "Bric-à-Brac," its title alone suggesting the nonessential clutterings of a nineteenth-century drawing room. The poem lists the "[l]ittle things that no one needs" unless they are "lonely folk" with nothing better to do than make miniature crafts with beads, thread, grass, or paper. The poem closes with another item no one needs: "Little verses, such as these."[89] The poem borders on self-parody; it delivers a joke on the light verse genre Parker used. Poetic littleness, however, is gendered feminine in the poem not because we read the speaker as Parker, but because the crafts in the poem are typically associated with women.

"Song of Perfect Propriety" and "For a Lady Who Must Write Verse" are two of Parker's Lady poems that more directly connect poetic littleness with feminine gender. The female speaker in "Song of Perfect Propriety" desires to be a "roaring buccaneer" who travels the seas, drinks, murders, takes captives and slaves—who determines her fate as well as the fate of others. Significantly, she would like to "stroll beyond the ancient bounds, / And tap at fastened gates," that is, move into areas normally occupied by men through their lived experience or their imagination. These desires, whether we read them literally or as metaphors for imaginative landscapes of the writer, stand in stark contrast with the speaker's reality. She sums up her situation in four lines appearing at the end of the second and fourth stanzas, respectively: "But I am writing little verse, / As little ladies do," and "But I am writing little songs, / As little ladies will."[90] "Song of Perfect Propriety" is a type of power fantasy poem Cheryl Walker identifies as part of the nightingale tradition, because its desire for agency, for an active rather than passive life, is juxtaposed against the speaker's passive reality. Not only does Parker negate her own poetry and women's poetry in general, but she invokes in 1926 the separate masculine and feminine spheres so prevalent in the nineteenth century.

Parker goes a step further in "For A Lady Who Must Write Verse," warning women away from the use of feeling in poetry, as well as from poetry publication:

> Unto seventy years and seven,
>   Hide your double birthright well—
> You, that are the brat of Heaven
>   And the pampered heir to Hell.
>
> Let your rhymes be tinsel treasures,
>   Strung and seen and thrown aside.
> Drill your apt and docile measures
>   Sternly as you drill your pride.
>
> Show your quick, alarming skill in
>   Tidy mockeries of art;
> Never, never dip your quill in
>   Ink that rushes from your heart.
>
> When your pain must come to paper,
>   See it dust, before the day;
> Let your night-light curl and caper,
>   Let it lick the words away.

Never print, poor child, a lay on
Love and tears and anguishing,
Lest a cooled, benignant Phaon
Murmur, "Silly little thing!"[91]

This instructional ballad suggests, in both form and content, how little had changed for women poets in the twentieth century. The Millaysian candle in this poem burns at one end, and consumes the literary record of passion. The requirement that poetry be impersonal—an imperative issued by nineteenth-century critics of women's poetry as well as by modernist ones—is as striking as the poem's bitter bifurcation of creativity into separate spheres: men produce art, women—specifically, ladies—produce "rhymes," "tinsel treasures," "docile measures," and "mockeries of art" devoid of Osgood's "feeling" that "feeds the fire divine." Similarly, the female speaker in Parker's "Daylight Saving" is "whittling rhyme" rather that writing a poem.[92] In the hands of men, poetry is both art and craft. Parker sees her own poems as craft alone, amounting to little more than a hobby.

Cheryl Walker argues that internalizing patriarchal attitudes leads women poets to "renounce not only the world but their own ambitions."[93] This seems to apply to Parker, yet her poems suggest that the issue is more complicated than the charge of complicity suggests. The woman poet's "double birthright" is that of the damned; neither docility nor revolt in the form of giving voice to one's pain, that is, expressing feelings in spite of the male editorial bias against them, will garner respect. Given the context in which Parker understood herself to be working, the light verse form in which she was so successful can be seen as a form of retreat, or at least a safe haven in which humor, irony, and satire could mask the feelings of pain often found there. This masking strategy is recognizably modernist, even though the poems Parker produces with it use conventional form.

If light verse were the only safe territory, where could she position herself to talk about the pain of others without mocking them? How could she write the political poem? Parker perceived a narrow field of options despite the number of women poets working at this time. But as Charlotte Nekola points out about political poetry in the 1930s, "revolutionary literary theory had a clearly masculine rhetoric" that alienated many women poets. In becoming a "weapon" of class struggle, poetry had even less room for subjective feeling. Even those women who continued to write political poems were excluded from revolutionary anthologies and canon-making accounts of important writers (which tended to be all white and all male). Furthermore, "gender, unlike class," writes Nekola, "did not constitute a worthy political or literary subject."[94] If the poetry written by women, and by Parker in particular, that had examined sexual politics was not deemed political, and if female political poets were not readily available as models, how might Parker have understood the nature of the political poem and poet? Genevieve Taggard, Lola Ridge, and Anne Spencer are a few of the poets who might have offered models for political or social reform poetry Parker could have used.[95] Isolated from that connection, Parker could only dissociate herself from her past. In "Sophisticated Poetry—and the Hell with It," Parker declared, "the songs of my time are as dead as Iris Murdoch."[96] A genuine desire for change met head on with patriarchal assumptions about art and politics. Parker followed her own advice, and let the fire of self-doubt "lick the words away."

CONCLUSION

Parker's poetics of shared conventions, her use of forbidden love, sanctuary, and suicide poetic types, and her thematic concern with renunciation and martyrdom suggests she fits neatly into Cheryl Walker's nightingale tradition. There are, however, some significant differences. In Parker's poetry, form itself provides a kind of sanctuary; the light or sophisticated verse she mastered enabled her to critique and condemn romantic love and women's emotional dependence on men from a safe distance. Her use of humor informs that distance, and provides both a link to and a break from Walker's nightingale tradition.

As Suzanne Clark writes of Edna St. Vincent Millay, love was Parker's "sentimental subject."[97] It was not only a subject unto itself in Parker's poetry, but often the motive behind her poems of martyrdom, suicide, and sanctuary. That Parker would use love as the primary poetic lens through which she experiences the world even though she clearly had other political and social interests says much about the literary culture in which she wrote. The topic of love sold magazines, newspapers, and books because the new sexual freedom for women with its attendant traps and anxieties warranted poetic discourse about love. Furthermore, love remained an acceptable focus for women's poetry. Even some of the more experimental women modernists admired by Pound and Eliot, such as H. D., Mina Loy, and Djuna Barnes, focused much of their work on the subject of love.

   In the broadest possible sense, love as a discourse of feeling, especially when contained in the light verse form, forges Parker's stron-
gest link to the nineteenth-century women poets. Love as a subject
embodies many of the contradictions built into women's poetic production as Parker and her nineteenth-century predecessors knew it:
universal and thus weighted with the importance of humanity, yet
highly personal and thus narrow; accessible and thus garnering a mass
audience, yet largely disregarded by the small intellectual audience
that would judge it; permissible as a subject for poetry in general and
women's poetry in particular, yet limiting for women in ways that a
poetics of "free love" did little to change. Love as a discourse of limitation no doubt enhanced Parker's belief that poetry was not worth
the trouble.

4

The Sentimental Connection II:
Dorothy Parker's Fiction
and the Sentimental Tradition

If Dorothy Parker's twentieth-century poetry seems at times enmeshed in nineteenth-century sensibilities, her fiction offers no less an enigma. Whether she is considered a marginal modernist or outside the canon entirely, whether she is being critically hailed or hammered, Parker is typically referred to as a "modern" writer, particularly where her fiction is concerned. The characterization applies not only to her use of irony and abbreviated form, but to her content as well. Thomas A. Guilason, for example, writes that Parker "used the short story to advance her modern ideas concerning the plight of oppressed people, especially women, struggling for their rights and their independence." He goes on to criticize Parker's fiction for its superficiality, unrelenting cynicism, one-dimensional characters, and reliance on "the standards set by the commercial magazines."[1] Guilason, his own standards apparently set by New Criticism, could be describing a nineteenth-century American woman writer of fiction.

Although Guilason does not use the term *sentimental* in relation to Parker, the characteristics he lists are often associated with the sentimental tradition. Furthermore, sentimental fiction shares many of the characteristics seen in sentimental poetry. Suzanne Clark and Joanne Dobson note the use of accessible language, style, and narrative conventions; Dobson and Jane Tompkins note the use of stereotypes (what Guilason calls "one-dimensional" characters). Passion and power are important and interrelated themes. The romance plot, argues Rachel Blau DuPlessis, subordinates female quest and adventure stories and is the dominant narrative for nineteenth-century

women. But if the subject of love masks a discussion of power in heterosexual relationships, as Alicia Ostriker has argued regarding poetry, then the romance plot in fiction may do the same. Intense female
feeling was also directed to women—mothers, sisters, friends. In either case, Tompkins and Nina Baym argue, sentimental heroines learn
to conquer passion or intense feeling out of recognition that unbridled
feeling can be destructive; the ethic of submission dominates. Not
surprisingly, female tears become a permissible outlet for woman's
rage. Nineteenth-century women writers, claims Tompkins, are concerned also with the general nature of power and who has it, a theme
often manifested in the reform or instructional nature of their work;
they often locate their own power center in the home and the maternal figure where the desire for human bonding is valued.[2] Passion
and power relate to another characteristic of sentimental fiction noted
by Dobson and Nancy Walker, and of particular relevance to Parker—
the presence of satire. The relationship between satire and sentimentalism dates back to the eighteenth century when, as R. F. Brissenden
tells us, "There was . . . a well established tradition of antisentimental
satire, often operating, paradoxically enough, in work which was ostensibly sentimental." The best authors, Brissenden continues, use
satire to critique the aspects of sentimentalism they often employed,
as when a man of sentiment turns out to be a fool or villain. Nineteenth-century women writers, however, tended to direct their satiric
venom at men, most often husbands and lovers, or at social and professional restrictions placed on women, rather than on the sentimental conventions they used. Thus, as in poetry, the use and critique of
"codified gender roles" typically occurs in these works. The desire to
impart a lesson or moral imperative—to convince the reader that the
fiction reflects real-world problems—occurs in satire as well as sentimental fiction, and as Robyn Warhol argues, is a strategy used by Victorian women writers to "engage" the reader.[3]

   We know from Marion Capron's interview with Parker a little about
Parker's early reading in the sentimental tradition at The Blessed
Sacrament School in New York:

> We couldn't read Dickens, he was vulgar, you know. But I read him and
> Thackeray, and I'm the one woman you'll ever know who's read every
> word of Charles Reade, the author of *The Cloister and the Hearth*.[4]

As part of the British sentimental tradition, Dickens and Thackeray
would have given the young Parker a taste for using fiction in the

service of instruction, much the way Adelaide Ann Procter did with poetry. Reade's recurring theme of the struggle against sexual feeling may have influenced Parker's use of sexual conflict in her stories. Reading Victorian novels was not in all cases simply an early, passing interest; Parker re-read *Vanity Fair* throughout her life: "I was a woman of eleven when I first read it—the thrill of that line 'George Osborne lay dead with a bullet through his head.'" Parker strongly identified with Becky Sharp, the novel's manipulative, self-promoting villain. And if we can assume that Parker read the authors she wrote about in her poem "A Pig's-Eye View of Literature," then Harriet Beecher Stowe's *Uncle Tom's Cabin* might have been added to her repertoire. All of these writers may have influenced what Lynn Z. Bloom calls "an implicit plea for reform" in Parker's work, which occurs not only in stories about heterosexual relationships, but in stories about racism and war.[5]

However "modern" aspects of Parker's fiction style and content may be, we can see in her stories a merging together of sentimental and modernist sensibilities and attributes—a personal and impersonal point of view, a reliance on but distrust of romance, a dissatisfaction with the status quo and submission to its reality. As with Parker's poetry, the patterns of connection, both aesthetically and culturally, between Parker's fiction and that of women writing in the nineteenth century are most efficiently and effectively revealed by grouping together observations made by the feminist critics working in this field. The categories—Narrative Form and Space, Bonding and Bound, A Plea for Reform, and In Defense of Feeling—provide critical frames through which new readings of Parker's fiction can be offered.

NARRATIVE FORM AND SPACE

Narrative Form and Space draws two connections between Parker's fiction and that of her predecessors in the nineteenth century. Her use of the sketch, while different in some respects from that of women writers of the nineteenth century, is nevertheless linked with the sketch tradition as outlined by Judith Fetterley, Elizabeth Ammons, Sandra A. Zagarell, and Josephine Donovan.[6] In terms of content, the sketch offers realistic depictions of time and place. It also was an appealing form for women writers of the nineteenth century, argues Judith Fetterley in her introduction to *Provisions*, because the novel, by virtue of its larger form and great literary importance, "received the most interference from the male literary establishment" in terms of acceptable themes and conventions.[7]

Parker's use of the sketch in the early twentieth century could suggest that "interference" was still present, though we may see it to some extent as a positive influence. Magazine editors liked the sketch format. With its brevity and quickness, the sketch looked and sounded modern—an MTV version of prose—against of a backdrop of overly rhetorical and descriptive nineteenth-century prose. Its concision was in keeping with the developing modernist aesthetic.[8] For nineteenth-century women writers, the form's brevity had also been an advantage: sketches could be written in between domestic duties. At the time Parker was writing many of hers in the teens and 1920s, she had none of these, but she did write for a living, producing longer play reviews and essays in addition to her fiction and poetry. Although she did not write quickly, the sketch may have been a way of maintaining her fictive voice while writing more commercial pieces to support herself.

The sense of smallness and limitation embodied in the sketch form provides a more significant connection: Parker's use of space, even in her longer stories, reflects the kind of confinement and limited movement associated with cultural restrictions that kept nineteenth-century women in the home. And as seen in some of the spatial metaphors in her poetry, Parker's stories often use domestic settings. There are far fewer references to "ladies" in Parker's fiction compared with her poetry, but those present tend to be pretentious society types within domestic settings. These are odd strategies, for two reasons: (1) Parker spent relatively little time at home, and (2) she was writing at a time when women's options were supposedly expanding outside of the home. Parker's use of these strategies suggests that New Women continued to face Old Values.

Parker's short stories fall into three groupings: interior and dramatic monologues, dialogues with a minimum of narration, and longer, more fully narrated stories involving more than two characters. The first two groupings are often referred to as "sketches." Two sketch types occur in nineteenth-century British and American literature; the one most relevant in terms of Parker's connection to the sentimental tradition is the village sketch, influenced in America by a British text, Mary Russell Mitford's *Our Village* (1832). The village sketch, sometimes called local color literature, is a form of realism used by early nineteenth-century American women such as Rose Terry Cooke, Harriet Beecher Stowe, and Catherine Sedgwick, and contin-

ued later in the century by Sarah Orne Jewett, Mary Wilkins Freeman, Kate Chopin, and others. Details of place and localized names
typically occur in these works; their realism, argue Josephine Donovan
and Sandra A. Zagarell, runs counter to the romance novel, or
"Cinderella script," so prevalent in the nineteenth century, and forge
a tradition of women's literary realism that continues into the twentieth century. Donovan thus sets the village sketch outside of the sentimental tradition, but as the above scholars have shown, sentimental
literature encompasses more than just romance; it features realism
and an emphasis on community, both of which occur in the village
sketch.[9]

The "village" in Parker's work is New York City, specifically Manhattan. Its particular localities include apartments, speakeasies, train
cars, and cabs. Parker's concentrated attention to the physical details
of character and place exemplifies her realism, as in the opening
sentence of "A Terrible Day Tomorrow": "The woman in the leopard-
skin coat and the man with the gentian-blue muffler wormed along
the dim, table-bordered lanes of the speakeasy." Parker wrote a number of sketches that are entirely descriptive, and thus closely aligned
to the nineteenth-century sketch.[10] Her dialogue sketches, however,
contain much less narrative; she renders her realism through conversation. While Parker's lack of narration is an aspect of modernist brevity, her ear for voice—whether of the sophisticated snob, the insensitive
clod, or the lovelorn individual—creates the strong sense of place so
crucial to the village sketch. The "clipped and fused" slang and clichés
of the 1920s, as Philip Furia points out, circulated through flappers,
fiction writers, light verse poets, and song lyricists. Ira Gershwin, for
example, cut his lyrical teeth on light verse poets like Parker who had
parodied flapperese, and then he returned the influence. A year after he wrote the song "S'Wonderful" for the musical *Funny Face* (1927),
Parker created two characters whose conversation relies largely on
the slang from Gershwin's song lyrics:

> ". . . What a party this turned out to be!"
> "And how!" she said.
> "And how is right," he said. "S'wonderful."
> "S'marvelous," she said.
> "S'awful nice," he said.
> "S'Paradise," she said.
> "Right there with the comeback, aren't you?" he said. "What a girl you
>   turned out to be! Some girl, aren't you?"
> "Oh, don't be an Airedale," she said.[11]

If the borrowed language in this excerpt from "The Mantle of Whistler" seems like a superficial device, it nevertheless points to the
superficiality of communication between the story's protagonists, Miss
French and Mr. Bartlett. The couple, in effect, is parodying a parody
of their own slang for communication. This verbal layering has its
price; their conversation, at once realistic and superficial, gets them
nowhere. Furthermore, the couple in this and other Parker sketches
either come together for superficial or convenient reasons, or break
apart, giving her work an element of anti-romance found in the village sketch tradition. The empty language used to linguistically capture the emptiness of heterosexual romance comments on both the
particularities of 1920s culture and the difficulties of love in general—
in any time and place. Ironically, Parker's success with this technique
was interpreted by critics who labeled her a "period" writer as a limitation.[12]

Another paradox concerns Parker's form. It has been said that
much of Parker's fiction is autobiographical in nature, an account of
her own experiences or the experiences of those she knew. Thus,
there is an element of movement and externality to her work, a sense
of the author/narrator as reporter moving about the world and recording its people and events. Yet the sketch form does not allow
Parker much room for narrative maneuvering; neither does Parker
allow her characters much movement or space. More than thirty of
Parker's stories have static settings and limited or no action. The stories take place in a variety of limited settings: in a room, at a table, or
on the couch at a party in someone's home ("The Mantle of Whistler," "Arrangement in Black and White," "A Young Woman in Green
Lace," "Travelogue," "Who Might Be Interested," "Oh, He's Charming," "But the One on the Right," "The Garter"); over a table in a
speakeasy or restaurant ("Just a Little One," "You Were Perfectly Fine,"
"The Last Tea," "Soldiers of the Republic," "A Terrible Day Tomorrow," "Dialogue at Three in the Morning,"); in the home ("The Sexes,"
"The Wonderful Old Gentleman," "I Live on Your Visits," "The Lovely
Leave," "Such a Pretty Little Picture," "Mrs. Carrington and Mrs.
Crane," "Advice to the Little Peyton Girl,"); in a bedroom ("Lady
with a Lamp," "The Little Hours," "Cousin Larry,"); in the back of a
cab ("Sentiment," "The Road Home"); in the confines of a telephone
call ("New York to Detroit," "A Telephone Call," "'Sorry, the Line Is
Busy'"); in a train compartment ("Here We Are"); and within a single
dance where movement is paradoxically confining ("The Waltz").[13]

Certainly the sketch form invites this kind of physical limitation, and yet even in Parker's longer, more heavily narrated stories, the change in location is typically from home to one or at most two external locations, and most of the story's action takes place in the home. Hazel Morse in "Big Blonde" moves from speakeasy to home; Mimi McVicker in "The Lovely Leave" briefly goes to her job and shops, but most of the action takes place in her small apartment; Miss Wilmarth, the begrudged home nurse in "Horsie," leaves the Cruger home at the end of the story to return to the small apartment she shares with an aunt where she sleeps on a couch. Four stories feature spacious homes—"Horsie," "The Custard Heart," "The Bolt Behind the Blue," and "Glory in the Daytime"—but in the latter two, activity is confined to one room.

Parker's settings prompt several observations. Their smallness can be attributed, in part, to their New York City realism; small apartments and hotel rooms, rather than spacious mansions, were the norm for Parker. The fact that so many of Parker's settings are home-based seems unusual, since she spent most of her time during the years she wrote the bulk of her fiction outside of her own small hotel room. Both of these attributes, however, have ties to social codes and narrative forms of the nineteenth century. A woman's place was in the home, claimed John Ruskin in "Of Queens' Gardens," an influential essay which, as Kate Millet and Gillian Rose argue, helped to restrict Victorian women to the domestic sphere. "Confinement," writes Rose in *Feminism and Geography*, "is a recurring image in women's accounts of their lives."[14] This is no less true in their fiction. Interpreting limited space as a positive, spiritual attribute, Jane Tompkins in *Sensational Designs* claims:

> all sentimental novels take place, metaphorically and literally, in the "closet." Sentimental heroines rarely get beyond the confines of a private space—the kitchen, the parlor, the upstairs chamber—but more important, most of what they do takes place inside the "closet" of the heart. For what the word "sentimental" really means in this context is that the arena of human action . . . has been defined not as the world, but as the human soul.[15]

Tompkins is referring specifically to Christian salvation, an irrelevant issue in Parker's fiction, although moral judgments are clearly implied in "Clothe the Naked," "Arrangement in Black and White," "Soldiers of the Republic," and "Who Might Be Interested." Yet Tompkins's emphasis on heart—on feeling—is certainly relevant to the stories in

Parker's oeuvre that focus on the heartbreak of relationships.
Significantly, a number of Parker's sketches, as well as several of her
longer stories, feature characters who suppress their emotions, desires, and conversation, who are as emotionally enclosed as they and
their narratives are physically enclosed. In "The Last Tea," a nameless woman won't confess her attraction or anger to a man who expresses interest in another woman. In "Here We Are," young
newlyweds are too embarrassed to discuss the upcoming consumma-
tion of their marriage, even though their conversation inevitably slides
toward it. In "The Road Home" and "The Sexes," conversation consists of ironic retorts designed to avoid open expressions of anger
and resentment, yet anger and resentment build, and in "The Road
Home," culminate in violence. The suppression of conversation in
stories relying heavily on dialogue is another paradox that Parker
works to her advantage. She focuses on what her characters say in
order to show what they cannot or will not say. Parker's suppression
of space, movement, and communication not only is an aspect of
modernist concision, but derives as well from gender-based behavioral suppression in the nineteenth century.

BONDING AND BOUND

Bonding and Bound looks at the ways in which some of Parker's stories about love adhere to certain characteristics of sentimental fiction,
or reflect cultural pressures associated with the nineteenth century.
Although similar to the Gender Rigidity category used to discuss
Parker's poetry, Bonding and Bound moves beyond the male-aggres-
sive/female-passive dichotomy. This category incorporates the observations of Jane Tompkins and Joanne Dobson regarding the desire
for human bonding found in sentimental fiction by women. "I think
it is accurate to say," writes Dobson, "that the sentimental imagination at its core manifests an irresistible impulse toward human connection; sentimentalism in its pure essence envisions—indeed
desires—the self in relation." In Parker's fiction, the "impulse toward
human connection" manifests itself in her portrayal of heterosexual
relationships, which are often governed by a code of behavior that
limits female autonomy and agency. This code of behavior imposes a
rigidity on heterosexual relationships in Parker's fiction that seems
reminiscent of Victorian courtship rather than of "free" or "modern"
love. Thus, Parker's female characters often find themselves bound

by the rules they follow in order to secure their desired bond, that is, the love of a man. Another level of bonding that connects Parker with women writers of the nineteenth century concerns formal qualities and audience. Parker shares with her predecessors "an emphasis on accessible language, a clear prose style, and familiar narrative conventions and character types" that "defines an aesthetic," argues Dobson, "whose primary impulse is also generated by a prioritizing of connection, an impulse toward communication with as wide an audience as possible."[16]

Parker focused on heterosexual bonding for good reasons; the world of romance had changed. Early twentieth-century dating was complicated by increased personal and political freedoms for women in general, and by the notion of "free love" in particular. If, on the one hand, "free love" suggested an alternative to the pitfalls of marriage that Emma Goldman defined in her 1917 essay "Marriage and Love," on the other hand it signified a lack of male obligation or responsibility to a female partner who could be damaged physically through pregnancy or venereal disease, or emotionally through society's sexual double standard and expectation of marriage.[17] The actual number of women participating in "free love" may have been relatively small, but the "free love" atmosphere is pervasive in the works of the period.

Romantic relationships in Parker's fiction nearly always fail, yet the very fact that Parker returns to that topic suggests that she places high value on relationships and human bonding. At the very least, the desire for bonding, for a relationship that has the potential for permanence, is important to many of her female characters. Jane Tompkins considers the desire for human bonding in sentimental novels a positive attribute, but in Parker's fiction the desire often degenerates into dependency and confinement. Whether the course of action is "free love," dating as a prelude to or part of a long-term relationship, or marriage, women in relationships with men are encumbered by rules that hint of Victorian rigidity, giving Parker's stories about "modern love" a sentimental twist. These rules concern the extent to which a woman can—or cannot—communicate her feelings to a man with whom she is romantically involved. At issue, of course, is the suppression and validation of women's feelings.

In Parker's "Advice to the Little Peyton Girl" and "A Telephone Call" the female protagonists know the courtship rules but show no ability to follow them. For all the irony this suggests, the rules nevertheless remain valid, for breaking them neither yields success nor eliminates the rules. Miss Marion, in "Advice to the Little Peyton Girl," advises Sylvie Peyton on how to hold onto Bunny Barclay. The advice places Sylvie in a paralyzing never-never land: she should never talk things over with Bunny, never stay home and wait for the phone to ring, never remind him of the sadness he caused her, never ask him where he's been, never start a fight, never make him feel guilty, never let him know how important he is to her.[18] Neither the Peyton girl nor Miss Marion follows these rules, and so to a certain extent the story satirizes the instructional fiction common in the nineteenth century. Yet the rules and their aura of propriety and female suffering remain in place.

These rules take on a near-cosmic proportion in an earlier story, "A Telephone Call." This artfully integrated interior monologue is also an extended prayer that moves from rationalizing, to anger, to irrationality. The speaker prays to God to let her lover "telephone me now" because the rules prohibit her from calling him or displaying her feelings: "I know you shouldn't keep telephoning them—I know they don't like that. When you do that, they know you are thinking about them and wanting them and that makes them hate you"; "He'll be cross if he sees I have been crying. They don't like you to cry"; "They don't like you to tell them they've made you cry. They don't like you to tell them you're unhappy because of them. If you do, they think you're possessive and exacting. And then they hate you. They hate you whenever you say anything you really think"; "They hate sad people." Within the frame of the story, the speaker abides by these rules, yet there is one rule she knows she has broken, described ambiguously as "that." The speaker's "that" could refer to sex; it more likely refers to adultery, given the speaker's defensive and then angry posturing with God—"We didn't hurt one single soul; you know that. . . . It was bad. I knew it was bad. All right, God, send me to hell."— and the fact that the lover never calls.[19] Thus, the telephone call is never received, and the prayer is never answered, enlarging the irony of the story's title and subject: the telephone call that never takes place, the communication made conspicuous by its absence as in "'Sorry, the Line Is Busy.'" Rules of romance and the punishment for rule-breaking are clearly associated with patriarchal authority, in both a human and godly sense.

Other pressures feed into this theme. Clock and time are repeated images, magnifying the speaker's desperation but also suggesting the ticking of the biological clock (Parker was thirty-five when the story was published). The lover was supposed to call by five, so the speaker tries to kill time by counting to five-hundred by fives. This occurs three times in the story, three being a biblical number and also suggesting the possibility of a love triangle between the speaker, the male lover, and the male lover's wife. The speaker lashes out irrationally at the telephone, the lover, God, and the "God damned lie" of romance novels that contain "people who love each other, truly and sweetly." Yet for all her anger and protest, the nameless speaker of "A Telephone Call," like Miss Marion, waits tearfully by the telephone.

Parker is clearly satirizing both the women and the rules, suggesting a modernist rejection of nineteenth-century rigidity; who would want to be with such desperate, dependent women? Their very dependency, however, reflects Parker's continuation of a nineteenth-century theme. In their desire for bonding, these characters subject themselves to rigid, gender-encoded rules that ultimately confine them physically and emotionally. Males are the active initiators of romance, while females remain passive—and at home. Parker may ultimately reject these rules via her satire, but her protagonists who strain against them do not.

"The Waltz" may be Parker's most famous example of gender-based rules of dating and their cost to women, and significantly the waltz was the preferred dance of Victorians. In this monologue by a woman who dances with a partner she secretly dislikes, we have a different rule—a woman never says "No," as explained by the narrator: "But what could I do? Everyone else at the table had got up to dance, except him and me. There was I, trapped. Trapped like a trap in a trap."[20] The narrator then suffers a series of humiliations during the dance, including awkward steps, an inappropriately fast pace, kicks to the shin, a stomped foot. "The Waltz" is famous for its combination of exterior and interior monologues to reveal the paradoxical nature of a woman's experience: the narrator conducts polite, congenial conversation with her partner during the dance, but mentally slays him, leaving us uncertain as to her true feelings. Complementing this aspect of the story is the paradoxical image of confinement in motion. Not only was the narrator "trapped" at the table and forced to dance with this undesirable partner, she is now trapped in the dance itself and all it potentially symbolizes—sex, love, marriage: "And here I've been locked in his noxious embrace for the thirty-five years this waltz has lasted." Read allegorically, this story turns a particular dancing incident into a commentary on the boredom, sexual dissatisfaction, and physical abuse found in twentieth-century marriage. The narrator's "movement" is as confining as the stasis endured by Miss Marion and the narrator of "A Telephone Call."

The desire for human bonding constructs the frame of Parker's "The Lovely Leave," a story set during World War II. Like "Advice to the Little Peyton Girl," "A Telephone Call," and "The Waltz," the protagonist in "The Lovely Leave" struggles to control emotion, passion, and desire, what Jane Tompkins calls "the sentimental heroine's vocation."[21] Mimi McVicker is devastated when her husband Steve's twenty-four-hour leave from the army is shortened to less than an hour, and he spends that time bathing, shining his belt buckle, and thinking about his troops. Her preparations for his arrival, as well as the ensuing argument during his brief visit, underscore Mimi's conventional femininity, as well as the active-male, passive-female roles we find elsewhere in Parker's work. Mimi perceives Steve as "her warrior"; in honor of his visit, she buys an expensive, seductive black dress, a delicate nightgown, perfume and toilet water, and flowers for the apartment. She is proud of him—"He was an American officer, and there was no finer sight than he"—but her role as the waiting wife is more problematic. The "rules" Mimi learned to follow are framed by the special conditions of being a soldier's wife, yet their emphasis on cheerfulness is similar to the rules of Miss Marion:

> Never say to him what you want him to say to you. Never tell him how sadly you miss him, how it grows no better, how each day without him is sharper than the day before. Set down for him the gay happenings about you, bright little anecdotes, not invented, necessarily, but attractively embellished. Do not bedevil him with the pinings of your faithful heart because he is your husband, your man, your love. For you are writing to none of these. You are writing to a soldier.[22]

The fact that Mimi had to "know the rules and abide by them," that "there were rules to be learned," tells us Mimi follows an expected code of suppression rather than choosing a strategy to protect herself from rejection.

If "letters were difficult" because "every word had to be considered and chosen," actual conversation pertaining to Mimi's feelings is worse, degenerating into an argument that further ruins the leave. Mimi breaks the rules, telling Steve how his absence affects her, and revealing her dependency: "'You have a whole new life—I have half an old one. . . . I can't get used to being so completely left out. You don't wonder what I do, you don't want to find out what's in my head—why, you never even ask me how I am!'" Uncomfortable with Mimi's discussion, Steve tries to dismiss it, asking her, "'But aren't you feeling fairly sorry for yourself?'" and suggesting she go out more. Mimi, however, does not want to go out, preferring to stay at home. The argument continues until Steve, on his way out the door, tells Mimi he wants to be with her, but adds, "'I can't talk about it. I can't even think about it—because if I did I couldn't do my job.'" Steve's retreat from feeling to the emotional desert of military duty may be emblematic of the rules he must follow, but it also manipulates Mimi into suppressing her feelings; she later tells a friend the leave was "lovely."[23] Like Miss Marion and the narrator in "A Telephone Call," Mimi strains at the codes that bind her, but ultimately submits to them. This war story reenacts, on a domestic level, the kind of breakdown in communication that leads to war in the first place.

Why the emphasis on rules of courtship and communication in these three stories? The rules found in "The Lovely Leave" may reflect official documentation. The armed services provide manuals to wives of soldiers that instruct them on both military and domestic issues. In general, however, dating rules were in circulation in magazines and books, and Parker read at least one of them. In a 1927 Constant Reader review for the *New Yorker* titled "Wallflower's Lament," Parker discusses *The Technique of the Love Affair* by an anonymous author signed "A Gentlewoman." Parker summarizes the book's rules regarding how women should behave around men as follows:

> You should always be aloof, you should never let them know you like them, you must on no account let them feel that they are of any importance to you, you must be wrapped up in your own concerns, you may never let them lose sight of the fact that you are superior, you must be, in short, a regular stuffed chemise.[24]

Parker concludes "bitterly" that the book makes "considerable sense." By this time she had already written "A Telephone Call"; "Advice to the Little Peyton Girl" and "The Lovely Leave" were yet to come. Ironically, reflecting the "modern" times in which she lived meant Parker had to draw on values from a previous era.

A PLEA FOR REFORM

A Plea for Reform shows how Parker's connection with her audience also embodies a desire for social change, a tendency found in women's fiction of the nineteenth century. Nancy Walker, Suzanne Bunkers,

and Emily Toth have discussed Parker's use of humor in the service
of social protest; my analysis focuses primarily on Parker's
nonhumorous use of stereotypes, a weakness as far as modernist criticism is concerned. Jane Tompkins offers the most useful approach to
reading stereotypes of nineteenth-century authors, not as a weakness,
but as a tool needed to accomplish the narrative's "'cultural work.'"
Stereotypes are useful, she maintains, because they "are the instantly
recognizable representatives of overlapping racial, sexual, national,
ethnic, economic, social, political, and religious categories; they convey enormous amounts of information in an extremely condensed
form." Thus, the one-dimensional characters Thomas Guilason criticizes become agents of cultural change, for they "tap . . . into a store-
house of community held assumptions, reproducing what is already
there in a typical and familiar form." Their presence in a text can
suggest that the author sees her work as something other than an
aesthetic object to be interpreted and appraised as such.[25]

As discussed in chapter 2, Parker's relationship with stereotypes,
particularly racial stereotypes, is a complicated matter. Part of the
complication stems from trying to write about Black culture with very
little first-hand knowledge of the culture, that is, through the bias of
White eyes. Another factor concerns aesthetics. Parker was writing
during a period when writers, critics, and editors were moving away,
though not completely breaking away, from prose forms that relied
on didacticism and stereotypes. By analyzing two of Parker's stories,
"Clothe the Naked" and "Big Blonde," through the lens of Tompkins's
concept of "cultural 'work,'" the conflicting literary values underlying Parker's fiction rise to the surface. In "Clothe the Naked," Parker
uses offensive racial stereotypes for a worthy cause—to explore racism and the economic plight of African Americans—that may seem,
at best, paternalistic to late twentieth-century readers. "Big Blonde,"
often interpreted autobiographically as the story of one of Parker's
suicide attempts, presents a different case. I argue that we can read
"Big Blonde" as a corrective response to Anita Loos's novel, *Gentlemen Prefer Blondes*, a novel by one of Parker's contemporaries that
helped to codify the "dumb blonde" stereotype. One story relies on
stereotypes, seeing them, if somewhat blindly, as agents for social
change. The other story sets out to examine and then negate a pervasive stereotype. One story focuses on race, the other on gender. Both
stories address economic issues and rely on realism and sentiment to
accomplish their "cultural 'work.'"

As pointed out in chapter 2, "Clothe the Naked" was ridiculed for its sentimentality; Parker's heart, the critics argued, got in the way of Parker's head where political issues were concerned. No one doubted that Parker's intentions with the story were political or that, in Tompkins's words, the story had "cultural 'work'" to do. We may never know if Parker read *Uncle Tom's Cabin* or ever took the novel as a model, but there are reasons to believe that she was familiar with the story. Her book reviews, as well as the allusions in her short story "The Little Hours," suggest she read widely in both popular and serious forms, and the fact that she wrote about Harriet Beecher Stowe in "A Pig's-Eye View of Literature" suggests that she might have read the novel.[26] In either case, a number of similarities between the two works invite comparison, and illustrate how *Uncle Tom's Cabin* and "Clothe the Naked" are involved in very similar "cultural work."

Perhaps it is best to first recognize the obvious differences between the two works. One is a novel with more room for action and a larger number of characters, the other is a short story with less action and fewer characters. Stowe uses what Robyn R. Warhol calls an "engaging" narrator, frequently addressing the reader directly and assuming the reader agrees with her moralistic commentary.[27] Parker's omniscient narrator offers no direct address. *Uncle Tom's Cabin* is about nineteenth-century American slavery. "Clothe the Naked" is about twentieth-century racism, though in many respects what Parker describes and enacts through her stereotypes resonates with an antebellum mentality. Stowe's protagonist is a Black man, Parker's is a Black woman; both are victims of an unjust system based on racial prejudice.

Parallels can be drawn between the characters and narrative structure of these works. Initially Tom, a slave belonging to the Shelby family, and Big Lannie, a laundress for several White families, are resigned to their positions and receive some form of compensation. Tom is trusted by the Shelby's to conduct family business across the Ohio River; Big Lannie is told by some of her customers that "she did her work perfectly," though her wages are barely adequate, reminding us that one need not literally be a slave to receive slave wages. Both protagonists go through a period of profound loss. Tom loses his home, his wife, and his children when he is sold to pay off Shelby family debts. Big Lannie, who had lost her husband and three of her children to death, loses her only remaining child, Arlene, who dies giving birth to an illegitimate child named Raymond. His "light-colored" skin suggests his father may have been White, offering a possible reference to miscegenation, a theme Stowe touches on with the mulatto Eliza. Out of their loss rises a period of salvation whereby Tom and Big Lannie are the saviors. Tom saves the life of the White and physically delicate Eva and becomes her companion when Eva's father buys him in gratitude. Big Lannie gives up her jobs—much to the consternation of her employers, who "dressed their outrage in shrugs and cool tones"—to raise the light-skinned Raymond, whose physical delicacy is blindness.[28]

Another period of loss, in which we meet the antagonists, then follows. In *Uncle Tom's Cabin*, Eva dies and Tom is later flogged to death by his new overseer, Simon Legree, a transplanted Yankee from Vermont. There is no murderer, and no literal murder in "Clothe the Naked," but there are modified versions of both. Where Simon Legree represents racial hatred at its most overt and deadly, Parker's Mrs. Delabarre Ewing enacts the upper/middle-class hypocrisy that masks racial hatred. Mrs. Ewing is perceived by Big Lannie just as she wishes to be perceived: the saving grace for giving Big Lannie work again when Raymond is older. Big Lannie subsists on a modern plantation of sorts, for without enough work or money, she is unable to buy winter clothes for Raymond, whose walks outside are one of his few daily pleasures. She begs Mrs. Ewing for clothing, which is begrudgingly offered in the form of an oversized suit of her husband's. The first time Raymond wears the suit on his walk, he is met with a ridiculing laughter that parallels Legree's whip:

> It was not the laughter he had known; it was not the laughter he had lived on. It was like great flails beating him flat, great prongs tearing his flesh from his bones. It was coming at him, to kill him. It drew slyly back, and then it smashed against him. It swirled around and over him, and he could not breathe. He screamed and tried to run through it, and fell, and it licked over him, howling higher.[29]

When Big Lannie comes home, she finds Raymond "on the floor in a corner of the room, moaning and whimpering," his clothes "cut and torn and dusty."[30] Her last act, and the story's conclusion, is the removal of the ill-fitting suit from Raymond's slight frame. Parker's moral lesson is not delivered by rhetoric but by the symbol of the suit, which points to the inappropriate response of Whites to the needs of American Blacks.

Two other points deserve attention. Stowe's novel takes up the fight for abolition while Parker's story deals with its aftermath. The economic issues Parker focuses upon are not just an aspect of her interest in communism in the 1930s; they are a key factor in twentieth-century race relations. A one-time gift cannot replace legitimate work, and only serves to further humiliate those who are made to depend upon it. Perhaps Parker believed that so general a truth needed the generalizing power stereotypes offer, or perhaps her limited exposure to Black culture did not allow her to see individuals. Either case leads to a second observation. Stowe's novel helped to create stereotypes, while Parker's story unfortunately helps to perpetuate them. "Clothe the Naked" was labeled sentimental in the pejorative sense of excessive emotion, but its true sentimental connection is in its use of feeling and stereotypes to achieve reform.

"Big Blonde" offers another opportunity to see the "cultural 'work" of Parker's fiction, but makes a profoundly different move where stereotypes are concerned. This 1929 O. Henry Prize winner, which traces a woman's decline through a disappointing marriage and divorce, a series of boyfriends, depression, and alcoholism, is often praised as one of her best. Yet discussions of it often point to its autobiographical nature; Parker, like her protagonist Hazel Morse, tried to kill herself by taking an overdose of sleeping pills but was discovered in time. While this aspect of the story's relationship to the "real" (in contrast to the fictional) world serves to validate a woman's experience, and thus reveals its "cultural 'work,'" I believe the story responds to another aspect of the "real" world, the "dumb blonde" stereotype codified in Anita Loos's *Gentlemen Prefer Blondes*.

Before examining Loos's novel and how Parker's story responds to it, we should consider the events leading up to this stereotype which incorporates feminine youth and beauty, a lust for material goods, and ignorance thinly veiled as pseudo-sophistication. While the stereotype has its origins in observed behavior among females, its role as a target for ridicule has its origins with members of the Algonquin Round Table. As early as 1914, Franklin Pierce Adams created and mocked the "Dulcinea" character, the feminine sweetheart whose conversation consisted of little more than clichés or "bromides." Though not necessarily blonde, she is necessarily inane. Dulcinea makes statements such as, "If only I could write I know I could fill a book." Adams's character, initially appearing in the *New York Herald Tribune* and *Vanity Fair*, later became the "Dulcy" of George S. Kaufman's and Marc Connolly's popular comedy play *Dulcy*, reviewed by Parker in 1921; she praised it for its comedic powers in both her review and in a poem, "Lynn Fontanne," titled for the actress who played Dulcy.

Meanwhile, another female type known for sexual independence, slang, and inane banter was on the horizon. F. Scott Fitzgerald, another friend of Parker's, had been publishing fictional and nonfictional accounts of flappers and their Jazz Age exploits in the *Saturday Evening Post*. They came out in book form in 1920 *(Flappers and Philosophers)* and in 1922 *(Tales of the Jazz Age)*. In 1922 Parker acknowledged flappers in one of her Figures in Popular Literature poems, "The Flapper," and then dismissed them in 1923 in "Ballade of a Not Insupportable Loss." In effect, the flapper was an Americanized version of the British import, the New Woman. She represented a radical change of values primarily among post–World War I youth. The fact that the flapper became the target of ridicule, not only by Algonquin Round Table members but by a number of writers, editors, and cartoonists like John Held, Jr., may reflect the anxiety felt by an older generation essentially schooled in Victorian values.[31]

During this period Parker also reviewed several comedies or bedroom farces featuring female characters who either marry for money or are suspected of doing so. As time goes by, Parker's attitude toward these productions changes. In 1919 she praises the abundant humor in Avery Hopwood's popular farce *The Gold Diggers*. By 1922, however, *The Gold Diggers* becomes an ironic touchstone in her review of *Lillies of the Field*. Parker claims the play's author, William Hurlbut, "evidently saw *The Gold Diggers* and thought it was great stuff." Hurlbut's play, argues Parker, has "a small and uniquely tedious plot" about a group of "ladies who lead the enviable life of Reilly at the expense of their gentlemen friends." Later that year, Parker is equally testy in her review of Gladys Unger's remake of a French play, *The Goldfish*. The play's heroine marries three times to improve her economic and social status, but "suddenly sees the hollowness of it all, and returns to her first husband and those glorious days of poverty that were hers in the first act."[32] Revealing her modernist inclinations, Parker objects to the play's moralistic and unrealistic turn of events.

With respect to the development of the "dumb blonde" stereotype, two transformations take place between 1914 and 1922. First, a dumb female type, blonde or otherwise, becomes associated with or evolves into the era's symbol of female independence, the flapper. The fact that the flapper or protoflappers such as Dulcinea seek economic gain is in keeping with a decade characterized by an economic boom, speculative spending, and a surplus of leisure items and advertising. But the merger of the dumb with the feminine, especially as it appears in pervasive, popular forms such as comedic theater and mass circulation magazines, will do little to help women gain a foothold as equals in a patriarchal culture. Second, and significant for reading "Big Blonde" as a response to *Gentlemen Prefer Blondes*, Parker's tolerance for the type, and for simple, comedic ridicule of the type, has decreased. Her rejection initially aims at the very nature of the stereotype, that is, its predictability. In "Big Blonde" her critique becomes much broader.

Born the same year as Parker, Anita Loos traveled in roughly the same circles as Parker and would have been exposed to the same cultural dialogue regarding Dulcies and flappers. As early as 1915, Loos published a satire in *Vanity Fair* about a rural girl who comes to New York and marries a rich man. Her character Nella of "The Force of Heredity, and Nella," who accepts a job as a manicurist with the confession that "she did not know how to cure manis," is a prototype of the protagonist in *Gentlemen Prefer Blondes*. In 1963, however, Loos will claim a different and very particularized origin for her 1925 novel. Her fiction, she argues in an introduction to a reissue of the novel, was based on observed fact: H. L. Mencken, a close friend of hers, at times paid more attention to uneducated but attractive blondes than he did to Loos, an educated, attractive brunette. Loos therefore set out to satirize the "witless blonde."[33]

Like *Uncle Tom's Cabin*, it is impossible to know if Parker read *Gentlemen Prefer Blondes*, but it seems highly likely. Parker knew Loos, who, though married to Round Table member John Emerson, was excluded from the group, though she attended other gatherings frequented by Round Table members. In any event, the novel would have been a difficult one for Parker to miss. When *Gentlemen Prefer Blondes* came out in 1925, it was enormously popular, going into sixteen printings between November 1925 and August 1926, and ultimately going into forty-five editions and thirteen translations after having been serialized in *Harper's Bazaar* in 1924. It would later inspire two stage productions and two films. Benét's *Reader's Encyclopedia* reports that some female readers read it as a valid how-to book for single women.[34]

Loos's novel is written in the form of a diary penned by Lorelei Lee, a blonde consolidation of the Dulcy and flapper female types. Her diary describes the events leading up to her marriage, many of them involving a friend who, significantly, is a sharp-tongued brunette named Dorothy. Although she has bobbed hair, Lorelei does not consider herself a flapper; she is instead "an old fashioned girl," one who doesn't say exactly what she thinks as does Dorothy. Lorelei is more calculating than Dorothy; she embodies the gold-digging, "dizzy" or "dumb blonde" stereotype that has remained in currency for most of this century. Loos clearly had urban, elitist intentions regarding her protagonist and narrative. Drawing on Mencken's bias against provincial America, Loos used Arkansas as her protagonist's place of origin because she "wanted Lorelei to be a symbol of the lowest possible mentality of our nation."[35] While Loos achieves a great deal of humor with this strategy, there are moments in the novel where her satire backfires. As I will show, when we consider Lorelei in light of the acquisitive economy that is both the subtext and the context of the novel, we realize she is far too successful to warrant our derision. These moments of satiric failure, as far as Loos's claimed intentions for the novel are concerned, open the way for Parker to respond with "Big Blonde."

Before focusing on these moments and Parker's response, it is worthwhile to consider what this underappreciated novel accomplishes. Its successful moments of satire go far beyond Loos's limited intentions. In her efforts to mock Lorelei, Loos satirizes a number of cultural pillars: highbrow notions of education, public institutions, and male vulnerability to female beauty, feminism and families, the diary form and literary authority, and romantic love, strands of which run through each of the other areas. For example, readers may define Lorelei's adventure as a quest for marriage, money, or happiness, but Lorelei defines it as a quest for education. The diary opens with Gus Eisman the Button King who, as Lorelei tells us, "is the gentleman who is interested in educating me, so of course he is always coming down to New York to see how my brains have improved since the last time." Gus convinces her to keep a diary ("he said that if I took a pencil and a paper and put down all of my thoughts it would make a book," writes Lorelei, echoing Franklin Pierce Adams's Dulcinea, who appeared the previous year), read books he sends her, and travel, all under the guise of "educating a girl," when in fact he is trying to keep her away from other men while he is out of town. Lorelei keeps her diary, but she avoids the books that bore her, and finds it "much more educational" to shop or talk with a small-time bootlegger than to visit the art museums of Munich. She equates education with monetary, rather than mental, assets, as her critique of Dorothy makes clear: "But Dorothy really does not care about her mind and I always scold her because she does nothing but waste her time by going around with gentlemen who do not have anything, when Eddie Goldmark of the Goldmark Films is really quite wealthy and can make a girl delightful presents."[36] Later in the novel, education and intelligence, insofar as they are represented by one of the great minds of the twentieth century, as well as psychoanalysis, are belittled when Lorelei meets Sigmund Freud and disproves his theories. By the time Lorelei closes her diary with a chapter titled "Brains Are Really Everything," a life of luxury is at hand, aligning education with the acquisition of wealth.

Loos also takes aim at male vulnerability to female beauty in her anti-romantic romp. Older men, such as Sir Francis Beekman, rich men such as Gus Eisman and Henry Spoffard, and powerful men in the form of judges, prosecutors, and police officers find themselves seduced by Lorelei's powers. Even two Parisian con men are out-conned by Lorelei as they try to retrieve the $7,500 diamond tiara given to Lorelei, after her careful planning and manipulation, by Sir Francis Beekman. The tiara with its crownlike appearance provides a fitting symbol for Lorelei's power over men. In addition to male vulnerability, several institutions are embodied in this ridicule: British aristocracy and royalty, capitalism, the American judicial system, and the American legal profession.

Feminism and families fare no better. As suggested by the diamond tiara, equality with men would be, for Lorelei, a step down. She pities Gerry Lamson, who felt pressure to marry a suffragette he doesn't love—"she was a suffragette and asked him to marry her, so what could he do?"[37] And Lorelei's future sister-in-law, having found a certain amount of autonomy during World War I, is now an anomaly at home:

> So it seems that Henry's sister has never been the same since the war, because she never had on a man's collar and necktie until she drove an ambulants in the war, and now they cannot get her to take them off. Because ever since the armistice Henry's sister seems to have the idea that regular womens clothes are effiminate. So Henry's sister seems to think of nothing but either horses or automobiles. . . . Henry's sister does not go to church because Henry's sister always like to spend every Sunday in the garage taking their Ford farm truck apart and putting it back together again. Henry says that what the war did to a girl like his sister is really worse than the war itself. [*sic*][38]

This portrait of Henry's sister, of course, is not one of a political being, but merely a caricature, a popular image of a feminist. At the same time, she seems odd in light of the conventional standards of feminine appearance and behavior that Lorelei uses to her advantage. By placing these two figures together, Loos unwittingly underscores an important point: In a market economy focused on consumers of youth and beauty, feminism is a hard sell. Henry's sister disappears both literally and figuratively from the novel; neither feminist nor conventionally feminine, her lack of identity and disappearance symbolizes the waning of feminist political activity after the passage of the nineteenth amendment. Furthermore, the novel seems to be suggesting that even if female self-assertion and feminist politics are as powerful as feminine wiles, they are far more frightening to men.

Other members of the family prove to be hypocrites. Beneath the twining veils of religious piety and old money, Henry's mother is a closet lush, his father a closet letch. Henry, a self-proclaimed moral censor, anxiously spends "all his time looking at things that spoil people's morals," suggesting that the gentleman protests too much. Lorelei concludes: "Life was really to short to spend it in being proud of your family, even if they did have a great deal of money" [sic].[39] The family, for Lorelei, is a kind of bank employing clerks and tellers no one else would hire.

Even the diary form itself, which in this case involves an actual author and a fictional author, is ridiculed. The novel forces the question: Which author is in control? While *Gentlemen Prefer Blondes* contains more wisdom than perhaps Loos intended, it withholds information and draws attention to its gaps, instead of providing the intimate disclosures we have come to associate with diary writing. Although Lorelei claims "to believe in the old addage, Say it in writing" [sic], her diary is significantly vague about whether she is sexually active or merely sexually promising. In her account of her trial, Lorelei tells us Mr. Bartlett "called me names that I would not even put in my diary." She refuses to provide the details of government secrets she later learns from Bartlett, not out of regard for national security, but because they are "to long to put in my diary" [sic]. Regarding her conversations with Lamson and Freud, Lorelei admits to saying "things I would not even put in my diary."[40] Lorelei appears morally tainted by implication, by what is *not* said, a strategy Loos possibly felt was necessary to get her work published, and also suggestive of the Victorian reticence seen in Parker's work. These omissions also can be read as Lorelei's attempt to protect herself, to maintain the stance of innocence that is so useful in her acquisition strategies—the very strategies that undercut Loos's intended satire of Lorelei. If so, we are left to believe that the fictional author wrote this diary self-consciously, with an eye toward publication and payment. Even the rules regarding signification and meaning are questioned. Lorelei's sentence-level errors provide one challenge to writing norms; her rhetoric, characterized by a lack of transitional phrases, provides another.[41] Most of Lorelei's sentences start with "I mean" and "So," implying that Lorelei is unable to connect her thoughts logically, or to render complex relationships among events and concepts. Yet these limitations do not prevent Lorelei from telling her story clearly, thereby seducing a reading public. On one level, the economy-conscious, fictional author of *Gentlemen Prefer Blondes* employs strategies that outwit the actual author.

It is in the area of Lorelei's intelligence, and its play with economics and romance, that Loos's satire falls short of her intentions. Lorelei thinks of herself and her life in economic terms. Recalling the attacks on her character by Mr. Bartlett, the district attorney who unsuccessfully prosecuted her for shooting Mr. Jennings, Lorelei notes, "A gentleman never pays for those things but a girl always pays."[42] As a single woman living in a time when being financially independent meant working in low-paying labor or clerical jobs, Lorelei's quest is to make the gentleman—any gentleman—pay. She uses flirtation, tears, and sexual blackmail to manipulate a series of men into providing her with the best in jewels, travel, and champagne.

Lorelei's rise from poverty and her ignorance regarding history, culture, politics, and current events become the focus of Loos's ridicule. Therefore, Lorelei can only assume a pseudo-sophistication as she reveals a number of "halfbrow" preferences and assumptions: she prefers shopping to reading Benvenuto Cellini, Coty and Cartiers to Place Vendome; she thinks books by Joseph Conrad are about ocean travel, and that "bird life is the highest form of civilization."[43] Lorelei's diary may be a catalog of misused diction, improper grammar, wrong or missing punctuation, and misspelled words, but significantly she knows how to spell "chandelier," "champagne," "emerald bracelet," "pearls," "diamond tiara," "the Ritz," and other words associated with upper-class acquisition, as well as the names of men who buy her such gifts.

Given the cultural context in which Lorelei must survive—a culture that values money and the acquisition of material goods without providing women the opportunity to achieve them on their own—she is highly intelligent. Lorelei wants material comforts without the confines of a marriage that would deter her continued acquisition and her ultimate goal of becoming a film star. This process leads her to invert one of capitalism's primary tenets. Men, rather than the material goods they provide, embody accelerated, built-in obsolescence. Most of these men, much older than Lorelei, are content to have her as a showpiece, to parade her in the jewels and clothing they have bought for her. By using an unmarried protagonist, Loos (perhaps unwittingly) modernizes a turn-of-the-century figure found in the novels of Edith Wharton: that of the married, leisure-class woman whose primary function is to display the wealth of her husband.[44] Unlike her married predecessors, however, Lorelei is aware of her commodity status, and she uses this knowledge to continue the acquisition of her own commodities. Falling in love, she declares, is dangerous for a woman, particularly if the lover in question cannot serve her financially: "When a girl really enjoys being with a gentleman, it puts her to a disadvantage and no real good can come of it."[45]

Another example of Lorelei's intelligence can be found in the ironic subtext of her refrain "Fate keeps on happening," for Lorelei leaves nothing to fate. She plans and executes a number of escapades, including assault, blackmail, espionage, theft, and pseudo-adultery before she finally marries Henry Spoffard, a rich, self-righteous man who agrees to launch her film career but who will more or less leave her alone. Lorelei's economic intelligence is thus aligned with the deromanticizing of love, making her a subversive figure in a patriarchal culture because she can manipulate rather than be manipulated by the passive, feminine role for women defined in the rules of courtship. At the same time, the novel offers the classic romantic ending: poor girl marries rich man. "Failure" is not a word in Lorelei's vocabulary; neither is "age." Outside of flashbacks, the diary covers less than a year in Lorelei's life; our vision of her also aligns success with perpetual youth and beauty. Loos objected to economic readings of her novel, but its economic context cannot be denied.[46] Loos's ridicule became a recipe because in a time of limited economic opportunities for women, Lorelei always won, and those she vanquished continued to love her. Youth, beauty, and money never faded.

The same cannot be said of Hazel Morse, the protagonist in Parker's "Big Blonde," published in 1929 four years after *Gentlemen Prefer Blondes*. Parker's story does share, however, several characteristics with Loos's novel before taking them in new directions. As mentioned previously, Parker's story has an autobiographical component. Hazel Morse, the blond protagonist, attempts suicide, as did Parker on more than one occasion. This feature, combined with Hazel's drinking and her sentimental love for animals has led biographers to put too much emphasis on the autobiographical elements of the story. Yet several characteristics of Hazel that differ from Parker, combined with a number of textual markers that link "Big Blonde" to *Gentlemen Prefer Blondes*, suggest that more was at stake than masked autobiography. Hazel was a large, blonde, full-figured woman; Parker was a petite brunette. Hazel associated with middle-class, traveling businessmen, not the writers and sophisticates Parker knew. Finally, Hazel's lack of an occupation after marriage and divorce is not at all parallel to Parker's experience as a writer in several genres. In terms of links to Loos's novel, "Big Blonde" includes, besides a blonde protagonist, the stereotyping of women, a series of affairs with men, economic concerns, jewels, clothing, drinking, and tears. When these elements are considered in conjunction with the story's suicide attempt, it becomes clear that Parker is offering a serious response to a particular situation.

"Big Blonde" has never been accused of stereotyping, but a type of woman certainly emerges in contrast to the slim, youthful, attractive Lorelei. During the period in which Hazel is working as a model, the narrator tells us, "it was still the day of the big woman." When the narrator tells us that Hazel's "ideas, or, better, her acceptances, ran right along with those of the other substantially built blondes in whom she found her friends," we are left with the impression that blondes, en bloc, think the same way. At one point shortly before her divorce, a male admirer affectionately calls Hazel a "dizzy blonde."[47] After her divorce, Hazel frequents a speakeasy called Jimmy's, where the women:

> looked remarkably alike, and this was curious, for, through feuds, removals, and opportunities of more profitable contacts, the personnel of the group changed constantly. Yet always the newcomers resembled those whom they replaced. They were all big women and stout, broad of shoulder and abundantly breasted, with faces thickly clothed in soft, high-colored flesh. . . . They might have been thirty-six or forty-five or anywhere in between.[48]

Some of these women had a child in boarding school; all were divorced, "matronly," and "fatalistic" about money, relying on a series of male admirers to pay their bills. Laughter was their calling card, but their evenings at Jimmy's would often end with "displays of kodak portraits and of tears."[49] This type of blonde characterized by the aging process has none of the glibness and glamour of Lorelei.

Before Hazel reaches this point, however, she exhibits the same kind of "good time" behavior with a number of men as does Lorelei, and is initially successful. But as we saw in "Advice to the Little Peyton Girl," "A Telephone Call," and "The Lovely Leave," rules of behavior regarding courtship govern Hazel's actions:

Men liked you because you were fun, and when they liked you they took you out, and there you were. So, and successfully, she was fun. She was a good sport. Men liked a good sport.[50]

Hazel must remain cheerful, suppressing any feeling to the contrary, if she is to attract and hold onto a man. Like her other blonde friends, Hazel never questions the rules behind her actions, hence the "Haze" of her name. Other words suggesting a lack of clarity—"hazy," "foggy," "blurred," "dream-like," "fogginess," "'Mud in your eye,'" "mist" and "misty-minded," "cloud," and "her days lost their individuality"—occur throughout the story. Hazel is thus doomed to suffer from her actions in a world that offers few alternatives. Instead of the successful calculation we see in Lorelei, Hazel allows events to push her along. The sexual freedom associated with flappers backfires in Hazel's case, and if we credit "Big Blonde" with a degree of realism, we have to wonder how carefree the Jazz Age was for women.

Parties, drinking, and marriage enter into both narratives, but the progression of these elements differs. Rather than end with a marriage, "Big Blonde" begins with one. Hazel is a full-figured dress model in her early thirties when she meets and marries Herbie Morse. As a model she has been on display, but in a context that distances her from wealth. Clothing is not a symbol of material acquisition for Hazel as it is for Lorelei. Hazel wears the clothes of others, not her own possessions. Furthermore, Hazel forces her feet into "snub-nosed, high-heeled slippers of the shortest bearable size," symbolic of the ill-fitting role of the "good sport" she is expected to play at all times.[51]

In the early days of her marriage, Hazel adopts a "terrific domesticity" that we never see in Lorelei, but it fails to offer a preferable alternative to Lorelei's actions. Married life for Hazel constitutes a reprieve from the rigors of single life: "It was a delight, a new game, a holiday, to give up being a good sport. . . . To her who had laughed so much, crying was delicious." Tears had been a useful tool of manipulation for Lorelei, but Hazel's tears for "kidnapped babies, deserted wives, unemployed men, strayed cats," in short, for "all the sadness there is in the world," repulse Herbie.[52] He increases his own drinking and encourages Hazel to drink, which leads to the further deterioration of their marriage. Hazel's tears, however, are not just the weeping of a sentimental figure, but a sign of dissatisfaction with the world as it is; as such, they have to be controlled, and they ultimately— and ironically—lead to the manipulation of Hazel. Herbie eventually leaves her, and Hazel becomes the kept woman of a series of men who insist that she drink and remain cheerful. Hazel obliges, not with champagne, but with the Scotch whiskey they buy her.

Like some of Lorelei's men, Hazel's men exhibit a certain pride of ownership. The nature of that ownership, however, differs greatly. When Ed, the first of Hazel's men after Herbie, "had a good year," he gave Hazel a sealskin coat, but such gifts were rare from middle-class men with wives and children. The typical "gift" was rent, food, drink, and other necessities. Where Lorelei modeled the wealth of her admirers in terms of jewels, Hazel the ex-model and kept woman was herself the sign of her keepers' success; she appealed to their middle-class sense of worldliness. Ed admired Hazel's "romantic uselessness"— she refused to do any housekeeping—"and felt doubly a man of the world in abetting it" by hiring a maid to clean Hazel's flat. In exchange for this support, Hazel provides not only sexual companionship, but the more difficult offering of constant gaiety. "'What you got to do,'" Ed tells her when she is depressed, "'you got to be a sport and forget it.'"[53] Excessive sentiment breaks the rules of courtship. All of Hazel's men agree, keeping her in a haze of alcohol and denial.

Both Lorelei and Hazel are dependent on men for economic survival, and neither of them possesses deep feelings for these men (with the exception of Hazel's initial passion for Herbie). But there is no diamond tiara in Hazel's closet; Lorelei controls her men, while Hazel is controlled by hers. Hazel's men are not Lorelei's millionaires, but traveling businessmen. Hazel's drinking is not Lorelei's champagne enhancement, but Scotch whiskey's escape. "Alcohol kept her fat," the narrator says of Hazel.[54] Older and overweight by the end of the story, Hazel takes an overdose of sleeping pills and alcohol, but does not die. Her botched attempt at suicide offers the harshest contrast to Lorelei's ongoing success.

Taken together, *Gentlemen Prefer Blondes* and "Big Blonde" suggest that if, indeed, gentlemen prefer blondes, they prefer them perpetually young, thin, attractive, and cheerful; here is where the thematic similarities of these two narratives end. On a related but more serious note, Loos's novel and Parker's story respond in different ways to an economic system that in the 1920s increasingly targeted women as consumers and as objects to be consumed.[55] In her attempt at ridiculing her female rivals, Loos both creates a figure who thrives in a capitalist economy, and ends up ridiculing many of the cultural and economic practices she means to protect from the likes of Lorelei. At the same time, the novel poses no real threat to these practices because

148

its point of view is that of an uneducated rube who succeeds. Lorelei is not a "symbol of the lowest possible mentality of our nation," but a cover girl for the American Dream. Parker, long before her declaration of communist sympathies in the late 1930s, may have appreciated the novel's humor, but must have recognized as well the danger of its false depiction of female success within patriarchal capitalism. Both Lorelei and Hazel play the commodities game with their male counterparts, but Hazel, through her physical, mental, and emotional decline, portrays the high price such a game exacts on the vast majority of women who play it. "Big Blonde" answers Lorelei's well-executed but glib success by offering a much harsher critique of the commodification of women.

Gentlemen Prefer Blondes effectively deromanticizes romance, but "Big Blonde" takes the process a step further by presenting a character in process, a character who ages and changes with the passing of time. Hazel is also a character who feels. Excessive sentiment constitutes a significant part of Hazel's story, and while Big Blonde the character is criticized for it, "Big Blonde" the story was not. Hazel had to withhold sentiment to be successful, but her story to a certain extent did not, pointing to the complicated response modernist readers and critics have to the sentimental. Unlike Lorelei, Hazel is unable to use or pervert the rules against expressing excessive feeling to her advantage. By the end of the story, she is aware of the price she pays, but she sees no alternative other than to take her life. Here is where the story's irony takes charge, and not just because the attempt fails, but because of the nature of the act. Suicide is not simply a tragic act; it can be read as a highly sentimental one since it is motivated by intense, uncontrolled feelings. It is also an act alluded to in nineteenth-century novels and paintings about "fallen" women, and in at least one well-known, late Romantic poem by a poet Parker must have read, "The Bridge of Sighs" by Thomas Hood.[56] Since Hazel's suicide attempt fails, we can see her as a character consistently denied expressions of sentiment (and it is this irony that no doubt makes the story's sentiment palatable to modernist readers). The result: Hazel returns to drink and a grim future. Although both narratives are grounded in realism and anti-romance, Lorelei Lee prompts our laughter, Hazel Morse, our sympathy.

Not surprisingly, "Big Blonde" received more critical acclaim than commercial success. It was published in the February 1929 issue of the *Bookman,* and later that year won the O. Henry Prize; there was talk of a film that never materialized. Four years later, in 1933, Parker would publish another short story, "From the Diary of a New York

Lady," in which she uses the diary form to ridicule the vacuous concerns of the upper class to which Lorelei Lee has ascended. By then, both Parker and Loos would be in Hollywood, a decade of speakeasy living and flappers behind them.

IN DEFENSE OF FEELING

In Defense of Feeling focuses on a key issue regarding sentimental texts: the influence of feminine feeling in the interpretation of a text. This has implications beyond that of reading Parker's—or any author's—work. As Joanne Dobson points out, "A gendered anxiety equating 'emotional' with 'feminine' and nervously rejecting both has . . . operated as a primary shaping factor in the construction of the American literary canon."[57] The nervous rejection Dobson refers to stems from the suspicion that tears and feeling have been used in texts to emotionally manipulate the reader. This is undoubtedly true in some cases, for as Susan Harris argues, sentimental texts, like any text, can be subjected to value judgments; there is good and bad sentimental writing.[58] Dobson, however, is pointing to a tendency among critics to consider all texts containing feminine emotion as sentimental in the pejorative sense without considering the cultural and aesthetic conditions under which they were written. Jane Tompkins, for example, has argued that tears became the acceptable substitution for female rage, an emotion deemed inappropriate for Victorian ladies. Nina Baym's remarks are perhaps more basic but no less valuable: "Need we say something in defense of women's tears?" she asks in *Women's Fiction*. "Women do cry, and it is realism in our authors to show it."[59]

Rage and realism constitute one part of the convention of tears; satire forms another. Sentimental authors are not above satirizing their own conventions. Thus, when we confront a text with female tears, we need to ask to what extent female emotion is being validated or vilified, as well as examine the critical assumptions behind our reading. We have already seen how the issue of sentiment pervades "Big Blonde" in such a way that a defense of women's feelings is implied. Other stories by Parker take a more direct approach and deserve fresh consideration.

In a *New York Times Book Review* assessment of Parker's second volume of fiction, *After Such Pleasures* (1933), an anonymous reviewer describes the relationship between Parker's fiction and sentimentality. Parker's stories are most humorous, writes this reviewer, when they "are concerned with the regrettable but undeniable tendency of most of us to sentimentalize our emotions." The reviewer suggests that Parker's work contains elements of anti-sentimentality when he writes, "She has the inestimable gift of jeering at sentimentality without utterly destroying it, so that though her love-sick girls may be ridiculous we can still regard them with sympathy and intense fellow-feeling." Mark Van Doren also praises this aspect of Parker's fiction.[60] The story these reviewers have in mind is "Sentiment," an interior monologue consisting of female tears and self-pity.

An understanding of the relationship between satire and sentimentalism provides a critical context against which we might read "Sentiment." Both the satiric and the sentimental are based in realism; they have the moral aim of improving society and produce an intense reaction in the reader. Ronald Paulson argues that the pairing of the satiric and the sentimental has its roots in the eighteenth-century novels of Mrs. Mary de la Riviere Manley and Eliza Haywood, who use romance conventions in their satires of government. An evil man raping a woman, for example, becomes the equivalent of a government's betrayal of its people. The merger of the two forms continues in the works of Sterne and Richardson, who often satirize the sentimental conventions they use, and reaches its peak in the nineteenth century novels of Dickens. In American women's fiction from the nineteenth century, Caroline Kirkland, Francis Whitcher, and Marietta Holley satirize sentimental women.[61]

Parker seems to be using the same technique in "Sentiment." The speaker is Rosalie, who is suffering the end of a relationship in the back seat of a taxi. "'Just keep driving,'" she tells the driver, though it is the reader who travels through the reminiscence and emotions of Rosalie.[62] Apparently consumed in self-pity, she snaps out of it in time to suspect that the taxi is driving through the neighborhood she shared with her ex-lover, which sends her on a new round of agony; she then discovers from the driver they are on a different street. One reading of this story is that Parker is mocking the sentimental; Rosalie's excessive emotion prevents her from dealing with reality at hand.

Yet Rosalie remains aware enough of her emotional state to analyze it. After observing "an old charwoman on the street" who she assumes "is done with hoping and burning" about love, she imagines how her ex-lover would have criticized her for her assumptions:

"Oh, for heaven's sake!" he would say. "Can't you stop that fool sentimentalizing? Why do you have to do it? Why do you want to do it? . . .

You don't have to dramatize everything. You don't have to insist that everybody's sad. Why are you always so sentimental? Don't do it, Rosalie."[63]

Afterward, she self-consciously critiques her responses, an act of self-reflection that suggests Parker's use of emotion involves more than manipulation of the reader or satiric rejection of the sentimental. When she hears the rhythm of the taxi wheels saying her lover will not return, she thinks, "That's sentimental, I suppose." When she ponders the sadness of returning to the places where she once knew happiness, she tells herself, "And that's sentimental, I suppose." But her self-analysis also leads her to criticize those people—or readers?—who might be critical of her, those for whom "sentiment" is a dirty word:

> I wonder why it's wrong to be sentimental. People are so contemptuous of feeling. "You wouldn't catch me sitting alone and mooning," they say. "Moon" is what they say when they mean remember, and they are so proud of not remembering. It's strange how they pride themselves on their lacks. . . . And why, why do they think they are right? Oh, who's right and who's wrong and who decides?[64]

Rosalie's question can be interpreted as a validation of female feeling, and resides at the heart of feminist efforts to set Harriet Beecher Stowe and Caroline Kirkland alongside Charles Dickens and Mark Twain. In effect, Rosalie redefines the sentimental by reversing its association with shallow people. She says of those who criticize her: "The shallow people, the little people, how can they know what suffering is, how could their thick hearts be torn?"[65] Rosalie's "shallow people" are not those who are sentimental, but those who reject the sentimental, who refuse to feel.

The fact that Rosalie's analysis of sentiment falls between her melodramatic opening—"Just keep driving"—and her sheepish recognition at the end that she is not in her old neighborhood, might have led readers to assume that her questions and comments comprise the sentimental rhetoric that Parker is rejecting. Yet the feeling of heartbreak in "Sentiment" is Parker's principal concern in story after story, and in many of her poems as well. She doesn't use the romance convention as a strategy to satirically attack a government, but her work in effect satirizes a period of history too often seen as carefree and glib as its titles indicate—the "Roaring Twenties," the "Jazz Age."

Through Rosalie Parker abundantly returns what a male-dominated criticism would diminish—the validity of a woman's tears.

Tears occur elsewhere in Parker's fiction—"The Wonderful Old Gentleman," "Lady with a Lamp," "Mr. Durant," "Soldiers of the Republic," and "Dialogue at Three in the Morning." With the exception of "Soldiers of the Republic," the tears in these stories tend to be an element of what Nina Baym calls "realism" rather than a strategy tied to what Jane Tompkins calls the story's "cultural 'work.'" Tears in these stories respond to a situation—a death, a lost love, an unexpected pregnancy, a punishment, a bruised ego—rather than offer a comment about the situation that generated them, or about tears themselves. War complicates somewhat the use of tears in "Soldiers of the Republic," written in 1938 after "Sentiment" and included in *Here Lies.* In this story, the contrast between a baby's blue hair ribbon and its location in a war zone brings the narrator to the point of tears. Yet the narrator struggles to control her emotions in a self-reflexive moment similar to those seen in "Sentiment":

> "Oh, for God's sake, stop that," I said to myself. "All right, so it's got a piece of blue ribbon in its hair. All right, so its mother went without eating so it could look pretty when its father came home on leave. All right, so its her business and none of yours. All right, so what have you got to cry about?"[66]

Given the narrator's location—a café in war-torn Spain crowded with soldiers and their impoverished families—the narrator is understandably wise in curbing her tears in the face of greater suffering by others. It is significant to note, however, that Parker at once acknowledges and limits female emotion in a story that Arthur F. Kinney compared favorably to works by Hemingway.[67] By 1938, Parker may have been responding to not only the Spanish Civil War, but to, in Suzanne Clark's words, "the modernist . . . invective against emotion" as well.[68]

CONCLUSION

Parker's fiction is shadowed by contradiction: she writes at a time when women's options seem to be expanding, yet locates her protagonists in the confined space of the home; she relies on dialogue yet often her characters fail to express themselves clearly; the early twentieth-century love affairs she describes are riddled with rules that her characters can neither follow to success nor reject; and the hard-boiled, cynical "Mrs. Parker" describes her political and cultural scene with stereotypes and tears. As this chapter has shown, when we examine Parker's fiction within the broader context of her sentimental predecessors and the new interpretations of that work offered by feminist scholars, these paradoxes reflect a collision of nineteenth- and twentieth-century literary values rather than a failure on Parker's part. In fact, the paradox of Parker may stem more from a reading of her that is grounded in—and therefore limited by—New Critical values that ignore the sentimental tradition.

In *Sentimental Modernism*, Suzanne Clark argues that early twentieth-century women writers were cut off from a rich female literary tradition that combined art and social activism by the modernist "revolt against the sentimental."[69] If women were discouraged from seeking models in their nineteenth-century predecessors, they nevertheless could not completely escape sentimental influences, as Parker's fiction clearly illustrates. If her themes are modern, if her prose tends to be sharper and more concise than the sometimes cumbersome rhetoric of nineteenth-century sentimental fiction, she maintains a connection through her narrative form and enclosure, her use of gender role rigidity, her desire for reform, and her emphasis on feeling. In Parker we have a merging, rather than a separation of, the modern and the sentimental. It would be wrong, however, to assume that sentimentalism alone exerted an influence on Parker's work, or that she embraced those values uncritically. Nor can we say that Parker is simply a sentimental writer in the nonpejorative sense. Other influences dominating the *fin de siècle*—decadence and feminism—would filter into her work, further complicating Parker's modernism.

5

Neither Cloister Nor Hearth: Dorothy Parker's Conflict with the Sentimental Tradition

In 1865, James Abbot McNeill Whistler painted *The Little White Girl,* a painting whose line of literary descendents runs from Algernon Charles Swinburne, through the decadents, and into twentieth-century modernism. The painting depicts a young woman in a white dress leaning against a mantel, whose troubled face is reflected in the mirror above the mantel. This image of a divided and conflicted self, which became so prevalent in the 1880s and 1890s, can serve to some extent as a paradigm for the aesthetic conflict we see in Dorothy Parker's work. While her conventional poetic forms, linear and realistic narrative, and impetus toward reform link her with nineteenth-century sentimentalism, certain elements in her work—decadent themes and images, and the feminist strategies of anti-domesticity and revisionist myth-making—can be read as rejections of the sentimental. And yet, the relationship between Parker's sentimentalism and her decadence is more complex than this one-on-one opposition suggests. At times, her decadent techniques and strategies serve an anti-sentimental project; at other times they overlap with sentimental tendencies.

To argue that Parker's decadence is a move away from nineteenth-century values poses some problems aside from the obvious issue of dating. First, the relationship of literary modernism to literary decadence has been subject to some debate. W. B. Yeats, Ezra Pound, T. S. Eliot, and Virginia Woolf considered decadence a Victorian influence that needed to be discarded, a move Linda Dowling calls an example of "the avant garde disavowing its past in order to regenerate itself and gain creative space." Dowling, along with Ian Fletcher, Karl

Beckson, and Thomas Reed Whissen see decadence as distinct from Victorian literary culture, and a precursor to modernism. On the other end of the spectrum, Malcolm Bradbury and James McFarlane fold the 1890s (including decadence and other literary influences) into their concept of the modernist period. Essays by Oscar Wilde, Walter Pater, and French poets influencing decadence are found in Richard Ellmann and Charles Feidelson's anthology, *The Modern Tradition*.[1] If certain elements of decadent literature, such as a preoccupation with death and excessive, destructive passion, seem reminiscent of Victorian themes, a greater number of elements—a world-weary attitude, the retreat from nature, the elevation of art, the use of masks, and the formal concision of the epigram and psychological sketch—move much closer to a modernist aesthetic.

Second, the relationship between decadence and women's literature has been problematic because the male writers associated with literary decadence and aestheticism were notoriously anti-feminist, if not blatantly misogynist. Yet as Elaine Showalter points out in her introduction to her anthology, *Daughters of Decadence: Women Writers of the Fin-de-Siècle*, many women writers in the 1880s and 1890s embraced the decadent aesthetic as a means of revising misogynist notions of women and sexuality. Women's writing in this period, however, is more complex than Showalter's anthology suggests. Her important but limited selections—all fiction—are no doubt designed to emphasize a feminist quality. Had she included, for example, the poetry of Olive Custance or the fiction of Evelyn Sharp, other ways in which women remained within the decadent aesthetic would be apparent. Much of Custance's poetry elevates art, and Sharp's "The Other Anna" portrays a male-female encounter in a bohemian setting that ends in traditional marriage.[2] Other scholars, Cheryl Walker in poetry and Ann Ardis in fiction, have argued that while women writers in the late nineteenth century were increasingly concerned with "modern" issues of female sexuality and empowerment, they often produced "boomerang" works representing a retreat to traditional roles or to despair about their situation. This tendency, they argue, continues in the opening decades of the twentieth century through the continuation of Walker's "nightingale tradition" in poetry, and the muting of anger through an emphasis on form in fiction.[3]

The conjunction of decadence and women's writing raises other issues. The great irony in literary decadence is that its proponents, who come to be known as effeminate, reject a sentimental tradition which itself is associated with the feminine. The decadent rejection of moralizing rhetoric and nature as an ideal seems to set them apart from the sentimental tradition. At the same time, certain elements of decadent aestheticism can be read as an intensification of motifs found in women's sentimental literature. For example, the aesthetic preoccupation with small objects, particularly gems, occurs in much of the poetry by mid-nineteenth-century women. As Ellen Moers points out, images of littleness are common in the works of Christina Rossetti and Emily Dickinson. Cheryl Walker includes several poets in her anthology who use the "language of gems." Somewhat paradoxically, decadent writers use these images as key symbols in their move to reject nature and its association with the feminine through the elevation of art. Yet the elevation of art is itself an act of renunciation and sanctuary—two key elements in women's sentimental literature—from the agonies of human imperfection and physical decay. Not surprisingly, death is a recurring image in decadent works just as it was in sentimental fiction and poetry. Decadent death tends to be eroticized, but there are times when it suggests little more than escape, as in Lionel Johnson's "Nihilism": "Of life I am afraid . . . / The eternal tomb / Brings me the peace, which life has never brought."[4]

Other parallels suggest themselves when decadence and women's literature are set side by side. The use of the psychological sketch by decadent writers can be seen as an outgrowth of the village sketch developed by Mary Russell Mitford. White and silver, important decadent colors via the influence of Whistler's paintings, are associated with the moon, virginity, and femininity. And the decadents' use of self-parody and satire can be found in sentimental literature as well. This brings us to perhaps the most surprising common ground: the impetus toward reform. Though decadents weren't reformers in the overtly political or social sense, they used wit and emphasized artifice to counter sentimental works and the middle-class values they represented. Earlier nineteenth-century feminists criticized marriage and relationships, often using parody and satire to counter sentimental notions of romance. Both decadent critiques and feminist critiques by mid-century women voice discontent with Victorian values and lay the groundwork for more radical, if not permanent, change. Parker's work as a whole embodies this conflict, caught in a struggle between an "old" emphasis on content and a "new" emphasis on form. Significantly, this conflict is inherent in both past and present debates on modernism's geography, its contents and boundaries.

Finally, decadence until recently has been read as degenerate, rather than as a comment on degenerating cultural values. A few critics have associated Parker and the Algonquin Round Table with a decadent aesthetic in this manner. In a 1939 review of *Here Lies: The Collected Stories of Dorothy Parker,* Ruth McKenney observes with disappointment that "there is a large and weighty school of thought which finds Mrs. Parker very fin de siècle, very decadent." Six years later, Herbert Marshall McLuhan would claim that Parker and Alexander Woollcott have "a more or less direct link with Swinburne, Wilde, and the 'nineties. . . . Real but less direct connections with the 'nineties exist also for such writers as Robert Benchley, James Thurber, Ogden Nash, and E. B. White." McLuhan goes on to argue that part of Parker's decadent influence comes through the filter of Housman's *A Shropshire Lad,* which he describes as "Dowson or Wilde 'gone to earth' and become yokel or folksy," and that "the staple conflict in Mrs. Parker's world is familiar fin de siècle boredom with convention."[5] For both McKenney, who admired the social protest in Parker's fiction, and McLuhan, who considered Parker and her cohorts a literary scourge, the decadent influence was far from positive.

More recently, scholars have examined the decadent elements in modernist women writers, such as Katherine Mansfield, Djuna Barnes, Elinor Wylie, and H. D., to ascertain the relationship between gender, modernism, and decadent literary influence.[6] A similar examination of Parker's work reveals her awareness of the decadent aesthetic. She makes reference to Whistler in the titles of two stories, "Arrangement in Black and White," and "The Mantle of Whistler"; and one of her poems, "Convalescent," contains Whistlerian gloom in its "night, beneath a sky of ashes." She includes a verse on Oscar Wilde in "A Pig's-Eye View of Literature," and reviews a 1918 production of his play *An Ideal Husband* for *Vanity Fair.* In her short story "The Little Hours," she mentions reading the French decadent poets Rimbaud and Verlaine. Also, during her tenure at *Vanity Fair,* a magazine that both celebrated and satirized women's accomplishments, Parker was surrounded by remnants of decadent aestheticism. Arthur Symons's essay "On the Value of a Lie: The Intellectual Somersaults of Oscar Wilde" appeared in November 1916. A page on "Vampire Women," including an illustration by Djuna Barnes, appeared in the July 1915 issue. *Vanity Fair* also ran a "hokku contest" in 1915, an extension of the interest in Oriental culture encouraged, among others, by Whistler. And Parker would not have missed the Beardsleyesque illustrations that filled the magazine's pages. Even Parker's notorious slowness in writing—"I can't write five words but that I change seven," she told Marion Capron—echoes an anecdote on fastidiousness by

Oscar Wilde: "I was working on the proof of one of my poems all morning, and took out a comma. . . . [And] in the afternoon? I put it back again."[7]

However slowly or fastidiously Parker wrote, her work presents a composite picture of modernist writing that conflicts with standard versions of modernism. This chapter examines the ways in which three elements converge in Parker's work: decadence, feminism, and a move away from values associated with sentimentalism. In Ideals and the Dark Side I examine poems and stories in which Parker more or less applies decadent techniques in a straightforward manner. The decadent influence becomes more complicated after this. Works where sentimental and decadent values overlap or appear compatible are examined in The Retreat into Form. The next section, Content and Contention, looks at the ways in which Parker's adaptation of decadent techniques serves her desire for reform. Finally, a reading of her feminist works, which at times reject the sentimental privileging of domesticity, and at other times offer new versions of old myths, and which are sometimes infused with decadent images, will be offered in Home Is Where the Hard-Hearted Are and Misreading and Mythreading.

IDEALS AND THE DARK SIDE

Decadents are known for rejecting rosy pictures of life and nature. As rooted as they are in the material world, they nevertheless, argues R. K. R. Thornton, seek the "eternal ideal," and exhibit a "faithfulness for the unattainable." Ernest Dowson's "Non sum qualis eram bonae sub regno Cynarae," in which the speaker remains true to his lost love in thought but not in deed, provides the best example of this.[8] Love, rather than the loved one, becomes the impossible ideal in many of Parker's poems as well. Despite "vows" and "prayers" in "Somebody's Song," the speaker "knows" that "Lovers' oaths are thin as rain, / Love's a harbinger of pain —" and laments: "Ever is my heart a-thirst, / Ever is my love accurst." Yet the speaker, in this and other poems, will continue her pursuit of love, for the loved one in the poem "is neither first nor last." Parker's famous and perpetual disappointment in love, as much as it offers a critique on modern relationships, stems in part from her pursuit of an ideal rather than of a person. "Every love's the love before / In a duller dress," she writes in "Summary," suggesting the impossibility of satisfying her desires as well as the continuation of them.[9]

The unattainable ideal, particularly when it is love, intertwines with two other characteristics associated with decadence—a tendency toward what Thomas Reed Whissen calls excessive and destructive passion, as played out, for example, in Wilde's play *Salome*, and the conflation of images suggesting love and death.[10] We see this intertwining in Parker's work as well. The notion of excess, of course, permeated the 1920s in general, and Parker's Algonquin circle of friends in particular. Drinking, poker, other types of games, affairs of the heart, consumption of material goods—all of these *sans* moderation signified modern urban life. F. Scott Fitzgerald's *The Great Gatsby* is a well-known testament to this experience. If we look at Parker's work as a whole, we see an almost manic pursuit of love despite its inevitable disappointment; in fiction, Parker's "A Telephone Call" and "The Waltz" provide the obvious examples. In her poem "Chant for Dark Hours" the speaker instructs a woman, "[you will] wait your life away // for some damn man!" In both cases, the passion destroys the woman's autonomy and sense of self-worth just as, in terms of the nineteenth-century sentimental tradition, it makes her a martyr. Often, when love is not a viable option, death becomes an attractive alternative. Not surprisingly, some of Parker's poems that describe the demise of a relationship carry titles suggesting death, such as "Threnody" and "Requiescat."[11]

If we look at Parker's work in relationship to literary decadence, these moves can be read as something other than just a singular, morbid self-dramatization. In fact, a decadent evolution of sorts occurs in her first published book, *Enough Rope*. Unlike *Sunset Gun* and *Death and Taxes*, the poems in *Enough Rope* are divided into two sections, and a decidedly different tone occurs in each section. Reviewer Genevieve Taggard attributed the difference to Parker's break, in section two, from the influences of Rupert Brooke, Edna St. Vincent Millay, and Elinor Wylie.[12] My reading of the book as a move from decadent love/death conflation in section one, to a decadent world-weary, not-caring attitude toward love in section two, is not completely incongruent with Taggard's analysis. Decadent themes and images occur in the works of both Millay and Wylie. While not discounting such influences, it is simplistic to accept at face value Parker's (and other critics') claim that she merely "was following in the exquisite footsteps of Miss Millay, unhappily in my own horrible sneakers."[13] The decadent attitude was prevalent during the post–World War I era, and Parker's received influence likely stemmed from a number of sources.

"Threnody," literally a funeral dirge, opens *Enough Rope* with a description of a failing love. Sixteen of the section's thirty-three poems associate love with death in some way, often by expressing a longing for death when love fails. In "Epitaph," the speaker dies twice, the first one an emotional death due to lost love ("between my ribs was a gleaming pain"), and the second one a physical death. The poet does not establish a rhetorical connection between the two deaths, but rather a formal one—the first three couplets describe the emotional death, the last three the physical death. Also, the speaker is a voice from the grave: "And I lie here warm, and I lie here dry, / And watch the worms slip by, slip by," she concludes. The proximity of the two deaths suggests that they are related. After "Love has gone a-rocketing" in "Wail," the speaker demands: "Dig for me the narrow bed"; and in "Testament" the speaker claims: "Kinder the busy worms than ever love."[14]

Three other poems in the first section use the subject of death in conjunction with other attributes of decadence. "The Satin Dress" offers a focus on costume, an important concern of the decadent dandy. Every fabric in the poem has a particular association: bright brocades with wantons, organdie with brides, gingham with plighted maids, wool with a miser's chest, crape with the old, velvet with the loveless, lawn with a bishop's yoke, linen with a nun. Satin, on the other hand, is "for the free!," "for the bold!," "for the proud!" in the speaker's mind, attributes that run parallel to the freedom, boldness, and pride feminists were experiencing in the teens and 1920s. But, she concludes, it has an even stronger association with death: "They will say who watch at night, / 'What a fine shroud!'"[15] Clearly, satin's positive associations are undercut by an image of ultimate confinement. This poem calls to mind Amy Lowell's "Patterns," in which clothing and confinement are similarly connected. If, as Susan Gubar argues, some "female modernists escaped the strictures of societally defined femininity by appropriating the costumes they identified with freedom," others such as Parker who didn't cross-dress recognized the traps associated with feminine costume.[16] Decadent imagery gave her techniques with which to express this in "The Satin Dress."

Two of Parker's Lady poems provide other variations on decadent themes and imagery. A version of the degraded decadent renders him so preoccupied with costume, self, and preciousness that he fades into insignificance. Parker's "Epitaph for a Darling Lady" offers a similar observation, opening with a line containing a color associated with the 1890s:

> All her hours were yellow sands,
> Blown in foolish whorls and tassels;
> Slipping warmly through her hands;
> Patted into little castles.[17]

Parker's "Darling Lady" accomplishes nothing in her life, but we are not to pity her when she dies because she carries her trivial concerns to the grave: "She is happy, for she knows / That her dust is very pretty." Here Parker critiques the decadent attitude of self-absorption. A different lady is revealed in "The White Lady," which on the surface seems to be about a female ghost who is bored with the underworld. The poem describes her restless wanderings, during which she is rejected and feared by the living. To a certain extent, "The White Lady" runs counter to the decadent attraction for death, concluding with:

> We cannot rest, we never rest
>   Within a narrow bed
> Who still must love the living best—
>   Who hate the pompous dead![18]

Yet the divided consciousness suggested by the poem matches that of the "white girl" portraits of Whistler, portraits that helped make white a color of mystery and purity for the decadent writers. Parker was likely aware of the symbolic potency of the white family of colors through the work of her friend Elinor Wylie, of whom she wrote: "It is impossible, I think, to write of [her] work without somewhere using the word 'silver.' It is her word, made for her."[19]

In the second half of *Enough Rope*, the difficulties of love continue, but now the speaker takes on a world-weary acceptance of the inevitable, frequently ending the poem with an epigram and/or a humorous twist. The closing lines alone of several of the poems—"Godspeed," "Love Song," "Indian Summer," "Philosophy," "Observation," "Ballade of Big Plans," and "Neither Bloody Nor Bowed," respectively—indicate a striking change in attitude toward lost love:

> Go take your damned tomorrow!

> And I wish somebody'd shoot him.

> To hell, my love, with you!

And what if I don't, and what if I do?

Because I do not give a damn.

And love is a game that two can play at.

Inseparable my nose and thumb![20]

This kind of wit also serves as a convenient distancing device from the pain of disappointing love, giving these rhymed and metered poems a modernist edge. Parker uses a second technique as well. The speaker in such poems as "A Certain Lady," "Symptom Recital," "Fighting Words," "Pictures in the Smoke," "Nocturne," and the book's closing poem, "The Burned Child," is just as likely to leave her lover or find another as were the men in section one. This attitude is not too far removed from one expressed by Walter Pater in his famous conclusion to *Studies in the History of the Renaissance* (1873): "Not the fruit of experience, but experience itself, is the end."[21] Pater's dictum became one of the driving philosophies behind decadent aestheticism, and Parker absorbs it in the first two lines of the second stanza of "Fragment," a poem about love published in *Life* magazine in 1922. The poem is worth quoting in full, however, because it embodies a second decadent attitude:

Why should we set these hearts of ours above
The rest, and cramp them in possession's clutch?
Poor things, we gasp and strain to capture love,
And in our hands, it powders at our touch.
We turn the fragrant pages of the past,
Mournful with scent of passion's faded flow'rs,
On everyone we read, "Love cannot last,"—
So how could ours?

It is the quest that thrills, and not the gain,
The mad pursuit, and not the cornering:
Love caught is but a drop of April rain,
But bloom upon the moth's translucent wing.
Why should you dare to hope that you and I
Could make love's fitful flash a lasting flame?
Still, if you think it's only fair to try—
Well, I'm game.[22]

The poem's understated ending, as well as its appearance in a humor magazine, leads to its dismissal as a "light verse" poem. Yet "Fragment" represents a version of what R. K. R. Thornton calls "the Decadent dilemma"—a simultaneous rejection of and desire for an eternal ideal.[23] The voice is clearly one of experience, one who has pursued and lost love in the past. If, taken as a whole, Parker's poems constitute a critique of modern love, they do so through a sensibility shaped by attitudes associated with literary decadence.

The settings in some of Parker's fiction also seem to conform to decadent taste, particularly that of the macabre. In "The Wonderful Old Gentleman," the Bain family waits out the death of their father in a living room filled with "objects suggesting strain, discomfort, or the tomb" with "the eventual result of transforming the Bain living-room into a home chamber of horrors."[24] Parker goes at some length to describe the room and its objects:

> It was a high-ceilinged room, with heavy, dark old woodwork, that brought long and unavoidable thoughts of silver handles and weaving worms. The paper was the color of stale mustard. Its design, once a dashing affair of a darker tone splashed with twinkling gold, had faded into lines and smears that resolved themselves, before the eyes of the sensitive, into hordes of battered heads and tortured profiles, some eyeless, some with clotted gashes for mouths.[25]

A sense of decay and decline is unavoidable in this room, where a "close, earthy smell came from its dulled tapestry cushions," and "furry, gray dust accumulated in the crevices." The room's furniture is "dark and cumbersome and subject to painful creakings," and its artwork includes pictures of the Crucifixion, the martyrdom of Saint Sebastian, a "Mother of Sorrows," and "a colored print, showing a railroad-crossing, with a train flying relentlessly toward it, and a low, red automobile trying to dash across the track before the iron terror shattered it into eternity." Nearby a "savage china kitten" is "about to pounce upon a plump and helpless china mouse."[26] This description does more than establish a particular setting; it reflects the conflicted aesthetic in which Parker was working. The images of a decaying Victorian drawing room—the dark, heavy furniture, the religious pictures, the bric-à-brac—collide with a modern depiction of potential collision, the red car and the train. This setting also assists in Parker's deromanticizing of family life. The physical decline suggested by the room and its objects not only runs parallel to the father's death; it suggests a sense of decline in the concept of family. The Bains, who allowed the father to live with them, naively believe in his goodness despite his ingratitude, selfishness, and mean-spirited personality; he willed his money to the daughter who cared the least for him. Using the shades of decadent imagery, Parker paints the dark side of family life.

The fact that many of Parker's poems create a search for or struggle with love might have contributed to Mark Van Doren's observation in 1934 that her "poetry is of a consistent and unvarying sort" and maintains a "refusal to cut any new paths." Van Doren also noted that in reading Parker, "there is the difficulty of separating the woman one has heard about from the woman one is reading."[27] Taken together, these observations imply that Parker is caught within an autobiographical, thematic rut. Yet if we frame our reading of Parker by a knowledge of the decadent influences in which she worked, the rut— one of reading rather than of writing—opens up to new possibilities. Love as an unattainable ideal may at first seem too general a category. After all, the convention of courtly love, also familiar to Parker, certainly envisions love as an unattainable ideal. What aligns Parker's ideal with that of the decadents, however, is not just her location on the cusp of that movement, but her conflation of love and death, her evolution toward a world-weary attitude without ever rejecting the ideal, and the presence of other images found in works by decadent authors. Given that the romance Parker describes often fails or leads to marriages that fail, the longing for death when love fails in poems from *Enough Rope* hints of Wildean humor.[28] In Parker's world, those who see any difference between love and death have experienced neither.

A RETREAT INTO FORM?

One of the points at which sentimentalism and decadence intersect in Parker's work is that of form. Earlier I argued that Parker's use of conventional poetic forms helped to make her work accessible, linking her with nineteenth-century women poets through a poetics of shared conventions. But as Karl Beckson points out in *London in the 1890s*, form for decadent aesthetes became an aspect of their emphasis on artifice, which was designed to move art away from Victorian masses and rhetoric.[29] Most of the poetry in Beckson's anthology, *Aesthetes and Decadents of the 1890s*, uses rhyme and meter, and many poets write ballads as did Parker. William Butler Yeats, whose early poetry was associated with decadent aestheticism, wrote of the ballad form: "My generation, because it disliked Victorian rhetorical moral fervor, came to dislike all rhetoric. . . . People began to imitate old ballads because an old ballad is never rhetorical." Yeats has in mind A. E. Housman's *A Shropshire Lad,* a series of ballads that, as Arthur F. Kinney points out, influenced Parker's poetry.[30] Although ballads have been used to convey overt political messages, the "old ballads" Yeats is referring to are those that focus on a story, leaving any rhetorical or political message, if present, to be inferred.

Parker's "The Dark Girl's Rhyme" offers an excellent example of how the sentimental and modern uses of form intersect. In chapter 2, I argued that this poem, through its use of the ballad form and the forbidden lover motif, fell within Cheryl Walker's "nightingale tradition," yet pushed against the boundaries of gentility through its theme of interracial love. As a ballad in Yeats's sense of the term, its connection to modern verse is further established. Like the questioning presence found in many poems of the Romantic period and in Yeats's poetry, "The Dark Girl's Rhyme" interrogates. It opens and closes with questions, the first casting doubt on the couple's potential as lovers, the second questioning her ability to love another. Yet Parker avoids the use of heavy-handed rhetoric. The conjunction of race, class, and economics and its impact on human relationships is inferred from or informed by her anecdotal description of different ancestries, yet there is no moralizing statement or summation; Parker does not violate the formal constraints of the nonrhetorical ballad.

Coinciding with the emphasis on form, and indirectly connected to the decadent movement, is Parker's use of older French forms—the ballade, the rondeau, and the triolet. These were highly popular forms among early twentieth-century poets, particularly those working in light verse. Austin Dobson, a popular British poet in the 1890s, is credited with having revived interest in all three forms, and his influence, Arthur F. Kinney claims, was passed on to Parker through Eugene Field and Franklin Pierce Adams.[31]

In her use of the forms, Parker focuses on the fickleness of love, using a world-weary attitude also common to the decadents. The three ballades in Parker's *Enough Rope*—"Ballade of Great Weariness," "Ballade at Thirty-five," and "Ballade of Big Plans"—illustrate Parker's skill with the form's demands: three eight-line stanzas with a refrain, iambic tetrameter, three-rhyme pattern, and an envoy that sums up the poem's message. The speaker's nonchalance is indicated in the refraining line of each: "Scratch a lover and find a foe!," "I loved them until they loved me," "And love is a game that two can play at." The two ballades in Parker's *Death and Taxes* use the same theme, refraining with "Women and elephants never forget" ("Ballade of Unfortunate Mammals") and "Poets alone should kiss and tell" ("Ballade of a Talked-Off Ear"). Parker's "Rondeau Redouble (And Scarcely Worth the Trouble, at That)" in *Enough Rope* and her uncollected triolets published in *Life* and the *Saturday Evening Post* follow the same thematic and attitudinal patterns.[32]

We can not discuss decadent form without including the epigram. Although this form dates back to ancient Greece and was used by a number of poets Parker likely read—Martial, Ben Jonson, Francois de La Rochefoucauld, Alexander Pope, Samuel Taylor Coleridge, and Walter Savage Landor—Oscar Wilde kept the epigram in vogue throughout his works and particularly in "Phrases and Philosophies for the Use of the Young." Twentieth-century poets ranging from W. B. Yeats and Ezra Pound to Robert Frost and Edna St. Vincent Millay used the form, as did Parker. Many of Parker's poems have an epigrammatic quality to them, often through the use of a pithy, closing couplet or line. "Inventory" reads like a collection of four such couplets, ending with: "Three be the things I shall have till I die: / Laughter and hope and a sock in the eye." Her most famous epigram, of course, is "News Item": "Men seldom make passes / At girls who wear glasses."[33] This poem seemingly functions on the level of observation, but it offers other items of news as well. In romance, men respond to appearances. Also, as mentioned in chapter 3, the male/active, female/passive dichotomy is recreated here, since it is the men who "make passes," and the poem infers instruction. Thus, in two lines we see a collision of sentimentalism (gender-based active/passive dichotomy and instruction), decadence (epigram form via Wilde's popularization of it), and modernism (elimination of rhetoric, and twentieth-century diction of "make passes").

Parker's fiction also contains traces of decadent influence in the form of the psychological sketch. As Clare Hanson summarizes in *Short Stories and Short Fictions 1880–1980*, the psychological sketch was largely developed by women writers associated with *The Yellow Book* "who were eager to explore what seemed to them unchartered areas of women's subjective experience."[34] These stories are typically characterized by a change of feeling or moment of realization, repeated symbols and imagery, and interior monologue. The narrator in Ella D'Arcy's "The Death Mask," for example, becomes mentally "lost . . . in mazes of predestination and free-will" after viewing the death mask of a famous poet, which has caused the narrator to contemplate the poet's genius and degeneracy. These stories, with their focus on the "delicate inner threads" of experience, as George Egerton calls it in "The Lost Masterpiece," paved the way for the modern short story's emphasis on an individual's epiphanic moment.[35]

Parker's mastery of the interior and dramatic monologue represents an extension of this development in form, and her work thus appears modernist. Yet as we have already seen, the stories within these forms often portray women who are bound by traditional notions of romance and behavior. That both of these traits are so clearly present in works like "The Waltz," "The Garter," "A Telephone Call," "But the One on the Right," "The Little Hours," "Sentiment," and "New York to Detroit" suggests a collision of modernist and sentimentalist values.[36] In all of these interior monologues, the speaker is limited by her dependence on male companionship, while the form permits a realization of her condition, either to the speaker, or ironically to the reader. The speaker realizes her entrapment and despair in "The Waltz," the cruelty of fate in "The Garter," the depth of her anger in "A Telephone Call," women's lack of power and authority in "The Little Hours," and the paradox of emotion in "Sentiment." Dramatic irony is used to reveal the hypocrisy of social occasions and the deception by a lover in "But the One on the Right" and "New York to Detroit," respectively. For writers in a culture recently bombarded by Freudian theory, the self-conscious turn inward was the new frontier, and interior monologue the vehicle. Parker's accomplishment with this vehicle in the short story was matched by her contemporaries in longer and different forms: Joyce used it in passages in *Ulysses*, Woolf in *The Waves*, and Eliot in "The Love Song of J. Alfred Prufrock."

The sense of eavesdropping on the thoughts of others that Parker creates in her interior monologues also occurs in her dramatic monologues and two-person dialogues. In these stories, such as "Lady with a Lamp," "Dialogue at Three in the Morning," "Arrangement in Black and White," "The Sexes," "The Road Home," "The Mantle of Whistler," "Here We Are," "A Terrible Day Tomorrow," and "The Last Tea," the reader "overhears" a dialogue between two people with minimal narration; thus, we see another break from the sentimental.[37] While not directly linked to decadent aesthetics, this technique nevertheless limits the narrator's role and denies the story any moralizing rhetoric. Characters tell their own stories of lost love, hypocrisy, miscommunication, or alcoholism. These stories, which contain radically less narrative than any of the decadent fiction, elevate dialogue to the level of artifice by virtue of being art forms constructed solely or predominantly of dialogue.

Other qualities in Parker's fiction suggest that formal considerations guided her writing. What Paula Treichler noted about "The Waltz" is also true of "Here We Are": the endings of both stories return the reader to the stories' beginning, trapping or encircling the reader within the form itself. "Too Bad" uses a sandwich narrative consisting of three sections. The story of a divorce is told in the middle section; it is sandwiched between the first and third sections in which two friends (*two* friends for the *two* sections in which they appear) of the divorced couple discuss the divorce. Both friends, having been deceived by the marriage's appearance of stability, fail to understand what went wrong, and sum up their concerns with the empty euphemism that gives the story its title, "Too bad."[38] The stability or sense of completion implied in the story's three-part structure is ironic given the instability of the marriage, and the inability of the friends to understand what went wrong.

Parody is an important tool of the decadents, often used in conjunction with the epigrammatic wit and verbal cleverness that Oscar Wilde made so popular. As we saw in chapter 4, Parker parodies the epigrammatic slang so popular in the 1920s in her story "The Mantle of Whistler." The story's title combines slang and a decadent allusion. "Whistler" was an expression used in the 1920s to describe someone who took love lightly and maintained a cavalier attitude. Parker's work contains several whistling lads and whistling girls. Another allusion is also at work here. The "mantle" in Parker's title is the mantle of wit that James McNeill Whistler established through his written defenses of his art and of himself in letters to editors and in his book *The Gentle Art of Making Enemies* (1892).[39] Parker admired true wit, but that offered by her two characters, Mr. Bartlett and Miss French, is a degraded form of wit, a slang designed to seduce or fend off would-be seducers. Rather than serve the intellect, this form of degraded wit that Parker parodies only serves to keep people at a distance from each other. It is Parker's version of modernist alienation.

Other stories focus on a particular type of slang expression that raises complicated issues for women. "The Last Tea," a dialogue story in which a woman realizes she has lost a man's affection to another woman, contains several slang phrases associated with dancing, drinking, and emotion, respectively: "Burn your clothes, baby," "I must have been pretty fried," and "Keep your hair on." "Baby" was the new slang word for a girl or young woman (and at times, though less frequently, for a man or object). While its use represents a modern sensibility during the twenties, it also connotes an infantile dependence and vulnerability on the part of the woman referred to as "baby." It may or may not be coincidental, but it seems highly significant that baby-talk, typically spoken by a female to a male in Parker's stories, became frequent in literary works of the period. Baby-talk offers several, sometimes opposing, levels of meaning. Its most obvious use is as a phrase of endearment, but it can also convert to contempt when addressed to adults, making it a useful tool of irony. Its diction diminishes the person being addressed, conferring to the speaker a sense of power, authority, or control. Yet because the speaker is using a language associated with children, dependence and vulnerability are also conferred to the speaker; if the speaker is female, these two traits can become conflated with the maternal role. Parker's nameless, displaced woman in "The Last Tea" addresses her nameless male companion with phrases such as, "Ah. Whadda matter?," "Was it feelin' mizzable?," and "Ah, I was mean, wasn't I, scolding him when he was so mizzable."[40] In this instance, we can read this language ironically, since the woman realizes throughout the story that her companion has lost interest in her; she's glad he is suffering from the hangover he describes.

In other stories, however, the female-to-male baby-talk is not used ironically by the speaker, and seems in fact highly inappropriate. Grace, the protagonist in "Too Bad," refers to her "daffy down lillies" when speaking to her husband; the story describes the break-up of their marriage. Miss Wilmarth, the unappreciated home nurse in "Horsie," speaks excessive baby-talk to an infant in front of adults, later thanks her employer for a "'lovely little cockytail,'" and comments on roses he gives his wife: "'Oh, the darlings! . . . Oh, the boofuls!'"[41] In "Travelogue," a nameless society woman who asks a male acquaintance about his travels but has no interest in hearing about them scolds him for his absence:

> "Aren't you ashamed? Answer Muvver. Izzun you tebble shame you'self? . . . You come soon! Now you mind Muvver! Don't you be bad, naughty, wicked, tebble boy ever adain. . . . Nighty-ni. . . . S'eet d'eams.'"[42]

Parker realistically captures the voices of her day, but the parody of this language must have a point behind it. Her pointed mockery of the women who use this language could represent an instance, in Ann Douglas's terms, of a matricidal modernist killing off of the Victorian Lady. Yet the baby-talk in these stories is to a large degree the language of modern femininity, and just as this language connotes weakness, these women have no real power. Their men leave or mock them, or they become the author's ironic target. When women address other women with baby-talk, as seen in "Lady with a Lamp," "The Bolt Behind the Blue," and "Glory in the Daytime," neither power nor authentic feeling is invoked. Did Parker realize that the popular slang she parodied served as a metaphor for female vulnerability and complicity? If she did, she wasn't above using the expression "baby" outside of the frame of parody discussed above. She refers to herself (or to a persona like herself) as "baby" in her interior monologue "The Little Hours," where a woman talks herself through a sleepless night, and in her poem "Directions for Finding the Bard."[43] In these pieces, the intention is to capture the modern aspects of the term, but its negative connotations as far as female image is concerned can never be ignored. And significantly, both females in these pieces are alienated.

Perhaps it is unfair to say that Parker retreats into form, or that she emphasizes form as much as the decadents or other modernists do. After all, many of Parker's stories are more fully narrated, and most of them contain some kind of social critique, be it gender, race, class, or a concern for simple human dignity. Still, the fact that all of her poetry aside from free verse parodies follows a formal pattern, and that two of her fictional types stress form over rhetoric, suggest formal considerations occupied her thinking to a significant extent. These tendencies also reveal the overlapping of sentimental and decadent values, and suggest that modernism is not a simple purging of either.

CONTENT AND CONTENTION

Even when Parker seems to adapt decadent techniques in a straightforward manner, a careful reading of her work reveals the complexity of her adaptation. Many of Parker's stories, whether they are dialogues or longer, more fully narrated stories, have similar opening sentences that give her work a formulaic quality. These sentences offer descriptive narration, introducing an often nameless character or characters by the clothes they wear. Yet some of these sentences, presented below, not only open her stories, but open as well inquiries about the content in both her fiction and poetry:

The young man with the scenic cravat glanced nervously down the sofa at the girl in the fringed dress. ("The Sexes")

"Plain water in mine," said the woman in the petunia-colored hat. ("Dialogue at Three in the Morning")

The woman with the pink velvet poppies twined round the assisted gold of her hair . . . ("Arrangement in Black and White")

The young man in the chocolate-brown suit sat down at the table, where the girl with the artificial camellia . . . ("The Last Tea")

The woman in the leopard-skin coat and the man with the gentian-blue muffler wormed along the dim, table-bordered lanes of the speakeasy. ("A Terrible Day Tomorrow")

The young man in the sharply cut dinner jacket crossed the filled room and stopped in front of the young woman in green lace and possible pearls. ("A Young Woman in Green Lace")[44]

These opening sentences prompt observations about the decadence embodied in two closely related aspects of her work: concept of self, and the use of costume and artificiality. First, namelessness is tied to Parker's concept of self in many of her stories. Nameless characters are often used to suggest universality; the story's events could be happening to any of us, or at least to a broad group of people. As stereotypes, these characters fall under New Critical fire. We might also read this technique, especially in its modern form, as an effacement of self, or in Vincent Pecora's terms, a "crisis of faith in the self."[45] The use of clothing to replace the naming of characters, or to suggest traits of named characters, would seem to support this reading, since clothing's temporary nature—we "change our clothes"—implies the lack of a permanent self or self-identity. Parker's emphasis on clothing whether characters are named or not, however, implies that the character's relationship to self is not one of effacement, but one of duality reminiscent of Wilde's Dorian Gray. Characters confidently exert an outer self while their inner or other self remains unknown to them. One of Parker's stories with a strong allusion to decadence, "Arrangement in Black and White,"offers the best example of this phenomenon. The female protagonist believes herself to be open-minded on matters of race. Yet as we "overhear" her conversations with and about a famous Black author, we learn the depths of her racism. Within what has been called the limited form of the dialogue or sketch, Parker implies a call to reform—recognition and rejection of racism—without reverting to political rhetoric. She completes a sentimental project within the decadence-derived form she privileges.

At other times, Parker uses nameless characters to draw attention to artificiality itself. The speaker in "Cousin Larry" tries to break up a marriage but blames the husband's wife for all their problems; significantly, she tells her version while sitting before a mirror. The narrow-mindedness of two would-be sophisticates in "The Cradle of Civilization" is revealed by their contempt for their host country, France. Parker seems to be elevating her characters into artifice via their artificiality. Their narcissism provides a barrier between them and the realities of their immediate situation. Thus, it is possible to read her characters' artifice—their pose—as an extension of decadent posing. It might even be described as a degenerate decadent posing, since the pose they aspire to is pseudo-sophisticated in the first place. Karl Beckson's observation in *London in the 1890s* is relevant here: the narcissistic, effeminate posing of Oscar Wilde was read as a protest to conventional notions of manliness by W. E. Henley, editor of the *National Observer*.[46] The posings of Parker's characters, however, do not aspire to such broad, cultural readings. They focus on more narrow concerns—a friend's husband, or ease and comfort in a foreign country—suggesting that the poses of Parker's characters are parodies of the decadent convention. Both the use of decadent posing and the parody of it link Parker to Wilde and his fellow aesthetes, and also suggest a rejection of decadent values that moves Parker closer to a high modernist aesthetic.

Closely related to decadent posing and the self are Parker's emphasis on clothing and the particularity of her detail, which have roots in the decadent aesthete's preoccupation with costume, cosmetics, and appearance. Some of the descriptions in the opening sentences above suggest the straightforward specificity of realistic fiction: a "fringed dress," a "chocolate-brown suit," a "gentian-blue muffler." Others stress an artificiality that, while being a realistic depiction of cheapness, nevertheless contains echoes of decadent imagery: the "artificial camellia," the "pink velvet poppies" and "assisted gold of her hair," the "possible pearls."

Artificiality embodied the decadent rejection of nature as an ideal to which the arts should aspire. "All bad art," wrote Oscar Wilde, "comes from returning to Life and Nature and elevating them into ideals."[47] This attitude influences some of Parker's poetry as well. In "Song of the Open Country," published in *Life* in 1921 but not included in her poetry volumes, the sentimental images of a "frail bud," "purling brook," and "tiny cottage" through which the speaker "dream[s] of the countryside" are dismantled by the closing couplet: "And I thank whatever gods look down / That I am living right here in town." The poem had enough popular response that *Life* reprinted it. In the two stanzas of "Woodland Song," another *Life* poem published in 1922, the speaker argues that "The hothouses' offerings, costly and rare" cannot match the beauty of flowers found in nature. The couplets following each stanza, however, reveal the speaker's true preference: "No matter how lovely these flowers may be, / Gardenias and orchids look better to me" and "But my favorite blossoms, I'm here to aver, / Are American Beauties at five dollars per." Here Parker desentimentalizes not only nature, but the connection between flowers and love by prioritizing the flowers' price. Parker's poem also can be read as a comic rendition, though not a satire, of Theodore Wratislaw's "Hothouse Flowers," an 1893 decadent poem which asserts, "I hate the flower of common wood or field. // I love those flowers reared by man's careful art."[48]

Decadent posing relates to Parker's work in another way; it suggests a particular form of self and self-creation, the dandy, that precedes and extends beyond 1890s decadence but is nevertheless irrevocably linked with the period. In *Gender on the Divide: The Dandy in Modernist Literature*, Jessica Feldman offers a synopsis of the male dandy's best known characteristics that is worth quoting at length. The dandy, she observes, is

> artificial in dress and deportment, always elegant, often theatrical. . . . He requires an audience in order to display his hauteur, his very distance from that audience. Aloof, impassive, vain, the dandy has a defensive air of superiority that shades into the aggression of impertinence and cruelty. Military in bearing and discipline, the dandy is also as fragile and whimsical as a butterfly. . . . [H]e pursues an ideal of charm and personal beauty which the dominant culture . . . labels feminine. . . . The hall of mirrors is the dandy's ancestral home.[49]

Such characteristics are immediately associated with Oscar Wilde, arguably the most famous figure associated with dandyism, who wrote, "The first duty in life is to assume a pose." Wilde successfully marketed his aesthetic—and his persona—on American soil during his 1882 lecture tour. Karl Beckson argues that Wilde's public persona consumed him; at the very least it consumed part of his literary reputation.[50] As we have seen, the Mrs. Parker persona—the witty but vic-

timized sophisticate of the Algonquin Round Table—had a similar
effect on Parker's career. She became frustrated with interviewers,
Randall Calhoun documents, who wanted to focus only on that aspect of her life. She also masked her early work with two pseudonyms;
one of these was Henriette Rousseau, suggested by *Vanity Fair* editor
Frank Crowninshield as a pun on three French historical figures. The
other pseudonym was Helen Wells, echoing as Randall Calhoun has
suggested "Hell on Wheels," and also a possible parody of the American parodist Carolyn Wells, who is described by Nancy Walker and
Zita Dresner as "the chief female humorist of the first two decades of
the 1900s."[51]

In the broadest possible sense, a dandy is a paradoxical figure who
challenges the sexual polarities of masculine and feminine ingrained
in western culture. The dandy figure is most often a male displaying
feminine attributes, such as elaborate costume and excessive sensibility and delicacy, but female types occur also. Theophile Gautier's
Madeline in *Mademoiselle de Maupin* offers a female version of the
dandy through her combination of personal beauty, physical power,
transvestism, refined tastes, and disdain for the "erotic clutches" of
others. Cross-dressing by women modernists, particularly by expatriates living in Paris, has been well documented by literary scholars
and works of the period.[52] Unlike Janet Flanner, Radclyffe Hall, Jane
Heap, and others, Parker did not dress in masculine clothing. In fact,
she was known in the 1920s for her feminine attire and her large,
stylish hats. Frank Crowninshield recalls her as "reticent, self-effac-
ing, and preternaturally shy."[53] Yet her famous and long-standing
comradery with the mostly male members of the Algonquin Round
Table represents a kind of behavioral cross-dressing, a rejection of
femininity's association with the domestic realm.

Decadence is not an aesthetic that Parker naively embraces in full
or subtly parodies; she also openly satirizes it in her essays and fiction
by showing how its American form degenerates. Two early pieces appear in the April and May, 1918 issues of *Vanity Fair*. Parker offers a
definition of "glossies" which resonates with dandyism in "Are You a
Glossy?":

> A glossy is any person who is just a little more refined than is really
> necessary. The glossies derive their name from the fact that their man-
> ners, morals, speech, shoes, and finger-nails are all a little too pol-
> ished. They venture just a step farther than anyone else among the
> narrow path of etiquette; they are just a trifle more punctilious than

anyone really has to be. They are full of superfluous little niceties—little elegancies of dress and manner and intercourse that separate them from the cruder herd. They are more than refined—oh, much more![54]

Glossies use only their "own purist vocabulary," never succumbing to "the low patois of mere ordinary people." Glossies are always formally and decoratively dressed, "heavily jeweled," and "refute any suggestion of vulgar intimacy" with their spouses by referring to them as "Mr." or "Mrs." Parker's glossies, however, are actually insecure aristocrats with no taste for fine art. This becomes painfully clear when she ventures into their homes in "How to Know the Glossies." "There is a sort of timidity about them that is almost pathetic," Parker writes. "They are always in dread of doing something that the best people aren't doing, of going some place that isn't quite refined, of being forced to associate with common people." They hide "offensively utilitarian" objects, like the telephone, "beneath the spreading skirts of an elaborately costumed lady." The paintings on their walls are conventional; their homes are decorated with "China ornaments," "artificial flowers," and sets of books arranged by the color of their bindings. They mix their Shakespeare and Tennyson with "Myrtle Read and Marion Crawford."[55] Parker's glossies are not just people she has observed and then converted into types for the purpose of ridicule; they are American versions of the British dandy whose aestheticism has degenerated into pretentious self-consciousness.

Parker's glossies can be read as satire directed against the decadent aesthete, but in one of her short stories the portrayal becomes more complicated. "The Custard Heart," written for inclusion in Parker's *Here Lies* (1939), at first appears to be another verbal harpoon directed at the vacuous New York society women with whom Parker often came in contact. But the story has more at stake than that. "The Custard Heart" interweaves two elements that speak of the confluence of decadent and sentimental values in a modernist story: the satiric portrayal of Mrs. Lanier who, like the glossies, is rich and feigns aestheticism but is not associated with cross-dressing; and a satiric rejection of female sanctuary and the sanctity of motherhood. Parker both satirizes decadent aestheticism, and uses it to dismantle conventional femininity and class-based insensitivity to the suffering of others.

Although strictly feminine in dress and demeanor, Mrs. Lanier embodies many of the characteristics associated with decadent aestheticism and the dandy. She is "dedicated to wistfulness"; white is her favorite color for evening apparel; she often studies herself before a mirror; and her relationship with her husband seems anything but carnal. Her daily "duty" was to select and be fitted for new clothes: "Such garments as hers did not just occur; like great poetry, they required labor." Intent as she is on her appearance, Mrs. Lanier in fact becomes an art object through the full-length portrait by Sir James Weir, whose first name and last initial allude to James Whistler. "Wistfulness rests, immortal," observes the narrator, "in the eyes dark with sad hope, in the pleading mouth, the droop of the little head on the sweet long neck, bowed as if in submission to the three ropes of Lanier pearls." He paints her in yellow, and to be true to the painting, Mrs. Lanier wears yellow in the evenings, hearing "comparisons to daffodils, and butterflies in the sunshine," but she soon returns to her preferred white.[56]

Another aspect of Mrs. Lanier's persona is her overly delicate nature. During her clothing excursions, she is unable to endure the sight of ragged strikers outside of shops, or of blind pencil-sellers on the sidewalk. Upon returning home, she must rest before descending to her "sanctuary"—a drawing room "suspended above life, a place of tender fabrics and pale flowers, with never a paper or a book to report the harrowing or describe it." In this room, the narrator tells us, "Mrs. Lanier sat upon opalescent taffeta and was wistful." Here Mrs. Lanier performs a ritual of seduction and rejection, entertaining a group of younger men, confessing to one of them her unfulfilled desire to have a baby, and finally rejecting him when he proposes marriage. The desire for motherhood, however, is another pose, one that Mrs. Lanier practices before the mirror. Meanwhile, she fails to realize that her maid Gwennie is pregnant, despite Gwennie's weight gain, episodes of illness, and the sudden disappearance of the recently hired, young chauffeur.

If the story's irony seems obvious, we might keep in mind that subtle irony may not have been the story's sole purpose. By depicting Mrs. Lanier as a degenerate aesthete, or in Parker's words, a "glossy," Parker deconstructs the home as moral haven to man and children; it is instead the location of superfluous flirtation and bastardy. The sanctuary in "The Custard Heart" is not only a narcissistic retreat from the world of harsh realities, but a center for emotional manipulation and cruelty as well. Mrs. Lanier is not concerned with fulfilling desires, such as the one for a baby, but with the creation of "wistful" poses that unfulfilled desires facilitate. Decadent aestheticism, at least in its degenerate American phase, and female sanctuary are interwoven, both signifying a rejection of often unpleasant physical, social, and political realities. Parker's ironic tone throughout the story underscores her disapproval.

Parker's response to the influence of literary decadence in the opening decades of this century can be loosely compared to a multifaceted crystal or cut gemstone. On one face we see a fairly straightforward adoption of a number of decadent themes, values, and images, as evidenced in *Enough Rope*, stories such as "The Wonderful Old Gentleman," and her preoccupation with verbal wit and form. On another face, we see how decadent techniques offered her an avenue away from sentimental ideals of love and nature, which seemed to have little relevance to modern urban life. Parker's rejection of sentimental values is not absolute, however, for she implies a lesson or message in works like "The Dark Girl's Rhyme" and "Arrangement in Black and White." On yet another face, Parker mocks the decadent aesthete, offering degenerate forms in "The Mantle of Whistler" and "The Custard Heart." Like her close friend Elinor Wylie, Parker would recognize the dangers and limitations of decadent aestheticism, or as Judith Farr puts it, "the folly of art loved for its own sake" without regard to human costs.[57] If Parker's political activity from the 1930s through the 1950s provides the concrete evidence that this recognition occurred, we can nevertheless see elements of feminist posturing, amounting at times to yet another rejection of sentimental values, in some of her "nonpolitical" work as well.

HOME IS WHERE THE HARD-HEARTED ARE

We have already seen, in "The Custard Heart" and "The Wonderful Old Gentleman," how Parker uses the figure of the female dandy and decadent death imagery to depict homes devoid of kindred spirit. It can be said of both of these stories that women take the rap. How then can they be considered feminist? Here it might be helpful to remember that what constitutes a feminist critique is always circumscribed by the historical context in which it is made. Feminism has always been somewhat divided on the issue of home: Is it the location of women's oppression, or a culturally significant location that has been degraded and devalued because of its association with feminine values? Included in this debate, of course, are critiques of woman's role as wife and mother in the traditional family. In the case of Parker, the opening decades of the twentieth century, as in the later 1960s and 1970s, followed a more conservative period that championed traditional domestic roles for women. To depict scenes of domestic discord—to depict what conventional domesticity made of men and women—was to challenge the supremacy of the domestic realm at a time when it was perceived to entrap rather than enrich. Within this context, Parker's antidomestic pieces, even when they criticize the women characters, constitute a feminist critique of gendered assumptions about behavior.

Another important contextual factor regarding Parker's often harsh critiques of women concerns her exposure to the popular Broadway shows. As a theater critic in the teens and twenties, Parker reviewed a number of plays that offered simplistic, saccharine versions of romantic love and domestic life. Parker often criticized playwrights for such unrealistic renditions, and some of her reviews link this flaw to a sentimental tradition she claims to reject. In her review of *The Famous Mrs. Fair* by James Forbes, Parker observes that the play's moral—a "woman's place is in the home"—is far from subtle. She then adds, "Mr. Forbes' work is called a comedy, but one wonders just why, for tears, gulps, and heart-throbs completely out-distance the laughs." She claims that Hubert Osborne's *Shore Leave*, a play about a New England seamstress, "is all just too Mary E. Wilkins Freeman for anything." And the problem with the plays of Rachel Crothers, Parker notes in her review of *Nice People*, is that they end with a "pollyanti-climax."[58] These are just three of many theater reviews in which Parker rejects—and acknowledges the popularity of—the sentimental, happy endings that dominated Broadway theater productions when she was a theater critic. Most of the bedroom farces she reviewed ended with a happy marriage. This not only demonstrates the presence of sentimental values and Parker's complicated response to them; it offers insight regarding her antidomestic pieces. Her harsh critique of women and domesticity are a form of realism designed to counter the fairy tales of Broadway.

Parker's stories and poems that openly mock domestic life and motherhood do so at times without decadent imagery, at other times with it. In either case they represent moves further away from sentimental versions of kith and kin, home and hearth. This is a theme Parker develops early and maintains throughout her career, beginning with "Such a Pretty Little Picture" (1922). The Wheelocks—a name that itself suggests never-ending entrapment—present a "pretty little picture" of domestic bliss to passersby, yet the reality of family life is anything but pretty to Mr. Wheelock. Parker creates in Mrs.

Wheelock the conscientious, well-organized, but dominant wife and mother, who teases her husband into domestic submission by poking fun at his "handyman" ineptness. "'Yes, we finally got Daddy to do a little work,'" she tells her neighbors while Mr. Wheelock is trimming the shrubs, adding that she stays near by "'to watch over him, for fear he might cut his little self with the shears.'" Yet Mrs. Wheelock is not entirely to blame for the charade. Early in their marriage, Mr. Wheelock "had even posed as being more inefficient than he really was, to make the joke better," but having tired of the joke as well as the marriage, doesn't know how to get out of either. His ability to abandon his home for a better life cannot quite match his desire. And the couple's offspring, called "Sister," is as careful and constrained as her mother is controlling or as her father is meek.[59]

Offspring fare no better in three other stories, "Little Curtis," "I Live on Your Visits," and "Lolita." In all three stories, children are treated in cruelly manipulative ways as a means of serving the selfish ends of the mother. Curtis, the adopted son of Mr. and Mrs. Matson in "Little Curtis," is more of a showpiece for his middle-class and stingy benefactors. He was adopted to keep the nieces and nephews from inheriting their money, and to carry on the Matson Adding Machine business. Curtis is paraded out before guests and expected to perform with flawless, adultlike manners. His sailor suit is a stylish fad that reflects the rigidity of his young life. He is expected to address the Matsons formally, is discouraged from acts of generosity, and is punished for "playing with a furnaceman's child" and for spontaneous outbursts of laughter—in short, for being a child.[60]

As the title of "I Live on Your Visits" suggests, emotional manipulation plays a role in the relationship between a divorced mother and her son. When Christopher, enroute from school to the home of his father and stepmother, stops to see his mother, he finds her brimming with alcohol and self-pity. Her mood swings back and forth, from the "charming, wheedling voice, the voice of a little, little girl" who asks her son, "'Well, aren't you going to kiss me?'" to one of cold self-martyrdom:

> A sharp change came over her. She drew herself tall, with her shoulders back and her head flung high. Her upper lip lifted over her teeth, and her gaze became cold beneath lowered lids. . . .
> "Of course," she said in a deep, iced voice that gave each word its full due, "if you do not wish to kiss me, let it be recognized that there is no need for you to do so. I had not meant to overstep. I apologize."[61]

For the duration of Christopher's short visit, he must endure his mother's sarcasm about his father's new life, a verbal assault that paints her as a victim, and that is designed to make Christopher feel guilty for visiting his father. At one point, she begs him to stay "just two more minutes," and finally ends the visit—and the story—with a melo-dramatic monologue:

> "And when you can, when they will release you for a little while—come to me again. I wait for you. I light a lamp for you. . . . I live on your visits."[62]

Parker mocks not only an individual mother's martyrdom, but broader assumptions about maternal instincts through the phrase, "I light a lamp for you." The "lady with a lamp" refers to Florence Nightingale, the nineteenth-century British nurse who epitomized the self-sacrificing nurturing of others; her image appeared in magazine ad-vertisements during the 1920s. Another variation of this phrase occurs in the title to Parker's earlier short story, "Lady with a Lamp," in which the friend of a woman who has lost her lover and aborted her preg-nancy proves to be a very inept and insensitive visitor. Clearly, Parker did not view maternal instincts as inherent or essential aspects of women.

Although this story was written in the mid-1950s, Parker supple-ments the image of Christopher's degenerate mother with decadent imagery, suggesting the longevity of decadent influence on Parker's work. The mother's hotel room is filled with mirrors—on walls, doors, picture frames, cigarette boxes, and jackets for match boxes—sug-gesting self-absorption. Mme. Marah, a visiting friend of the mother, is a large, overweight woman with an interest in astrology and palm reading. Dressed in sequined but shabby black tweed, she wears on her wrists "bands and chains of dull silver, from some of which hung amulets of discolored ivory, like rotted fangs."[63] She also wears a mauve veil through which she drinks and smokes. When Marah reads Christopher's palm, she sees illness, an unhappy love affair, marriage, a dead offspring, and little money. With such a reading, she offers Christopher no relief from his mother's barbs. Marah's shabby dis-play is a degenerate form of fin de siècle occultism that complements the mother's degenerate maternalism.

"Lolita," also written in the mid-1950s, offers an antidomestic mes-sage but without the decadent imagery. Mrs. Ewing, the separated, then widowed mother in "Lolita," has not degenerated into alcoholism and self-pity, in part because she sets herself up in contrast to her plain daughter. Thin, pale, mousey, and inept at domestic skills and fashion, Lolita becomes the butt of jokes between Mrs. Ewing and Mardy, her housekeeper and cook. But Mrs. Ewing's laughter turns to jealousy when John Marble, a handsome and successful business-man from New York, falls in love with Lolita and marries her. Mrs. Ewing takes to slamming doors and adopting a smug "We'll see" atti-tude about Lolita's future. Significantly, "Lolita" and "I Live on Your Visits" offer stinging critiques of motherhood during a decade when, as Lois W. Banner points out in *Women in Modern America: A Brief History,* housewifery and motherhood were again being lionized as the highest occupations for women.[64] Parker, whose writings to a certain extent are based on observations of friends or overheard conversations, is in some respects a "journalist" of the period, "reporting" that all is not well on the domestic front. Parker's stories suggest that motherhood, whether in 1850 or 1950, is not the highest calling for all women.

Three of Parker's poems also take a very pointed antidomesticity stand. The speaker in "Story of Mrs. W——" describes her garden of "blossoms pink and white" and "trees . . . amiably arranged" where she walks and listens to her neighbors' chatter. But in the final stanza, her home is a metaphorical coffin she wishes were real:

> My door is grave in oaken strength,
>   The cool of linen calms my bed,
> And there at night I stretch my length
>   And envy no one but the dead.[65]

"Day-Dreams" offers a more humorous rendition of the same mes-sage. Addressing her lover, the speaker describes the life they would live in their "little bungalow / If you and I were one." Her version, in which both find bliss in domestic life, is both highly romanticized and terrifyingly realistic:

> I'd buy a little scrubbing brush
> And beautify the floors;
> I'd warble gaily as a thrush
> About my little chores.
> But though I'd cook and sew and scrub,
> A higher life I'd find;
> I'd join a little women's club
> And cultivate my mind.[66]

The poem closes with a rejection of this lifestyle: "And so I think it best, my love, / To string along as two." People do attempt to live the domestic fantasy, and as noted in such Parker stories as "Such a Pretty Little Picture," "I Live on Your Visits," "Mr. Durant," "Glory in the Daytime," and "The Banquet of Crow," they often fail to either be happy or hold the marriage together. Parker also deconstructs the dream of domestic bliss in "The Whistling Girl," whose speaker prefers to have a succession of lovers rather than a husband. Her answer to the married women who "gabble and honk and hiss" behind her back is that married life is confining, boring, and loveless. "Better a heart a-bloom with sins," she argues, "than hearts gone yellow and dry" in a long and loveless marriage.[67] Decadence resides, Parker implies in this 1928 poem, in the institution of marriage, rather than in those who would do without it but are themselves labeled "decadent."

The antiromantic treatment of domesticity, and of heterosexuality in general, is a repeated theme in the works of women modernists. In fiction, Katherine Mansfield dissects marriage and family life in stories such as "Prelude," "At the Bay," and "Bliss," as do Djuna Barnes in *Ryder* and Virginia Woolf in *Mrs. Dalloway*. Among the poets, Mina Loy ("Love Songs to Johannes") and Marianne Moore ("Marriage") offer similar critiques. Lesbian texts by Gertrude Stein, Charlotte Mew, Radclyffe Hall, and Djuna Barnes form another aspect of this challenge to heterosexual norms. Such works, whether they are formally experimental or conventional, support Judith Kegan Gardiner's observation in "On Female Identity and Writing by Women," that modernist women's texts not only deny convention, but indicate a breakdown in secure gender boundaries.[68] Parker's stories and poems discussed above certainly fit into this category, and she shares with her modernist contemporaries a second strategy.

MISREADING AND MYTHREADING

As we saw in chapter 3, Parker relinquished her poetry because she could not see it as a vessel for political issues, nor could she recognize the inherent politics of her "light" verse. Her poem "A Well-Worn Story" implies that her poetry's source is a broken heart. Neither the source nor the poem has value because when a lover leaves she will "spoil a page with rhymes." In "Directions for Finding the Bard," Parker associates the poet with "Trouble," "Gloom," and death, but names no particulars. Again, the poetry is devalued because it consists of "gibbering and squealing."[69] Yet in other poems Parker was also participating in a tradition with feminist underpinnings that began prior to and permeated through the nineteenth century, and that has continued through the twentieth: women's revisionist mythmaking.

It is not surprising that Parker uses this strategy even if she failed to recognize its subversive nature as politically inclined. A number of her modernist contemporaries—Yeats, Pound, Eliot, H. D., Millay, Wylie, to name a few—were employing mythology in their poems. For women in particular, and especially for a poet like Parker who had so little regard for her own work, mythical figures offered a special advantage. As Alicia Ostriker points out in *Stealing the Language*, mythical material stemming from myth, legend, history, the Bible, or any religious text "confers on the writer the sort of authority unavailable to someone who writes 'merely' of the private self." The power conferred in any revision can be substantial, even when mythical figures are only alluded to. Consider Parker's one-stanza poem, "The Flaw in Paganism," which on the surface seems designed to reflect the famous Parker persona and the carefree aura of the twenties:

> Drink and dance and laugh and lie,
> Love, the reeling midnight through,
>   For tomorrow we shall die!
> (But, alas, we never do.)[70]

Yet this poem also responds to and deflates the philosophy behind the male carpe diem poets who not only used the fear of death as a seduction technique, but whose poetry is part of the vers de société tradition in which Parker participates. Thus, Parker's brief poem takes on a much broader significance. The revisionist strategy as Ostriker defines it has a feminist agenda as well: "The core of revisionist mythmaking for women poets lies in the challenge to and correction of gender stereotypes embodied in myth," often by using "hit and run attacks" and by "turning Other into Subject."[71] A number of Parker's poems contain allusions to female mythical figures. Some of these figures are used conventionally; others take on a more radical nature.

Mythical figures not only provide a source for revisionist strategies and assertions of power; they also provide a "highbrow" contact point. In other words, among educated readers, mythical figures convey familiar representations of larger or more general themes based on actions done by or to them and the consequences of those actions. As such, they possess a utility similar to that of the stereotype: immediate recognition to the reading public. Parker made use of this aspect of mythology in several of her poems. Rather than revise the conventionalized readings of these figures, she capitalizes on them. "Reuben's Children," a one-quatrain poem, uses the curse laid upon the biblical Reuben for sleeping with his father's concubine as a way of describing the curse—and irony—of twentieth-century romance. The offspring of Reuben are essentially "dead" in terms of reputation or historical importance because, as a result of the curse, they fail to capitalize on opportunities or give rise to significant leaders. In terms of twentieth-century romance, Parker's descendents of Reuben are in a similar state. Those who "seek to find monogamy" must pursue "it from bed to bed"; the speaker concludes "they would be better dead." In a sense she has delivered the very curse she describes. "Reuben's Children" refers to lovers of both genders, but Parker focuses on mythical women in other poems. In "Rainy Night" the speaker is too busy living to be bothered with the "ghosts" of her "lovely sins"; she orders them to "Roam with young Persephone" instead. Both "Renunciation" and "Song of One of the Girls" offer catalogs of history's beautiful, seductive women—Helen, Hebe, Hero, Chloe, Sappho, Salome, Dido, and Eve, among others—as a way of pointing to the speaker's relative shortcomings. "Partial Comfort" uses the same strategy but with a shorter list. Helen and Sappho are also included in the ironic comparison of sexual prowess in "Words of Comfort to be Scratched on a Mirror." The female prophet in "Cassandra Drops into Verse" predicts the destruction of a relationship due to sentimental domesticity rather than the destruction of a regal family.[72]

The conventional meanings behind these figures facilitate Parker's cynical, self-deprecating poetry about the travails of romance. Given the humorous edge to these poems, the seriousness with which these mythical women are normally regarded gets undercut, so to a limited extent a kind of revisionism is implied. But in order for the poems to work at all, readers must be aware of the beauty and seductive power these mythical women conventionally embody. Inherent in these poems as well is the collision of "high culture" mythologies with "low culture," mass-market publishing in popular magazines.

Parker uses revisionist strategies in five other poems focused more directly on myth or legend: "Iseult of Brittany," "Guinevere at Her Fireside," "Salome's Dancing Lesson," "Penelope," and "From a Letter from Lesbia." All five legends center on romance, ranging from patient faithfulness to lust. To varying degrees, Parker revises the legend in each of them, often by giving voice to the female character. "Iseult of Brittany" probably remains closest to its original story, the medieval love triangle between Tristan and the two Iseults—the one who is queen of Cornwall and with whom he has adulterous affairs, and the one in Brittany he later marries. Unable to consummate his marriage because of his vow of devotion to the queen, Tristan tells his wife he vowed one year of chastity to the Virgin. She learns of his deceit, however, when, mortally wounded, he calls for the queen of Cornwall who has the power to save him. Iseult of Brittany is known for killing Tristan in a fit of jealousy by announcing that the queen has not arrived when in fact she has. In her thoughtful analysis of this poem, Ruthmarie H. Mitsch has called "Iseult of Brittany" "true poetry" because Parker's "two quatrains . . . capture so many tones of so many layers of the myth." Mitsch points to the poem's focus on Iseult's white, "delicate," and "lovely hands," which symbolize her beauty, her unconsummated marriage, and her weakness, for she can neither win Tristan's love nor resist the jealousy that leads to his death.[73] But in addition to capturing the essence of the myth, Parker offers a subtle ironic comment: Feminine beauty can fail to win a suitor, and come to symbolize female, rather than male, suffering instead. Iseult's "lovely hands" become her "bitterness."

Like "Iseult of Brittany," "Guinevere at Her Fireside" and "Salome's Dancing Lesson" also follow their original stories, which incorporate the love/death theme of interest to decadent writers. The Guinevere of Arthurian legend is linked to King Arthur's—her husband's—death through her affair with Sir Launcelot; as a result, she lives out her remaining life as a nun. Parker's Guinevere speaks from the convent, looking back on her life and her choices not with guilt, but with ironic detachment. The six-quatrain poem opens and closes with the same stanza:

> A nobler king had never breath—
> I say it now, and said it then.
> Who weds with such is wed till death
> And wedded stays in Heaven. Amen.[74]

Although this stanza reads like a kind of prayer, we can suspect a pun of "Amen"—"Ah! Men!" stated in perplexity or exasperation—when we consider the rest of the poem. Guinevere's wedded state was anything but heavenly. She overhears the knights and King Arthur "talk of love," yet she had "naught to do but think, at night," and her bed was merely "a thing to kneel beside." Arthur's lack of attention, the poem implies, leads Guinevere to have an affair with Launcelot, though only because "Tristram was busied otherwise." This is a thoroughly modern Guinevere, a strong woman in contrast to Launcelot's previous lover, "that chalky fool from Astolat / With all her dying and her pains!"[75] The men in the poem are also weak. Though noble and brave, one cannot deliver sexually, and the other falls short intellectually. Parker offers hard-edged justification and implied sexuality rather than apology for Guinevere's actions in order to mock the convention of unconsummated courtly love.

"Salome's Dancing Lesson" can be read as a response to the biblical Salome, but it more likely responds to Oscar Wilde's dramatic version which helped give rise to the image of the veiled, vampiric, and destructive woman, an image that remained popular in the United States throughout the teens and twenties. In Wilde's version, Salome agrees to dance for King Herodias in exchange for the head of John the Baptist (Jokanaan in the Wildean version). After dancing and kissing the severed head, Salome is put to death by Herodias, an act that lays most of the blame for Jokanaan's death on Salome. Parker takes the story in a different direction. The double entendre of the title of Parker's poem forces the question: Is this a lesson given to Salome or a lesson Salome gives? The voice of the poem is that of an experienced woman, and if we take it as Salome's voice, then she has escaped the death sentence of Wilde's play. The "lesson" offered by Parker's Salome, however, concerns the foolishness of powerful men. Ask for little and you get little, she argues in the first stanza, but "What's impossible to kings?" Since "Kings are shaped as other men," and "Veils are woven to be dropped," kings can be easily, sexually manipulated into providing death— "the rarest prize of all." Parker spends no time discussing Salome's motivations; her point is that Herodias's foolish lust is equally to blame for the death of Jokanaan. "Scratch a king and find a fool!" Salome chants at the close of the poem.[76]

By altering the moral frame of the story—that is, by making both parties, rather than just the woman, accountable in the story's deadly seduction—Parker deconstructs the exaggerated powers of the veiled woman. Unveiled female sexuality cannot be evil, then, without an equally evil and willing partner at hand. Salome is still dancing at the close of Parker's poem, suggesting that the dance of fools continues, and reminiscent of the ongoing cycle we see in her story "The Waltz."

Like "Guinevere at Her Fireside," Parker shows little compassion for powerful patriarchs.

"Penelope" and "From a Letter from Lesbia" offer more pointed responses to the myths upon which they draw. Penelope, the long-waiting, long-suffering wife of Ulysses, offered modernist women writers a bone of contention where female roles and behavior are concerned. Edna St. Vincent Millay wrote about Penelope in "An Ancient Gesture," a poem that contrasts Penelope's authentic emotion with Ulysses's "gesture" of emotion.[77] Though the poet's sympathy resides with Penelope, the mythical figure has no voice, and the poem retains the emphasis on weaving, patience, and faithfulness. In contrast, Parker's "Penelope" uses an element of humor and lets the voice of Penelope ring with sardonic wit at her condition:

> In the pathway of the sun,
>   In the footsteps of the breeze,
> Where the world and sky are one,
>   He shall ride the silver seas,
>   He shall cut the glittering wave.
>
> I shall sit at home, and rock;
> Rise, to heed a neighbor's knock;
> Brew my tea, and snip my thread;
> Bleach the linen for my bed.
>   They will call him brave.[78]

On a literal level, "Penelope" suggests that facing the dull routine of domestic life requires more courage than sailing "the silver seas," but a close examination yields other twists to the story. Parker's poem downplays the importance of the traditional Penelope's weaving and unweaving of a tapestry, a ruse to keep suitors at bay. "Snip my thread" can be read as a reference to unweaving the tapestry at night, though it is vague enough to suggest any kind of domestic sewing. Curiously, "snip" could also imply the completion of a sewing project, putting into question Penelope's faithfulness and patience. The fact that she must "bleach the linen for my bed" could suggest another dull domestic routine, or the possible removal of stains from love-making; given the numerous references to illicit love throughout Parker's work, such a reading is not entirely out of range. In Parker's Penelope, whether we read her as impatiently promiscuous or merely sarcastically humorous, we see the dismantling of a romanticized icon of feminine patience and domesticity. Two other poems by Parker, "A

Certain Lady" and "Chant for Dark Hours," while not alluding to
Penelope directly, offer a counterpoint to the kind of patience the
traditional Penelope represents.

"From a Letter from Lesbia" provides an even stronger, more direct rejection of a canonized romance—Catullus's love for Lesbia.
The poem can best be described as a response to Catullus's poem no.
3, which tells of the death of Lesbia's sparrow, although it addresses
in general Catullus's love for Lesbia.[79] It is a love that Parker's Lesbia
rejects out of hand from the first stanza:

> . . . So, praise the gods, Catullus is away!
>   And let me tend you this advice, my dear:
> Take any lover that you will, or may,
>   Except a poet. All of them are queer.[80]

As Catullus's poem no. 11 attests, Lesbia has other lovers in addition
to Catullus, and thus becomes the source of his martyrdom and disil-
lusion. To a certain degree, then, Parker remains true to the original
story; her re-vision lies in the altered point of view, from Catullus to
Lesbia. In Parker's poem, Lesbia is not the voiceless being of desire
and denial, but a woman with an argument. Catullus's romanticized
suffering for the sake of love seems melodramatic against Lesbia's
complaint—that Catullus treats events in Lesbia's life and his feelings toward her as little more than grist for his poetic mill:

> It's just the same—a quarrel or a kiss
>   Is but a tune to play upon his pipe.
> He's always hymning that or wailing this;
>   Myself, I much prefer the business type.
>
> That thing he wrote, the time the sparrow died—
>   (Oh, most unpleasant—gloomy, tedious words!)
> I called it sweet, and made believe I cried;
>   The stupid fool! I've always hated birds . . .[81]

By mocking and questioning the extent to which Catullus's affections
are genuine, Parker's Lesbia illustrates the way in which Catullus's
Lesbia has been victimized. Parker's Lesbia is more than the woman
who, in Catullus's words, is "blind to the love that I had for you /
once, and that you, tart, wantonly crushed."[82] Instead, her rejection
of Catullus is in fact a rejection of being made the object of his art.
This strategy points to the flaws in Catullus's nature, and complicates

the notion of unrequited love in his poem. Read in this way, "From a Letter from Lesbia" is more than an exercise in humorous verse; it rejects the romanticized notion of the female object d'art.

All five of these poems challenge or debunk sentimentalized notions of legendary romance. Particularly in "Penelope," "Guinevere at Her Fireside," "Salome's Dancing Lesson," and "From a Letter from Lesbia," Parker gives her mythical women a modern, cynical voice with which to offer their point of view, and thus revise their story. By giving, for example, Lesbia this voice, Parker's "From a Letter from Lesbia" answers Catullus the way, Ostriker argues, Denise Levertov's "The Fountain" answers T. S. Eliot's "The Waste Land," or Sharon Olds's "The Language of the Brag" answers the boasts of Walt Whitman and Allen Ginsberg.[83] The nursery-rhyme quality of Parker's rhyme and meter adds another level of irony to her versions, for her women are anything but innocent and childlike. It should be pointed out, however, that Parker, in moving her female figures from passive victim or object to cynical victimizer, is merely shifting them from one patriarchal convention to another. Yet in doing so, she presents the flaws and culpability of the male figures who have traditionally overshadowed the female ones. In contrast to the legends as they are conventionally understood, Parker's poems suggest that it takes two to make history, to make legend. Her male and female character remakes, with their flaws, are infused with a realism that bears a feminist message. To the extent that we can define women's "traditions" by individual strategies, these poems of Parker's belong in a tradition of revisionist mythopoesis.

CONCLUSION

Parker's embrace of decadence was not a preferable alternative to sentimentalism, but an unavoidable and in many ways productive influence that, despite its limitations, appealed to a number of modernists.[84] Decadence, feminism, and a rejection of sentimental values converge to form a complicated and conflicted rubric in Parker's work. The fact that sentimentalism embodies a plea for reform intersects nicely with Parker's feminist concerns, yet the sentimental privileging of the domestic sphere becomes a target for Parker's feminist attack. At times, the decadent aesthetic informs or assists Parker's feminism and antisentimentalism through her use of domestic images suggesting death and decay; at other times it stands in conflict with them because of the disregard for human suffering and inequity that "art for art's sake" embodies. If decadent imagery and themes provided avenues through which Parker could challenge sentimental constrictions, they could at the same time put her at odds with her own humanity-based aesthetic. Parker's recognition of this no doubt contributed to her parodies of decadent conventions.

Given the sentimentalism and decadence in her texts, where is the "modern" in Dorothy Parker's modernism? If modernism is that narrowly defined concept used to create the traditional canon, then we could point to the concision of much of her fiction, but not without acknowledging the nineteenth-century sketch tradition. We could point to the sense of alienation found among Parker's characters, who miscommunicate or fail to make relationships and marriages last, but not without acknowledging the alienation inherent in the sanctuary and forbidden lover poems of nineteenth-century women, and in the elevation of art promoted by the decadent aesthetes. We could point to the lack of polemic in much of her work in the teens and twenties, but not without acknowledging the inherent feminist critique in many of those poems and stories that has its roots in the satires and complaints of women writers in the nineteenth century. Significantly, the traits that assured her exclusion from the high modernist canon—her popularity and sentimentalism—also stem from nineteenth-century literature.

Parker's modernism is the collision of these diverse conventions, themes, and attitudes in the early twentieth century. This reading of Parker adds to the growing body of work cited throughout this study that attempts to redefine modernism as a complex literary period rather than as a collection of aesthetic principles. As Parker's work and the popular and critical responses to it suggest, the period's complexity is largely a function of the continuation of literary norms associated with women writers during a period in which a male-dominated critical establishment was rejecting them. While the gendered collisions in her work mark her as a writer of the modernist period, she is not a "period" writer. Her themes and concerns—romantic love, generational conflict, abortion, racism, war, economic disparity—are timeless and relevant across cultures. Viewed in this context, Parker's work, like literary modernism, is more complex than many critics have allowed.

If we can trace competing and conflicting influences in Parker's poetry and fiction, we have to wonder how they might have contributed to her sense of herself as a writer, and to her level of productivity. Parker was in her late thirties when she moved to Hollywood, took up screen writing, and focused her energy on more overt political activities. By the time she reached forty—a time when careers often reach or approach their peak—Parker had rejected poetry and was writing virtually no fiction. Was she shifting her career or rejecting it? The argument that she was seduced away from literature by Hollywood money and political interests no doubt has its place, though it should not negatively influence the way we read what work she did produce. The red scare tactics of the 1950s, such as blacklisting, may have also discouraged her from writing, although they did not discourage her from political activity. Yet the literary influences to which Parker responded offered little encouragement to her, in spite of her popularity. On the one hand, the critical rejection of the sentimental tradition denied her a sanctioned outlet for her humanity-based aesthetic. On the other hand, decadent aestheticism, which served as a direct conduit to modernist values, became for Parker as well as Elinor Wylie a dead end. And, if women's poetry consisted of "little verses," it could not be significant. The gendered collision so prevalent in Parker's work may have produced psychological shrapnel that contributed to Parker's move away from poetry and fiction.

Coda

Although she alluded to some of her literary values in her book and theater reviews, Dorothy Parker never defined her own aesthetic. How might we define it?

She wrote in more than one genre, and an interesting aspect of her work is the appearance of similar characteristics in both her poetry and fiction. We can observe spatial metaphors, particularly those involving domesticity and sanctuary, in her poetry, and images of spatial confinement, also involving domestic scenes, in her fiction. A concern with form is apparent—triolets, roundeaus, ballades, ballads, sonnets, and the general use of rhyme and meter in her poetry; experimental sketches, monologues, dialogues, and more fully narrated stories in her fiction. Brevity or concision characterizes the vast majority of her poems and many of her short stories, most notably her monologues and dialogues. She also tends to generalize in both genres, to talk about types of people and types of behavior that are grounded in both genders and in the dominating social codes for both. Yet in her fiction, her nameless characters are often described with such exquisite detail that they possess a particularity that moves against the grain of generalization. Upon common ground, this technique seems to imply, stand myriad individuals. Her poems often close with reversals, creating a comic and sometimes epigrammatic effect, but reversal as a form of closure is also seen in the blues music that was growing in prominence during the twenties, and thus seems appropriate in a body of work that so often is "singing the blues" about its subject. We see similar kinds of reversals in her monologues "The Garter" and "But the One on the Right." While her fiction is more typically open-ended, at times her stories use a circular closure, bringing us back to the beginning, as in "The Waltz," "Here We Are," and "Cousin Larry." Her world-weary, long-suffering persona appears most clearly in her poetry and theater and book reviews, though we get a taste of it in many of her monologues. This choice runs parallel to the realism and critique found in her work. We might understand Parker's aesthetic in terms of a mosaic, creating a distinctive voice out of a complex of strategies used fairly consistently.

Notice I have not mentioned humor or satire as descriptors of her work, as categories of her aesthetic. These elements are of course an important presence in her work, and are well examined by Nancy Walker, Emily Toth, and Suzanne Bunkers in essays cited previously in this study. However, when we focus exclusively on Parker as a humorist, we risk missing the rich interaction of theme and technique, and of history and contemporaneity she displays. In much of her work, humor is a tool rather than a goal. My point is that in addition to this well-established aspect of her work, we need to consider other elements as well. As old-fashioned as it may sound, we need to continue the kind of close and careful reading of Parker's style that Arthur F. Kinney conducted in his 1978 and revised 1998 studies, also mentioned previously in this study. This kind of reading in conjunction with a consideration of issues concerning context outside of the Algonquin Round Table, and tradition outside of modernism, yield a much richer sense of Parker's range and accomplishments.

Where do we locate Parker in terms of literary tradition? This study has focused on the collision of nineteenth-century sentimentalism and twentieth-century modernism in her work and the tensions and conflicts such a collision produces, but clearly the influence of other literary periods appears in her work. We have seen conversations with or allusions to biblical, Greek, and Roman literature and mythology; to medieval romance; to Shakespeare, Donne, and Cavalier poets; to John Milton; to eighteenth-century satirists such as Pope and Prior; and to other literary movements in the nineteenth century besides sentimentalism, involving rejections, at least in terms of content, of Romanticism and elements of Victorianism and Decadence. That many of these conversations, allusions, or rejections are presented in terms of conflict between sexes, races, or socio-economic classes suggests that Parker was not only modernizing the terms of the debate. She was participating in an evolving construction of tradition—a tradition that, once defined as more or less static by New Criticism, left her and a host of other writers out. Unfortunately, she had no sense of tradition as an evolving construction, or as an evolving, ongoing conversation. She did not know that other women in other periods had voiced similar concerns, but were cut from the record of the conversation. Her parenthetical subtitle to her poem "Verses in the

Night"—"After an Evening Spent Reading the Big Boys"—offers not only humor (she includes Gertrude Stein along with E. E. Cummings and T. S. Eliot in her parody of "the Big Boys" of literature), but a definition of who creates tradition-worthy works. In that regard, Parker was a victim of her times; she could not see the implicit and explicit feminism and politics of much of her work.

Instead, Parker would see how her work was perceived by anthologists in her lifetime. Parker's work would not appear in anthologies that were in the process of defining a generalized American canon— Conrad Aiken's *American Poetry, 1671–1928 (1929);* Harriet Monroe's and Alice Corbin Henderson's *The New Poetry* (1932); Louis Untermeyer's *Modern American Poetry* (1950); or Cleanth Brooks and Robert Penn Warren's *Understanding Poetry* (actually, a poetry textbook, but a highly influential one, 1951). Her work did appear, however, in these anthologies: J. B. Mussey's *The Cream of the Jesters* (1931); Louis Kronenberger's *An Anthology of Light Verse* (1935); and Bennett Cerf's *An Encyclopedia of Modern American Humor* (1954). Without a doubt Parker's work belongs in both categories of anthologies.

Parker was unable to discover the value of her work, but we now have the critical tools with which to recover it. If reading Parker's work in a broader historical and literary context yields its complexity, reading the *reception* of her work within the prevailing cultural and critical contexts proves equally valuable. It can be no coincidence, for example, that Parker's critique of domesticity was lost in the late 1940s and the 1950s when domesticity reigned in that post-Depression, post-war era. Likewise, new appreciation of her work surfaced as a result of the second wave of feminism in the 1970s.

Our next step is to trace Parker's influence, in terms of genre, style, and content, on the writers following her, thus delineating her role in the process of literary tradition(s). Nancy Walker already has demonstrated the link Parker's work provides between pre-twentieth- and late-twentieth-century American women's humor; Sondra Melzer examines the feminism in a selection of her stories. I want to suggest some other directions, in terms of both literary techniques and literary descendants, these kinds of studies can take. As a book reviewer and fiction writer who combined humor and feminist critique, she may have served as a model for Gloria Steinem, Nora Ephron, and Fran Lebowitz. Even Norman Mailer might have been intrigued with the contradictions embedded in her work. The relatively frank discussions of sex in some of her poems may have inspired Erica Jong.[1] And we have to wonder if Anne Sexton and Sylvia Plath read Parker's suicide poems. Finally, Parker's poetry and fiction may have offered significant influence overseas. Her collected works have been published in England since the late 1930s; as recently as 1992, Duckwork published *The Sayings of Dorothy Parker.*

Stevie Smith, the mid-twentieth-century British poet and novelist whose work shares a number of similarities with Parker's, may have read an American edition of Parker's fiction that influenced the rhythm of her first novel, *Novel on Yellow Paper* (1936)[2] Parker's "The Waltz," with its use of stream-of-consciousness and interior monologue techniques, may have provided that rhythmic influence. Parker and Smith also share a number of personal and professional elements that suggest the need for comparative study: both had difficult births and estranged relationships with their fathers; both were preoccupied with death, attempted suicide, and wrote about it; both directed their caustic wit at friends and male partners; both critiqued the limitations of heterosexual love and marriage, focusing in particular on gamesmanship and rules; both used a childlike or nursery-rhyme technique, clothing imagery, and masking in their fiction and poetry; and both wrote in a variety of genres, enjoyed commercial success, and have been categorized as humorists. Unlike Parker, Stevie Smith left behind a substantial record of correspondence that speaks of her literary values. The Stevie Smith papers at the McFarlin Library, University of Tulsa, contain no reference to Parker, but they do refer to a number of writing and muse-related issues—obscenity, sophistication, sadness, alcohol—that we can see in Parker's work. Other connections between the works of Smith and Parker have been investigated by Laura Severin.[3]

On a more contemporary note, Wendy Cope's use of humor and form—triolet, ballade, roundeau redouble—as well as her closing reversals and caustic critique of male lovers and authorities, certainly suggest an affinity with Parker. Cope's poem "Some More Light Verse," published in *Serious Concerns* (1992), has the staccato, declarative sound, and cataloguing effect of several of Parker's poems, such as "Résumé," "Interview," "Men," and "General Review of the Sex Situation," all found in *Enough Rope.* Also like these poems by Parker, Cope's "light verse" deals with the difficulty of maintaining happiness and of the problems generated by male–female relationships.

Several of the comparisons described above draw heavily on the use of humor. While these comparisons are valuable, we might also consider other formal and thematic techniques as a basis for investigation. Given the formal quality of Parker's poetry, where does her work stand with respect to that of the poets included in Anne Finch's anthology, *A Formal Feeling Comes: Poems in Form by Contemporary American Women* (1994)? Can the critique of domesticity found in Parker's fiction be linked with the 1970s consciousness-raising novels analyzed by Lisa Maria Hogeland in *Feminism and Its Fictions: The Consciousness-Raising Novel and the Women's Liberation Movement* (1998)? Can the sympathy for political and social underdogs found in Parker's poetry, fiction, and essays be usefully compared or contrasted with protest literature of the 1960s and early 1970s? Clearly, investigating the connections between Parker's work and that of later writers will lead to useful readings of individual works and of the process of, in particular, female-to-female influence.

For a writer whose work seems, on first reading, so direct and accessible, Dorothy Parker throws a number of assumptions about literary tradition, production, and influence into the air. Even the play of popular culture and serious literature that we associate with postmodernism was occurring in the works of modernists, Parker among them. Thus, she raises questions about how we write and how we read. She is not the only female modernist to do so; Edna St. Vincent Millay comes to mind, particularly where the intersection of sentimentalism and modernism is concerned. Parker's work is a significant factor in our understanding of that intersection, and of women's literary and cultural work. Further studies of Parker's work can only increase that understanding.

Notes

Preface

1. Margo Jefferson, "By Dorothy Parker, Moods from A to Z," *New York Times*, 23 Nov. 1994, sec. B, p. 3.

2. William Grimes, "The Two Dorothy Parkers at Breakfast," *New York Times*, 15 Oct. 1994, sec. B, p.12.

3. Alan Rudolph, dir., *Mrs. Parker and the Vicious Circle*, Fine Line Features, 1994.

4. William Grimes, "Wit at the Round Table: Was It, Er, Um, Square?" *New York Times*, 28 June 1944, sec. B, p. 1.; Anthony Lane, "Etherized," *New Yorker*, Dec. 1994, p. 128.

5. Janet Maslin, "So Witty, So Sophisticated, and So Very Lonely," *New York Times*, 23 Nov. 1994, sec. B, p. 3.

Introduction

1. "Paths," in *The Portable Dorothy Parker* (New York: Viking Press, 1973), 84-85.

2. "'Sorry, the Line Is Busy,'" *Life* 77:2007 (21 Apr. 1921): 560.

3. Arthur F. Kinney, *Dorothy Parker* (Boston: Twayne, 1978), 37.

4. Dorothy Parker, "A Piece about Christmas," *Life*, 1 Dec. 1927, 56.

5. "Any Porch," in Stuart Y. Silverstein, ed., *Not Much Fun: The Lost Poems of Dorothy Parker* (New York: Scribner, 1996), 70.

6. Alexander Woollcott, "Our Mrs. Parker," in *While Rome Burns* (New York: Viking Press, 1934), 149.

7. Ann Douglas, *Terrible Honesty: Mongrel Manhattan in the 1920s* (New York: Noonday Press/Farrar, Straus and Giroux, 1995), 168. In *Paris Was a Woman: Portraits from the Left Bank* (San Francisco: HarperSanFrancisco, 1995), Andrea Weiss discusses the dual identities of female expatriates. See also Shari Benstock, *Women of the Left Bank* (Austin: University of Texas Press, 1986).

8. Malcolm Bradbury and James McFarlane, eds., *Modernism: A Guide to European Literature, 1890–1930* (New York: Penguin Books, 1976).

9. For the feminist debate regarding the value of women's sentimental literature, see the following: Nina Baym, *Women's Fiction: A Guide to Novels by and about Women in America, 1820—1870* (Ithaca and London: Cornell University Press, 1978); Myra Jehlen, "Archimedes and the Paradox of Feminist Criticism," in *Feminisms*, eds. Robyn R. Warhol and Diane Price Herndl (New Brunswick, N. J.: Rutgers University

Press, 1991); Ann Douglas, *The Feminization of American Culture* (1977; reprint, New York: Anchor Press, 1988); Jane Tompkins, *Sensational Designs* (Oxford and New York: Oxford University Press, 1985); Mary Kelley, *Private Woman, Public Stage: Literary Domesticity in Nineteenth-Century America* (New York and Oxford: Oxford University Press, 1984).

10. Tompkins, *Sensational Designs,* p. xv.

11. Cheryl Walker, *Masks Outrageous and Austere: Culture, Psyche, and Persona in Modern Women Poets* (Bloomington: Indiana University Press, 1991); Suzanne Clark, *Sentimental Modernism: Women Writers and the Revolution of the Word* (Bloomington: Indiana University Press, 1991).

12. Norman Friedman, "E. E. Cummings and the Modernist Movement," in *Critical Essays on E. E. Cummings,* ed. Guy Rotella (Boston: G. K. Hall, 1984), 39–46; Carol T. Christ, *Victorian and Modern Poetics* (Chicago: University of Chicago Press, 1984); Howard W. Fulweiler, *"Here a Captive Heart Busted": Studies in the Sentimental Journey of Modern Literature* (New York: Fordham University Press, 1993).

13. Andreas Huyssen, *After the Great Divide* (Bloomington: Indiana University Press, 1986), 55.

14. "In Broadway Playhouses: The Force of Example," *Ainslee's,* May 1922, 155–57.

15. Cary Nelson, *Repression and Recovery: Modern American Poetry and the Politics of Cultural Memory, 1910–1945* (Madison: University of Wisconsin Press, 1989), 6–7.

16. Astradur Eysteinsson, *The Concept of Modernism* (Ithaca: Cornell University Press, 1990), 14–28, 97.

17. Thomas Reed Whissen, *The Devil's Advocate: Decadence in Modern Literature* (New York: Greenwood Press, 1989), xix.

18. See Cassandra Laity, "H. D. and A. C. Swinburne: Decadence and Modernist Women's Writing," *Feminist Studies* 15:3 (Fall 1989): 461–84; Sydney Janet Kaplan, *Katherine Mansfield and the Origins of Modernist Fiction* (Ithaca: Cornell University Press, 1991), 19–35; Louis F. Kannenstine, *The Art of Djuna Barnes: Duality and Damnation* (New York: New York University Press, 1977), 100; Judith Farr, *The Life and Art of Elinor Wylie* (Baton Rouge: Louisiana State University Press, 1983), 61–74.

19. Wyndham Lewis, with input from Ezra Pound, edited the two-issue journal *Blast* in 1914 and 1915; facsimile editions were published in 1992 and 1993, respectively, by Black Sparrow Press. With regard to Parker's place in the canon, it is interesting to note that at this writing, the fourth and fifth editions of the *Norton Anthology of American Literature,* vol. 2, include Parker in the section on modern literature, whereas the second and third editions of the *Heath Anthology of American Literature,* vol. 2, do not.

20. Elaine Showalter, "Feminist Criticism in the Wilderness," in *The New Feminist Criticism,* ed. Elaine Showalter (New York: Pantheon, 1985), 263; Sandra M. Gilbert and Susan Gubar, *No Man's Land: The Place of the Woman Writer in the Twentieth Century, Vol. 1: The War of the Words* (New Haven and London: Yale University Press, 1987).

21. Suzanne Bunkers, "'I Am Outraged Womanhood': Dorothy Parker as Feminist and Social Critic," *Regionalism and the Female Imagination* 4 (1978): 25–34; Emily Toth, "Dorothy Parker, Erica Jong, and New Feminist Humor," *Regionalism and the Female Imagination* 3 (1977/78): 70–85; Nancy Walker, *A Very Serious Thing: Women's Humor and American Culture* (Minneapolis: University of Minnesota Press, 1988).

CHAPTER 1: SEX AND CONTEXT

1. Three full-length biographies have been published: Marion Meade, *Dorothy Parker: What Fresh Hell Is This?* (New York: Villard Books, 1987); Leslie Frewin, *The Late Mrs. Dorothy Parker* (New York: Macmillan, 1986); and John Keats, *You Might as Well Live: The Life and Times of Dorothy Parker* (New York: Simon and Schuster, 1970; reprint, New York: Paragon House, 1986). In addition, Arthur F. Kinney and Randall Calhoun have chapter-length biographies in their studies of Parker: Arthur F. Kinney, *Dorothy Parker* (Boston: Twayne, 1978; second edition , 1998); and Randall Calhoun, *Dorothy Parker: A Bio-Bibliography* (Westport, Conn.: Greenwood Press, 1993). Calhoun's book includes three biographical essays by Richard E. Lauterbach, Wyatt Cooper, and Joseph Bryan III. Another useful essay is William Shanahan, "Robert Benchley and Dorothy Parker: Punch and Judy in Formal Dress," *Rendezvous* 3 (1968): 23–24. See also Margaret Case Harriman, *The Vicious Circle: The Story of the Algonquin Round Table* (New York: Rinehart, 1951); and James R. Gaines, *Wit's End: Days and Nights of the Algonquin Round Table* (New York: Harcourt Brace Jovanovich, 1977).

2. Tompkins, *Sensational Designs* 8, 23-24; Cary Nelson, *Repression and Recovery*, 6–7.

3. "Dorothy Parker," interview by Marion Capron, in *Writers at Work: The Paris Review Interviews*, ed. Malcolm Cowley (New York: Viking Press, 1958), 72.

4. Gaines, *Wit's End*, 124.

5. Meade, *Dorothy Parker*, 108.

6. "One Perfect Rose" is included in *The Portable Dorothy Parker*, 104; the rest of the poems appear in Silverstein, *Not Much Fun*: "Rhyme of an Involuntary Violet," 168; "Ballade of Understandable Ambitions," 145; "The Temptress," 170; "The Far-Sighted Muse," 116. "One Perfect Rose" might be usefully read as a reply to Edmund Waller's "Go, Lovely Rose," a poem in the carpe diem tradition. The first and last stanzas read: "Go, lovely Rose — / Tell her that wastes her time and me, / That now she knows, / When I resemble her to thee, / How sweet and fair she seems to be. / / Then die — that she / The common fate of all things rare / May read in thee; / How small a part of time they share / That are so wondrous sweet and fair!" (from Arthur Quiller-Couch, *The Oxford Book of English Verse 1250–1900* [1900; reprint, Oxford: Oxford University Press, 1931], 310; see also my discussion of Parker's "The Flaw in Paganism" in chapter 4).

7. Wyatt Cooper, "Whatever You Think Dorothy Parker Was Like, She Wasn't," *Esquire*, July 1968, 56–57, 61, 110–14; the article is reprinted in Calhoun, *Dorothy Parker*, 131–50.

8. Parker reviewed the first four plays in the following issues of *Ainslee's* magazine: respectively, Dec. 1920, 155–56; Aug. 1920, 156–57; Dec. 1920, 158–59; and Mar. 1922, 157–58; *Abraham Lincoln* was reviewed in *Vanity Fair*, Feb. 1920, 41.

9. "Oh, Look—I Can Do It Too," Silverstein, *Not Much Fun*, 76–77; "Verses in the Night," in Parker's *Sunset Gun* (New York: Boni and Liveright, 1928), 57–59. The fact that Parker did not include "Verses in the Night" in *The Portable Dorthy Parker* editions could suggest she felt the weight of critical approval for the experimental modernists.

10. See Ronald Bush's introduction to Pound in *The Gender of Modernism*, ed. Bonnie Kime Scott (Bloomington: Indiana University Press, 1990), 353–59; Andreas Huyssen, *After the Great Divide* (Bloomington: Indiana University Press, 1986), vii–ix.

11. S. N. Behrman, "An Introductory Reminiscence," in *The Smart Set: A History and Anthology* by Carl Dolmetsch (New York: Dial Press, 1966), xix–xx.

12. David Perkins, *A History of Modern Poetry from the 1890s to the High Modernist Mode* (Cambridge: Belknap/Harvard University Press, 1976), 98–99; Frederick J. Hoffman, Charles Allen, and Carolyn F. Ulrich, *The Little Magazines* (Princeton: Princeton University Press, 1947), 1; Gaines, *Wit's End*, 36–39.

13. Frank Luther Mott, *A History of American Magazines, 1885–1905* (Cambridge: Harvard University Press, 1957, 11–12; Edwin Emery, *The Press and America* 2^d ed. (Englewood Cliffs, N. J.: Prentice-Hall, Inc., 1962), 525–26.

14. Philip Furia offers a useful discussion of this phenomenon in *Ira Gershwin: The Art of the Lyricist* (New York and Oxford: Oxford University Press, 1996).

15. Frank Crowninshield, quoted in Keats, *You Might as Well Live*, 33.

16. The Stein satire in the December 1916 issue of *Vanity Fair* appears on p. 76. For an anthology of *Vanity Fair* pieces ranging from serious to popular subjects, though without advertising, see Cleveland Amory and Frederic Bradlee, eds., *Vanity Fair: A Cavalcade of the 1920s and 1930s* (New York: Viking Press, 1960).

17. Gaines, *Wit's End*, 36.

18. "Are You a Glossy?" *Vanity Fair* (Apr. 1918, 57, 90; "How to Know the Glossies," *Vanity Fair*, May 1918, 59, 89; "Good Souls," *Vanity Fair*, June 1919, 47, 94; "Is Your Little Girl Safe?" *Vanity Fair*, Sept. 1918, 46, 86; "The Christmas Magazines," *Vanity Fair*, Dec. 1916, 83.

19. "The New Order of Musical Comedies," *Vanity Fair*, May 1918, 49; "The Dramas that Gloom in the Spring," *Vanity Fair*, June 1918, 37, 84; "The New Plays," *Vanity Fair*, Dec. 1918, 39, 84.

20. See Robin Lakoff, "Talking Like a Lady," in *Language and Woman's Place* (New York: Harper, 1975), 8-19.

21. "Hymn of Hate: The Younger Set," *Life*, 30 Mar. 1922, 8; "Ballade of a Not Insupportable Loss," *Life*, 21 June 1923, 9; both reprinted in Silverstein 224 and 157, respectively. "Professional Youth," *Saturday Evening Post*, 28 Apr. 1923, 14, 156–57; is reprinted in Colleen Breese, ed., *Dorothy Parker: Complete Stories*, (New York: Penguin Books, 1995), 437–47.

22. Gaines, *Wit's End*, 81–84; Ann Douglas, *Terrible Honesty*, 5–9.

23. See Capron, "Dorothy Parker," 74.

24. "The Far-Sighted Muse," *Life*, 9 Mar. 1922, 3; see also Silverstein, *Not Much Fun*, 116.

25. See Tompkins, *Sensational Designs*, 123; see also Baym, *Women's Fiction*, 11–21.

26. See Capron, "Dorothy Parker," 75.

27. Willard Huntington Wright, in Dolmetsch, *The Smart Set*, 34–35.

28. Dolmetsch, *The Smart Set*, 36.

29. Ibid., 57, 62.

30. See Robert E. Drennan, *The Algonquin Wits* (New York: Citadel Press, 1968), 122.

31. Meade, *Dorothy Parker*, 137.

32. Perkins, *The History of Modern Poetry*, 98; Dolmetsch, *The Smart Set*, 79–80; *The Smart Set* pieces can also be found in Burton Rascoe and Groff Conklin, eds., *The Smart Set Anthology of World Famous Authors* (New York: Halcyon House, 1934).

33. *Merrily We Roll Along* appears in George S. Kaufman and Moss Hart, *Six Plays by Kaufman and Hart* (New York: Modern Library, 1942), 123–32; see especially pp. 148, 160, 174–75, and 214–15 for the portrayal of Parker.

34. For discussions of Dr. Barach, see Meade, *Dorothy Parker,* 158–62, and Gaines, *Wit's End,* 116. Parker publicly denounced her poetry in "Sophisticated Poetry—and the Hell with It," *New Masses,* 27 June 1939, 21. She denigrates her fiction during her interview with Marion Capron; see Capron, "Dorothy Parker," 75.

35. Randall Calhoun records the printing history of Parker's *Enough Rope* in *Dorothy Parker,* 43. For reviews of *Enough Rope,* see J. F., *Bookman,* Mar. 1927, 80; Edmund Wilson, "Dorothy Parker's Poems," *New Republic,* 19 Jan. 1927, 256; Marie Luhrs, "Fashionable Poetry," *Poetry* 30:1 (Apr. 1927): 52–54; Genevieve Taggard, "You Might as Well Live," *New York Herald Tribune Books,* 27 March 1927, 7; "The Phoenix Nest," *Saturday Review of Literature,* 1 Jan. 1927, 492; (no title or author), *Nation,* 25 May 1927, 589. In his introduction to *Not Much Fun,* Silverstein downplays the significance of Parker's publishing numbers relative to other authors. Nevertheless, for a first book of poetry by a woman author, the numbers are impressive.

36. For the printing history of Parker's *Sunset Gun,* see Calhoun, *Dorothy Parker,* 43. For reviews of *Sunset Gun,* see Garreta Busey, "A Porcupine's View," *New York Herald Tribune Books,* 15 July 1928, 7; William Rose Benét, "New Moon Madness," *Saturday Review of Literature,* 9 June 1928, 943; Herschel Brickell, *North American Review* 226:adv (Aug. 1928): 230w; Edith Walton, "New York Wits," *New Republic,* 27 June 1928, 155; H. M. Robinson, *Bookman,* Sept. 1928, 96; R. A. Simon, *New York Evening Post,* 2 June 1928, 8; Edwin Clark, "Six Rhymesters in Cap and Bells," *New York Times Book Review,* 1 July 1928, 10.

37. For the printing history of Parker's *Death and Taxes,* see Calhoun, *Dorothy Parker,* 45. For reviews of *Death and Taxes,* see Franklin Pierce Adams, *New York Herald Tribune Books,* 14 June 1931, 7; Horace Gregory, "Dorothy Parker, Lady Wit," *New York Evening Post,* 20 June 1931, 12; "Books in Brief," *Nation,* 23 Sept. 1931, 315; Percy Hutchison, "Satire and Epigram in Dorothy Parker's Versicles," *New York Times Book Review,* 14 June 1931, 4; "Dorothy Parker's Poems," *Springfield Republican,* 21 June 1931, 7e.

38. For the printing history of Parker's *Not So Deep as a Well,* see Calhoun, *Dorothy Parker,* 46. For reviews of *Not So Deep as a Well,* see Louis Kronenberger, "The Rueful, Frostbitten Laughter of Dorothy Parker," *New York Times Book Review,* 13 Dec. 1936, 2, 28; William Rose Benet, "Deep, at That," *Saturday Review of Literature,* 12 Dec. 1936, 5.

39. Gilbert and Gubar, *No Man's Land, Vol. 3: Letters from the Front.* Brendan Gill's remark occurs on p. xix of his introduction to *The Portable Dorothy Parker.*

40. Fanny Butcher, "Dorothy Parker's Stories Given Praise as a Book," review of *Laments for the Living, Chicago Tribune,* 21 June 1930, 6. For the printing history of Parker's volumes of fiction, see Calhoun, *Dorothy Parker,* 44–48.

41. Scott, *The Gender of Modernism,* 4.

42. The reviews cited include the following: Morrie Ryskind, "Man's Words, Women's Voice," review of *After Such Pleasures,* by Dorothy Parker, *New York Herald Tribune Books,* 12 Nov.1933, 7; review of *After Such Pleasures, Forum,* Jan. 1934, 5; Ogden Nash, "The Pleasure Is Ours," review of *After Such Pleasures, Saturday Review of Literature,* 4 Nov. 1933, 231; T. S. Matthews, "Curses Not Loud but Deep," review of *Laments for the Living, New Republic* 64 (1930): 133; "Shorter Notices," review of *After Such Pleasures, Nation,* 20 Dec. 1933, 715; Edgar Johnson, "Technique and Tantrum," review of *Here Lies, Kenyon Review* 1:3 (Summer 1939): 348–51; Gladys Graham, "Cut-Outs from Life," review of *Laments for the Living, Saturday Review of Literature,* 5 July 1930, 1172; Herschel Brickell, "Hemingway and Parker," review of *After Such Plea-*

sures, North American Review, Jan. 1934, 94; Fanny Butcher, "Short Stories Still Live as Works of Art," review of *After Such Pleasures, Chicago Daily Tribune,* 28 Oct. 1933, 16.

43. "Irony and Sympathy," review of *Laments for the Living, Springfield Sunday Union and Republican,* 21 Sept. 1930, 7e; John Mair, "New Novels," review of *Here Lies, New Statesman and Nation,* 21 Oct.1939, 583–84.

44. Ryskind, "Man's Words, Women's Voice." For a similar treatment of women's writing by a male critic during this period, see the review of Solita Solano's first novel, *The Uncertain Feast,* quoted in Andrea Weiss, *Paris Was a Woman: Portraits from the Left Bank* (San Francisco: HarperSanFrancisco, 1995), 180–81.

45. Adrienne Rich, "When We Dead Awaken: Writing as Revision" (1971), in *On Lies, Secrets, and Silence: Selected Prose 1966–1978* (New York: Norton, 1979), 33–49.

46. Gaines, *Wit's End,* 54–55.

47. For reviews of the 1944 edition of *The Portable Dorothy Parker,* see Edward Weeks, *Atlantic,* July 1944, 125; *Kirkus* 12 (1 May 1944): 202; Kenneth Fearing, "Review of Distinctive New Fiction," *New York Herald Tribune Weekly Book Review,* 6 June 1944, 6. For reviews of the 1973 edition, see Clive James, "Nickel and Ivory," *New Statesman,* 27 Apr. 1973, 623–24; "Low Spirits," *Times (London) Literary Supplement,* 6 Apr. 1973, 395.

Chapter 2: The Sentimental Infection

1. A number of studies have examined aspects of the sentimental in literature; see R. F. Brissenden, *Virtue in Distress* (New York: Macmillan, 1974), 15–16; Fred Kaplan, *Sacred Tears: Sentimentality in Victorian Literature* (Princeton: Princeton University Press, 1987); Janet Todd, *Sensibility: An Introduction* (London and New York: Methuen, 1986); Ann Douglas, *The Feminization of American Culture* (New York: Anchor Press, 1988). Kaplan and Douglas interpret nineteenth-century sentimentality as largely a feminine phenomenon.

2. I. A. Richards, *Practical Criticism* (London, 1929), 255; John Frederick Nims, *Western Wind: An Introduction to Poetry* (New York: Random House, 1974), 128, 140.

3. Nims, *Western Wind;* John Crowe Ransom, "The Poet as Woman," in *The World's Body* (1938; reprint, Port Washington, N. Y.: Kennikat Press, 1964). Amy Kaplan examines the sentimentalism of male authors in *The Social Construction of American Realism* (Chicago: University of Chicago Press, 1988), 2.

4. Lionel Trilling, *The Liberal Imagination* (New York: Viking Press, 1950), 221–22. Amy Kaplan discusses his argument in her *Social Construction.*

5. Mary Ross, "Thirteen Manhattans," review of *Laments for the Living, New York Herald Tribune Books,* 15 June 1930, 7.

6. Butcher, "Stories Given Praise," 6.

7. Kinney, *Dorothy Parker,* 1978, 1, 165; and Kinney, "Dorothy Parker's Letters to Alexander Woollcott," *Massachusetts Review* 30:3 (Autumn 1989): 488.

8. Keats, *You Might as Well Live: The Life and Times of Dorothy Parker* (New York: Paragon, 1986), 139. "Verse for a Certain Dog" can be found in *Enough Rope* (New York: Sun Dial Press, 1940), 67; "To My Dog " can be found in Silverstein, *Not Much Fun,* 94–95. For an examination of Parker's satire, see Martha Denham Bone, "Dorothy Parker and *New Yorker* Satire," diss., Middle Tennessee State University, 1985.

9. The two "Hymns of Hate" and the "Hate Song" can be found in Silverstein, *Not Much Fun,* 230–36 and 187–89, respectively. "Day-Dreams" and "The Story of

Mrs. W___" are both in *Enough Rope*, 63 and 36, respectively. "Such a Pretty Picture" can be found in *Complete Stories*.

10. Kinney, "Letters to Alexander Woollcott," 497 and 504; Robert Drennan, *The Algonquin Wits* (New York: Citadel Press, 1968), 122. Kinney's observation appears in his *Dorothy Parker*, (1978), 39.

11. Meade, *Dorothy Parker*, 180.

12. "Men" (*Vanity Fair*, February 1917, 65); "Slackers," (*Vanity Fair*, December 1917, 83); "Bohemians," (*Vanity Fair*, October 1918, 46). All of these poems can be found in Silverstein, *Not Much Fun*, 190, 198, 201, respectively.

13. For Parker's criticism of patriotic drama, see "The Star-Spangled Drama," *Vanity Fair*, Aug. 1918, 29, 66; and "The Fall Crop of War Plays," *Vanity Fair*, Oct. 1918, 56, 104, 106. Her comment regarding Forster appears in E. M. Forster, *Commonplace Book*, ed. Philip Gardner (Stanford, Calif.: Stanford University Press, 1985), 200.

14. "The New Plays—If Any," *Vanity Fair*, Oct. 1919, 41, 112; "The Union Forever," *Vanity Fair*, Oct. 1919, 37, 84; "Poem in the American Manner," *Life*, 11 May 1922, 9 (also in Silverstein, *Not Much Fun*, 122).

15. Meade, *Dorothy Parker*, 180–86; Keats, *You Might as Well Live*, 130.

16. "Who Might Be Interested," in *Voices Against Tyranny: Writing of the Spanish Civil War*, ed. John Miller (New York: Charles Scribner's Sons, 1986), 192–97; "Incredible, Fantastic . . . and True," *New Masses*, 23 Nov. 1937, 15–16; "Not Enough," *New Masses*, 14 Mar. 1939, 3–4; "Sophisticated Poetry—and the Hell with It," *New Masses*, 14 Mar. 1939, 21; Diane Johnson, *Dashiell Hammett: A Life* (New York: Random House, 1983), 156, 166; Meade, *Dorothy Parker*, 337–38. Useful accounts of Parker's political activities are also found in Kinney's, *Dorothy Parker* and "Letters to Alexander Woollcott," (pp. 487–515); and in Calhoun's introduction to *Dorothy Parker*.

17. Keats, *You Might as Well Live*, 192–93; Silverstein, *Not Much Fun*, 44–50; Dixie Tighe, "Dorothy Parker Returns from Spain with Tears in Her Soul," *New York Post*, 22 Oct. 1937, 17.

18. Edmund Wilson, "A Toast and a Tear for Dorothy Parker," review of *The Portable Dorothy Parker* (1944), *New Yorker*, 20 May 1944, 67–68; Lillian Hellman, *An Unfinished Woman: A Memoir* (Boston: Little, Brown, 1969), 218; Kinney, *Dorothy Parker*, 1978, 59; "Letters to Alexander Woollcott," 500.

19. "Lillian Hellman Walking, Cooking, Writing, Talking," interview by Nora Ephron in Jackson R. Bryer, ed., *Conversations with Lillian Hellman* (Jackson: University Press of Mississippi, 1986), 136.

20. Meade, *Dorothy Parker*, 15; Dorothy Rothschild, "Relatives," *Vanity Fair*, Aug. 1917, 39 (also in Silverstein, *Not Much Fun*, 196–97).

21. See, for example, the cartoons in *Life* 75:2045 (12 Jan. 1922): 3; and 79:2065 (1 June 1922): 19. Chinua Achebe's essay "An Image of Darkness: Conrad's *Heart of Darkness*" is instructive here. Achebe's argument that *Heart of Darkness* is a racist text is based on the fact that W. E. B. Du Bois had previously identified "the problem of the color line" as the most pressing issue of the twentieth century; Conrad should have been aware of this argument and avoided the used of stereotypes. As the *Life* cartoons and Parker's work at times illustrate, the acknowledgment and application of racial equality was a slow and complicated process. Achebe's essay is in *Hopes and Impediments: Selected Essays* (1988; reprint, New York: Anchor Books, 1990).

22. Douglas, *Terrible Honesty*, 77; for Parker's comments on blackface and on Al Jolson, see these reviews from her "In Broadway Playhouses" column in *Ainslee's*:

"National Institutions," Sept. 1920, 156–59; "The Season's Greetings," Nov. 1920, 155–59; "Hard Times," Feb. 1922, 155–59.

23. "In Broadway Playhouses," review of *Come Seven* by Octavus Roy Cohen, *Ainslee's*, Oct. 1920, 157.

24. Ibid., 158.

25. "Broadway Playhouses," review of *The Emperor Jones*, by Eugene O'Neill, *Ainslee's*, Mar. 1921, 157–58.

26. James D. Hart, ed., *The Oxford Companion to American Literature*, 5th edition (New York and Oxford: Oxford University Press, 1983), 147, 205. For a discussion of Augustus Thomas, see Brooks Atkinson, *Broadway* (New York: Macmillan, 1970), 72–74.

27. "The Dark Girl's Rhyme," *The Portable Dorothy Parker*, 78. Emerson's "The Rommany Girl" was published in the Nov. 1857 issue of *The Atlantic Monthly;* it can be found in *Atlantic Unbound*. Online. October 1990, <theatlantic.com/atlantic/atlweb/poetry/poetpage.htm>. A number of anonymous English ballads that speak of forbidden love also offer useful comparisons and may have served as models. See, for example, "The Gypsy Laddie," in John Frederick Nims, ed., *The Harper Anthology of Poetry* (New York: Harper and Row, 1981), 44–45; or "Lord Thomas and Fair Annet," in Francis B. Gummere, ed., *Old English Ballads* (Boston: Ginn, 1894), 231–32. Another interesting comparison comes from a poet Parker read: Samuel Taylor Coleridge's unfinished "The Ballad of the Dark Ladie." The poem can be found in David Perkins, ed., *English Romantic Writers* 2[d] ed. (New York: Harcourt Brace College Publishers, 1995), 545–46.

28. This assumption became one of many perverse outcomes of, as well as a justification for, slavery in America. See Anne Firor Scott, *The Southern Lady: From Pedestal to Politics, 1830–1930* (Chicago: University of Chicago Press, 1970), 52–53; and Angela Y. Davis, *Women, Race, and Class* (New York: Vintage Books, 1983), especially chaps. 1–3.

29. "The Dark Girl's Rhyme," *The Portable Dorothy Parker*, 78.

30. "Arrangement in Black and White," *The Portable Dorothy Parker*, 19–23; Arthur F. Kinney, *Dorothy Parker, Revised* (New York: Twayne, 1998), 16.

31. "A Terrible Day Tomorrow," *Complete Stories*, 86–91.

32. "The Compleat Bungler," review of *The Art of Successful Bidding*, by George Reith, and *Home to Harlem*, by Claude McKay, in *The Portable Dorothy Parker*, 501–3. For a discussion of the Harlem Renaissance, see David Levering Lewis, *When Harlem Was in Vogue* (New York: Oxford University Press, 1982), especially chap. 6.

33. Alain Locke and Montgomery Gregory, eds., *Plays of Negro Life* (1927; reprint, Westport, Conn.: Negro Universities Press, 1970); Alain Locke, ed., *The New Negro* (1925; reprint, New York: Atheneum, 1968); Douglas, *Terrible Honesty*, 81, 378; Sascha Feinstein, *Jazz Poetry from the 1920s to the Present* (Westport, Conn.: Praeger, 1997).

34. "Mrs. Hofstadter on Josephine Street," *The Portable Dorothy Parker*, 155–64.

35. See Kinney, *Dorothy Parker*, 1978, chap. 3, n. 83, 190; and the original story in the *New Yorker*, 4 Aug. 1934, 20–26, especially pages 21, 25, and 26.

36. Kinney, *Dorothy Parker*, 1978, 111–15.

37. John O'Hara, "Dorothy Parker, Hip Pocket Size," review of *The Portable Dorothy Parker, New York Times Book Review*, 28 May 1944, 5, 29.

38. Meade, *Dorothy Parker*, 303–4; Keats, *You Might as Well Live*, 223; Florence Haxton Britten, "Devastating, Tender and Witty," review of *Here Lies, New York Herald Tribune Books*, 7 May 1939, 3; Kinney, *Dorothy Parker*, 1978, 141–42. Kinney claims it is

"the laughter of the exploitative construction workers" that destroys Raymond; Meade claims Raymond "is almost beaten to death by white workmen." However, there are no construction workers in the story.

39. Kinney, "Letters to Alexander Woollcott," 507, 510.

40. Montgomery Gregory, "The Drama of Negro Life," *The New Negro*, 153–60.

41. Sandra A. Zagarell, "The Conscience of Her Age," review of *Harriet Beecher Stowe: A Life*, by Joan D. Hendrick, *Women's Review of Books*, (Apr. 1994): 13–15.

42. Kinney, *Dorothy Parker*, 1978, 166; Ross Labrie, "Dorothy Parker Revisited," *Canadian Review of American Studies* 7 (1976): 55; Meade, *Dorothy Parker*, 21, 142.

43. Gilbert and Gubar, *No Man's Land, Vol. 1: The War of the Words,* 151.

44. Ernest Hemingway, "To a Tragic Poetess," in *88 Poems*, ed. Nicholas Gerogiannis (New York: Harcourt Brace Jovanovich, 1979), 87–89.

45. Meade, *Dorothy Parker*, 106, 160.

46. Keats, *You Might as Well Live,* 90–91; Meade, *Dorothy Parker,* 105–7.

47. Hemingway, "To a Tragic Poetess."

48. Ibid.

49. Kronenberger, "The Rueful, Frostbitten Laughter," 2, 28.

50. Wilson, "Dorothy Parker's Poems," 256.

51. Taggard, "You Might as Well Live"; Robinson, *Bookman*; and Walton, "New York Wits"; Lynn Z. Bloom, "Dorothy Parker," in Vol. 5 of *Critical Survey of Poetry*, ed. Frank N. Magill (Englewood Cliffs, N. J.: Salem Press, 1982), 2167.

52. Kronenberger, "The Rueful, Frostbitten Laughter," 2; Alexander Woollcott, "Our Mrs. Parker," in *While Rome Burns* (New York: Viking Press, 1934), 149, 144.

53. Benét, "New Moon Madness."

54. Henry Seidel Canby, "Belle Dame sans Merci," review of *Death and Taxes, Saturday Review of Literature,* 13 June 1931, 891.

55. Harold Rosenberg, "Nor Rosemary nor Rue," review of *Death and Taxes, Poetry,* Dec. 1939, 159–61.

56. "Book Notes," review of *Death and Taxes, New Republic* 67 (1931): 348–49; Herbert Marshall McLuhan, "The New York Wits," *Kenyon Review* 7 (1945): 12–28; Brendan Gill, "Introduction," *The Portable Dorothy Parker,* xviii.

57. T. S. Matthews, "Fiction by Young and Old," review of *After Such Pleasures, New Republic,* 15 Nov. 1933: 24–25.

58. Mina Curtiss, "Dorothy Parker's Idle Rich," review of *Here Lies, Nation,* 15 July 1939, 76–78.

59. Ibid.

60. Mark Van Doren, "Dorothy Parker," *English Journal,* Sept. 1934, 535–43.

61. Margaret Lawrence, *The School of Femininity* (1936; reprint, Port Washington, N. Y.: Kennicut Press, 1966), 173–74.

62. Clark, *Sentimental Modernism,* 9.

63. Edmund Wilson, "A Toast and a Tear," 67–68.

64. Hellman, *An Unfinished Woman,* 219.

65. Kinney, *Dorothy Parker*, 1978, 5, 6, 80, 141; Ann Springer, review of *Here Lies, Boston Evening Transcript,* 27 May 1939, 2.

66. Clark, *Sentimental Modernism,* 5–6.

Chapter 3: The Sentimental Connection I

1. Louise Bogan, *Achievement in American Poetry, 1900–1950* (Chicago: Regnery, 1951), 24; David Perkins, *A History of Modern Poetry from the 1890s to the High Modernist Mode,* vol. 1 (Cambridge: Belknap/Harvard University Press, 1976), 91.

2. E. C. Stedman, ed., *An American Anthology 1787–1900* (Boston: Houghton Mifflin, 1900). Emily Stipes Watts reports that Stedman draws from the following texts: Rufus Griswold, ed., *The Female Poets of America* (Philadelphia: Carey and Hart, 1849); Caroline May, ed., *The American Female Poets* (Philadelphia: Lindsay and Blakiston, 1848); Thomas Buchanan Read, ed., *The Female Poets of America* (Philadelphia: E. H. Butler, 1849). See Watts, *The Poetry of American Women from 1632 to 1945* (Austin: University of Texas Press, 1977).

3. Capron, "Dorothy Parker"; Margaret Drabble, ed., *The Oxford Companion to English Literature,* 5th ed. (Oxford and New York: Oxford University Press, 1985), 792.

4. Adelaide Ann Procter, *Legends and Lyrics,* vol. 1 (London: Bell and Daldy, 1865), 157. A useful introduction and ten of her poems can be found in Angela Leighton and Margaret Reynolds, eds., *Victorian Women Poets: An Anthology* (Oxford: Blackwell, 1995), 303–38.

5. *The Portable Dorothy Parker.*

6. Procter, *Legends and Lyrics,* 155–56.

7. "Ballade at Thirty-five," and "The Thin Edge," *The Portable Dorothy Parker,* 105 and 106 respectively.

8. "Prologue to a Saga," *The Portable Dorothy Parker,* 316.

9. Watts, *The Poetry of American Women,* 66–67; 74–75; 108–9, 144; 125–27, 133.

10. Sandra M. Gilbert and Susan Gubar, *The Madwoman in the Attic: The Woman Writer and the Nineteenth-Century Literary Imagination* (New Haven: Yale University Press, 1979), 50–51, 584, 564, 559; see also Suzanne Juhasz, *Naked and Firey Forms, Modern American Poetry by Women: A New Tradition* (New York: Colophon Books, 1976).

11. Cheryl Walker, *The Nightingale's Burden: Women Poets and American Culture before 1900* (Bloomington: Indiana University Press, 1982), xi, 152, 82–84, 104; Cheryl Walker, ed., *American Women Poets of the Nineteenth Century: An Anthology* (New Brunswick, N. J.: Rutgers University Press, 1992), xxiii–xxiv, xxv.

12. Cheryl Walker, *Masks Outrageous and Austere: Culture, Psyche, and Persona in Modern Women Poets* (Bloomington: Indiana University Press, 1991), 114, 177.

13. Nancy Walker, *A Very Serious Thing: Women's Humor and American Culture* (Minneapolis: University of Minnesota Press, 1988), 132. For discussions of Parker's humor, see also Kathy MacDermott, "Light Humor and the Dark Underside of Wish Fulfillment: Conservative Anti-Realism," *Studies in Popular Culture* 10:2 (1987): 37–53; Nancy Walker, "The Remarkably Constant Reader: Dorothy Parker as Book Reviewer," *Studies in American Humor* New Series 3, no. 4 (1997):1–14; Laity, "H. D. and A. C. Swinburne"; Kaplan, *Katherine Mansfield;* Kannestine, *The Art of Djuna Barnes;* and Farr, *The Life and Art of Elinor Wylie.*

14. Walker, *American Women Poets,* xxviii.

15. Ibid.

16. "The Veteran," *The Portable Dorothy Parker,* p. 101. This poem first appeared in *Enough Rope.* It was never published in a magazine or newspaper.

17. Kinney, *Dorothy Parker,* 1978, 87.

18. "Recurrence," *The Portable Dorothy Parker*, p. 88.

19. Aviva Slesin, dir., "The Ten-Year Lunch: The Wit and Legend of the Algonquin Round Table," PBS's *American Masters*, 1987.

20. *An Informal Hour with Dorothy Parker*, read by the author, New York: Westminster Spoken Arts, 1956, audiotape.

21. Gilbert and Gubar, *The Madwoman in the Attic*, 3–20.

22. T. S. Eliot, "The Waste Land," in *Collected Poems, 1909–1962* (New York: Harcourt Brace Jovanovich, 1963), 51–70; Edna St. Vincent Millay, "Spring," in *Collected Poems* (New York: Harper and Row, 1956), 53; Parker's poems "Song of the Wilderness," "Wanderlust," "Song of the Open Country," "Song for an April Dusk," "Monody," and "Somewhat Delayed Spring Song" can be found in Silverstein, *Not Much Fun*, 148, 150, 87, 160, 136, 137, respectively.

23. "The Dramatists," *The Portable Dorothy Parker*, 89–90.

24. Alicia Suskin Ostriker, *Stealing the Language: The Emergence of Women's Poetry in America* (Boston: Beacon Press, 1986), 34; Maureen Honey, Introduction to *Shadowed Dreams: Women's Poetry of the Harlem Renaissance* (New Brunswick, N. J.: Rutgers University Press, 1989), 2–7.

25. Steven Seidman, *Romantic Longings: Love in America 1830–1980* (New York and London: Routledge, 1991), 4; Clark, *Sentimental Modernism*, 69.

26. Ostriker, *Stealing the Language*, 36.

27. The poems by Parker can be found in the *The Portable Dorothy Parker*. For an example of Pope's satires, see "The Rape of the Lock" or "Epistle 2. To a Lady" in *The Norton Anthology of English Literature*, vol. 1, 6th ed., ed. M. H. Abrams (New York: Norton, 1993), 2233–52, 2270–77. Another selection of Lady satires can be found in Dennis Davison, ed., *The Penguin Book of Eighteenth-Century Verse* (New York: Penguin Books, 1973), 21–46.

28. Joanne Dobson, "The American Renaissance Reenvisioned," in *The (Other) American Traditions: Nineteenth Century Women Writers*, ed. Joyce W. Warren (New Brunswick, N. J.: Rutgers University Press, 1993), 170–71.

29. "Garden-Spot," *Death and Taxes*, 34.

30. Henry Wadsworth Longfellow, "God's-Acre," *The Poetical Works of Henry Wadsworth Longfellow*, Cambridge ed. (Boston: Houghton Mifflin, 1975), 16.

31. Harold Bloom, *The Anxiety of Influence* (Oxford and New York: Oxford University Press, 1973).

32. "The Maid-Servant at the Inn," *The Portable Dorothy Parker*, 225,

33. Robert Pinsky, "Tidings of Comfort and Dread: Poetry and the Dark Beauty of Christmas," *New York Times Book Review*, 4 Dec. 1994, 37–38.

34. "The Gentlest Lady," *The Portable Dorothy Parker*, 224.

35. "Prayer for a New Mother," *The Portable Dorothy Parker*, 310.

36. Frederick Locher-Lampson, Preface to *Lyra Elegantiarum*, quoted in *Princeton Encyclopedia of Poetry and Poetics*, enlarged ed., ed. Alex Preminger (Princeton: Princeton University Press, 1974), 446–47.

37. "Sophisticated Poetry—and the Hell with It," *New Masses*, 27 June 1939, 21; an edited version appears in *Fighting Words*, ed. Donald Ogden Stewart (New York: Harcourt Brace, 1940), 38–39.

38. Calhoun, *Dorothy Parker*, 12.

39. "Rainy Night," *The Portable Dorothy Parker*, 86.

40. "Interview," *Enough Rope*, 106. Parker evidently changed the contraction in the last line to "I have" for *The Portable Dorothy Parker* (1944 and 1973), making the

line's meter more regular. Why she felt compelled to do this is unclear, though she might have been responding to New Critical values.

41. Ostriker, *Stealing the Language*, 36.

42. Lizette Woodworth Reese, "To Life," in Walker, *American Women Poets*, 388.

43. "Fair Weather," *The Portable Dorothy Parker*, 229.

44. H. D. (Hilda Doolittle), "Oread" in *Collected Poems 1912–1944*, ed. Louis L. Martz (New York: New Directions, 1983), 55; Susan Stanford Friedman, *Psyche Reborn: The Emergence of H. D.* (Bloomington: Indiana University Press, 1981), 57–58.

45. Walker, *The Nightingale's Burden*, 91.

46. "Landscape" and "Two-Volume Novel," *The Portable Dorothy Parker*, 232 and 238, respectively.

47. See discussions in Watts, Cheryl Walker, and Gilbert and Gubar; see also Richard D. Altick, *Victorian Ideas and People* (New York: Norton, 1973), 50–59.

48. Dobson, "The American Renaissance Reenvisioned," 167.

49. Phoebe Cary, "Was He Henpecked?" in Walker, *American Women Poets*, 199–203.

50. Phoebe Cary, "Dorothy's Dower," in Walker, *American Women Poets*, 203–5.

51. Lucy Larcom, "Getting Along,"in Walker, *American Women Poets*, 217–19.

52. "I Know I Have Been Happiest," *The Portable Dorothy Parker*, 91.

53. Baym, *Women's Fiction*, 25; Tompkins, *Sensational Designs*, 45.

54. "Chant for the Dark Hours," "Men," and "News Item," in *The Portable Dorothy Parker*, 95, 109, and 109, respectively.

55. Walker, *The Nightingale's Burden*, 2.

56. "Renunciation," *The Portable Dorothy Parker*, 100.

57. Perkins, *A History of Modern Poetry*, 4-5.

58. Larcom, "Fern-Life," in Walker, *American Women Poets*, 231.

59. Cheryl Walker argues that the unfulfilled desire in Larcom's poem is a woman writer's freedom of expression; see *Nightingale's Burden*, 45.

60. "Landscape," *The Portable Dorothy Parker*, 232. In the first edition of *Sunset Gun* (1928) the third line reads: "The field is white *with* flowering lace."

61. "Midnight," *The Portable Dorothy Parker*, 311.

62. "A Portrait," *The Portable Dorothy Parker*, 94.

63. Walker, *Masks Outrageous and Austere*, 10.

64. Elinor Wylie, "Sanctuary," in *Collected Poems of Elinor Wylie* (New York: Knopf, 1934), 14.

65. "Sanctuary," *The Portable Dorothy Parker*, 297.

66. "The Homebody," *The Portable Dorothy Parker*, 228.

67. "Hearthside," *The Portable Dorothy Parker*, 85.

68. "Interior," *The Portable Dorothy Parker*, 215.

69. Walker discusses Dickinson's sanctuary poems and letters in *Nightingale's Burden*, 103–4; and Louise Bogan's retreat to the mind in chap. 7 of *Masks Outrageous and Austere*, 165–90. See poem no. 652 in Thomas H. Johnson, ed., *The Complete Poems of Emily Dickinson* (Boston: Little, Brown and Co., 1955), 324–25.

70. "Lyric," in Silverstein, *Not Much Fun*, 96.

71. "Now at Liberty," *The Portable Dorothy Parker*, 96. John Keats also observed the influence of Thomas Hood in the poem; see Keats, *You Might as Well Live*, 138.

72. Frances Osgood, "Forgive and Forget," in Walker, *American Women Poets*, 117.

73. Frances Osgood, "He Bade Me Be Happy," in Walker, *American Women Poets*, 113.

74. Watts, *The Poetry of American Women*, 133.

75. "Résumé," *The Portable Dorothy Parker*, 99.

76. "Swan Song," *Sunset Gun* (New York: Boni and Liveright, 1928), 44.

77. "Cherry White," *The Portable Dorothy Parker*, 299.

78. "Rhyme Against Living," *The Portable Dorothy Parker*, 239.

79. Gilbert and Gubar, *The Madwoman in the Attic*, 628; Walker, *Nightingale's Burden*, 83.

80. Ostriker, *Stealing the Language*, 34.

81. "Fighting Words," *The Portable Dorothy Parker*, 114.

82. Walker, *Nightingale's Burden*, 136.

83. "Philosophy," *The Portable Dorothy Parker*, 107.

84. "Observation," *The Portable Dorothy Parker*, 112.

85. Caroline May and Rufus Griswold, quoted in Watts, *The Poetry of American Women*, 70–71.

86. Frances Osgood, "Ah! Woman Still," in Walker, *American Women Poets*, 133.

87. "Tombstones in the Starlight," *The Portable Dorothy Parker*, 300.

88. Samuel Taylor Coleridge, "The Nightingale," in Perkins, *English Romantic Writers*, 544–45.

89. "Bric-à-Brac," *The Portable Dorothy Parker*, 215. Ellen Moers has commented on the frequent use of "the metaphor of littleness" by women writers in *Literary Women: The Great Writers* (Oxford and New York: Oxford University Press, 1976), 244–45.

90. "Song of Perfect Propriety," *The Portable Dorothy Parker*, 103.

91. "For a Lady Who Must Write Verse," *The Portable Dorothy Parker*, 238.

92. "Daylight Saving," *The Portable Dorothy Parker*, 226.

93. Walker, *Nightingale's Burden*, 7.

94. Charlotte Nekola, "Worlds Moving: Women, Poetry, and the Literary Politics of the 1930s," in *Writing Red: An Anthology of American Women Writers, 1930–1940*, ed. Charlotte Nekola and Paula Rabinowitz (New York: Feminist Press, 1987), 127–34. Parker's work is not included in this anthology.

95. Louise Kertesz discusses the reform poetry of Genevieve Taggard and Lola Ridge in *The Poetic Vision of Muriel Rukeyser* (Baton Rouge: Louisiana State University Press, 1980), 78–84. Maureen Honey discusses the radical content/conventional form strategy used by Anne Spencer and other Harlem Renaissance women poets in her Introduction to *Shadowed Dreams*, 1–41. All three poets are discussed by William Drake in *The First Wave: Women Poets in America 1915–1945* (New York: Collier, 1987), 170–210, 211–38, 239. Edna St. Vincent Millay also would write political poetry and suffer critically for it; see Nelson, *Repression and Recovery*, 41–43.

96. "Sophisticated Poetry—and the Hell with It."

97. Clark, *Sentimental Modernism*, 69.

CHAPTER 4: THE SENTIMENTAL CONNECTION II

1. Thomas A. Guilason, "The Lesser Renaissance: The American Short Story in the 1920s," in *The American Short Story 1900–1945*, ed. Philip Sterick (Boston: Twayne, 1984), 92–94.

2. Clark, *Sentimental Modernism*, 22; Dobson, "The American Renaissance Reenvisioned," 164–82; Tompkins, *Sensational Designs*, xvi, 178; Rachel Blau DuPlessis, *Writing Beyond the Ending: Narrative Strategies of Twentieth Century Women Writers* (Bloomington: Indiana University Press, 1985), 3–4; Ostriker, *Stealing the Language*, 34; Baym, *Women's Fiction*, 144.

3. R. F. Brissenden, *Virtue in Distress* (New York: Macmillan, 1974), 65, 135; Dobson, "The American Renaissance Reenvisioned," 167; Robyn R. Warhol, *Gendered Interventions*, 40–41.

4. Capron, "Dorothy Parker," 76.

5. For Parker's comments about reading Victorian novels, see Capron, "Dorothy Parker," 78; Lynn Z. Bloom, "Dorothy Parker," in *Critical Survey of Short Fiction*, vol. 5, ed. Frank N. Magill (Englewood Cliffs, N. J.: Salem Press, 1981), 2055; "A Pig's-Eye View of Literature," *The Portable Dorothy Parker*, 219–22.

6. Judith Fetterley, Introduction to *Provisions: A Readers from 19ᵗʰ-Century American Women*, ed. Judith Fetterley (Bloomington: Indiana University Press, 1985), 1–40; Judith Fetterley and Marjorie Pryse, Introduction to *American Women Regionalists 1850–1910*, ed. Fetterley and Pryse (New York: Norton, 1992), xv; Elizabeth Ammons, Introduction to *"How Celia Changed Her Mind" and Other Stories* by Rose Terry Cooke, ed. Elizabeth Ammons (New Brunswick, N. J.: Rutgers University Press, 1986), ix–xxxv; Sandra A. Zagarell, Introduction to *A New Home, Who'll Follow?* or *Glimpses of Western Life*, by Caroline M. Kirkland (New Brunswick, N. J.: Rutgers University Press, 1990), vii–xxi; Sandra A. Zagarell, "'America' as Community in Three Antebellum Village Sketches," in *The (Other) American Traditions: Nineteenth Century Women Writers*, ed. Joyce W. Warren (New Brunswick, N. J.: Rutgers University Press, 1993), 143–63; Josephine Donovan, *New England Local Color Literature: A Woman's Tradition* (New York: Frederick Ungar 1983).

7. Fetterley, Introduction to *Provisions*, 14.

8. Kinney, *Dorothy Parker*, 126. Kinney observes that Parker's sketches use the concision found in Hemingway and Joyce.

9. Donovan, *New England Local Color Literature*, 22–23, and see her discussion of Mitford's work, p. 32. See also Zagarell, Introduction to *A New Home*.

10. "A Terrible Day Tomorrow," *Complete Stories*, 86–91. Also see the nine pieces labeled as "Sketches" in *Complete Stories*, which rely on the type of descriptive narrative found in many nineteenth-century sketches.

11. "The Mantle of Whistler, *Complete Stories*, 96–98; Furia, *Ira Gershwin*, 10–11, 66–67.

12. Wilson, "A Toast and a Tear," 67–68.

13. All of the stories mentioned can be found in the *The Portable Dorothy Parker*, except the following: "The Mantle of Whistler," "A Young Woman in Green Lace," "Travelogue," "Oh, He's Charming," "But the One on the Right," "The Garter," "Mrs. Carrington and Mrs. Crane," "Advice to the Little Peyton Girl," and "The Road Home," *Complete Stories*; "'Sorry, the Line Is Busy'" *Life* 77:2007 (21 Apr. 1921): 560; "Who Might Be Interested," in *Voices against Tyranny: Writing of the Spanish Civil War*, ed. John Miller (New York: Scribner, 1986), 192–97 (the story originally appeared in a 1986 issue of *Mother Jones* magazine).

14. Kate Millett, *Sexual Politics* (New York: Avon, 1971), 126–51; Gillian Rose, *Feminism and Geography: The Limits of Geographical Knowledge* (Minneapolis: University of Minnesota Press, 1993), 144–46.

15. Tompkins, *Sensational Designs*, 150.

16. Dobson, "The American Renaissance Reenvisioned," 170–71.

17. Emma Goldman, *"The Traffic in Women" and Other Essays on Feminism* (New York: Times Change Press, 1970).

18. "Advice to the Little Peyton Girl," *Complete Stories*, 184–90.

19. "A Telephone Call," *The Portable Dorothy Parker*, 119–24.

20. "The Waltz," *The Portable Dorothy Parker*, 47-51; see also Paul Treichler's valuable discussion of this story in "Verbal Subversions in Dorothy Parker: 'Trapped Like a Trap in a Trap,'" *Language and Style* 13 (1980): 46–61.

21. "The Lovely Leave," *The Portable Dorothy Parker*, 3-18; Tompkins, *Sensational Designs*, 178.

22. "The Lovely Leave," *The Portable Dorothy Parker*, 5–6.

23. Ibid., 6, 11, 17, 18.

24. "Wallflower's Lament," *The Portable Dorothy Parker*, 522.

25. Tompkins, *Sensational Designs*, xv–xvi; Guilason, *The Lesser Renaissance*, xi, xvi.

26. Some of Parker's book reviews can be found in the 1973 edition of *The Portable Dorothy Parker* and in *Constant Reader* (New York: Viking Press, 1970); see also "The Little Hours," *The Portable Dorothy Parker*, 254–59. "A Pig's-Eye View of Literature" is included in *The Portable Dorothy Parker*, 219–22.

27. Warhol, *Gendered Interventions*, 33–34.

28. "Clothe the Naked," *The Portable Dorothy Parker*, 360, 361, 361.

29. Ibid., 368.

30. Ibid.

31. Franklin Pierce Adams, "Have You a Little Dulcinea in Your Home?" *Vanity Fair*, Sept. 1914, 39; "Comic Relief," review of (with others) *Dulcy* by George S. Kaufman and Marc Connolly, *Ainslee's*, Nov. 1921, 154–59; both "The Flapper" and "Ballade of a Not Insupportable Loss" are in Silverstein, *Not Much Fun*, 105, and 157, respectively. Ann Ardis discusses the anxiety created in Britain by the New Woman in *New Women, New Novels: Feminism and Early Modernism* (New Brunswick, N. J.: Rutgers University Press, 1990), 10–28. Dulcinea was originally the sweetheart of Cervantes' Don Juan.

32. "The First Hundred Plays Are the Hardest," review of (with others) *The Gold Diggers*, by Avery Hopwood, *Vanity Fair* 13:4 (Dec. 1919): 37, 108, 110; "Take Them or Leave Them," review of (with others) *Lillies of the Field*, by William Hurlbut, *Ainslee's*, Jan. 1922, 155–59; "The Comedy Blues," review of (with others) *The Goldfish*, adapted by Gladys Unger, *Ainslee's*, July 1922, 155–59.

33. Anita Loos, "The Force of Heredity, and Nella" (1915), in Cleveland Amory and Frederic Bradlee, eds., *Vanity Fair: A Cavalcade of the 1920s and 1930s* (New York: Viking Press, 1960), 16; Anita Loos, "The Biography of a Book," (1963), introduction to *Gentlemen Prefer Blondes*, (1925; reprint, New York: Penguin, 1992), 11–16.

34. For Loos's relationship to the Algonquin Round Table, see Gaines, *Wit's End*, 82; and Meade, *Dorothy Parker*, 103. For publishing record and reader response to Loos's novel, see *Benét's Reader's Encyclopedia*, 3ᵈ ed. (New York: Harper and Row, 1987), 373, 580.

35. Loos, *Gentlemen Prefer Blondes*, 106, and "The Biography of a Book," 106 and 13, respectively. Regarding the character of Dorothy, Gary Carey, in *Anita Loos: A Biography* (New York: Knopf, 1988), claims that Dorothy is a composite of Loos and Connie Talmade (p. 100), but the name "Dorothy" as well as the hair color and the sharp wit she exhibits ("Dorothy said 'paste' is the name of the word a girl ought to do to a gentleman that handed her one" [p. 78] is one of numerous examples) suggest Parker as well. If Loos had intended Parker as part of her "composite" por-

trait, she would have been wise not to admit so publicly, as Parker's rebuttal could have been devastating.

36. Loos, *Gentlemen Prefer Blondes*, 20, 19, 114, 43.

37. Ibid., 29.

38. Ibid., 144–45.

39. Ibid., 106, 145.

40. Ibid., 126, 48, 48, 29, 126.

41. A *few* examples include the following: misused diction, "So when he introduced us to each other I dropped her a courtesy" (123); improper grammar, "all of we real friends of his . . ." (23); wrong or missing punctuation, "womens clubs" (35), "others ways" (111); misspelled words, "authrodox" (22), "riskay" (31), "anteek" (63), "Eyefull Tower" (79).

42. Loos, *Gentlemen Prefer Blondes*, 59.

43. Reportedly a "direct transcription" of actress Lillian Gish; see Carey, *Anita Loos*, 101.

44. See Elizabeth Ammons, "Edith Wharton's Hard-Working Lily: *The House of Mirth* and the Marriage Market," in Edith Wharton, *The House of Mirth* (1905; reprint, New York: Norton Critical Edition, 1990) 345–57. Ammons refers to Thorstein Veblen's 1899 study, *The Theory of the Leisure Class: An Economic Study of Institutions*.

45. Loos, *Gentlemen Prefer Blondes*, 63.

46. Ibid., 13.

47. "Big Blonde," *The Portable Dorothy Parker*, 187, 187, 194.

48. Ibid., 198.

49. Ibid.

50. Ibid., 187.

51. Ibid.

52. Ibid., 189.

53. Ibid., 199, 197, 199.

54. Ibid., 197.

55. I am indebted to Cheryl Walker who applies this argument to Edna St. Vincent Millay in *Masks Outrageous and Austere*, 135–64. She cites another useful source: T. J. Jackson Lears, *The Culture of Consumption: Critical Essays in American History, 1880–1980* (New York: Pantheon, 1983).

56. See, for example, Charles Dickens's *Bleak House* and George Eliot's *The Mill on the Floss*. Often the death of a heroine occurs in a context that suggests the possibility of suicide. Thomas Hood, "The Bridge of Sighs," in *Selected Poems of Thomas Hood*, ed. John Clubbe (Cambridge: Harvard University Press, 1970), 317–20.

57. Dobson, "The American Renaissance Reenvisioned," 169.

58. Susan K. Harris, "'But is it any good?': Evaluating Nineteenth-Century American Women's Fiction," in *The (Other) American Traditions*, ed. Joyce W. Warren (New Brunswick, N. J.: Rutgers University Press, 1993), 267–79.

59. Tompkins, *Sensational Designs*, 178; Baym, *Women's Fiction*, 144.

60. "Dorothy Parker's Stories and Other Recent Works of Fiction," review of *After Such Pleasures*, New York Times Book Review, 29 Oct. 1933, 6; Mark Van Doren, "Dorothy Parker," *English Journal* 23:7 (Sept. 1934): 540–41.

61. Ronald Paulson, *Satire and the Novel in Eighteenth-Century England* (New Haven: Yale University Press, 1967), 220–24. See also Brissenden, *Virtue in Disstress*; and Introduction to *Redressing the Balance: American Women's Literary Humor from Colonial Times to the 1980s*, ed. Nancy Walker and Zita Dresner (Jackson: University of Mississippi Press, 1988), xxv.

62. "Sentiment," *The Portable Dorothy Parker*, 354–59.

63. Ibid., 355.

64. Ibid., 356.

65. Ibid., 357.

66. "Soldiers of the Republic," *The Portable Dorothy Parker*, 165.

67. Kinney, *Dorothy Parker*, 1978, 142–43.

68. Clark, *Sentimental Modernism*, 5.

69. Ibid., 32–33.

CHAPTER 5: NEITHER CLOISTER NOR HEARTH

1. Dowling, quoted in Ian Fletcher, *Decadence and the 1890s* (London: Arnold, 1979), 8; see also Linda Dowling, Introduction to *Aestheticism and Decadence: A Selected Annotated Bibliography* (New York: Garland, 1977); Karl Beckson, ed., Introduction to *Aesthetes and Decadents of the 1890s* (Chicago: Academy Chicago, 1981), xxi–xlvi; Malcolm Bradbury and James McFarlane, eds., *Modernism: A Guide to European Literature 1890–1930* (New York: Penguin Books, 1976); Thomas Reed Whissen, *The Devil's Advocates: Decadence in Modern Literature* (New York: Greenwood Press, 1989); Richard Ellmann and Charles Feidelson, eds., *The Modern Tradition* (New York: Oxford University Press, 1965).

2. Elaine Showalter, Introduction to *Daughters of Decadence: Women Writers of the Fin-de-Siècle* (New Brunswick, N. J.: Rutgers University Press, 1993), x. Olive Custance's poetry appears in Beckson, *Aesthetes and Decadents*, 74–78; Evelyn Sharp's "The Other Anna" appears in Stanley Weintraub, ed., *The Yellow Book: Quintessence of the Nineties* (New York: Anchor Books, 1964), 323–43.

3. Walker, *The Nightingale's Burden*; Ann Ardis, *New Women, New Novels: Feminism and Early Modernism* (New Brunswick, N. J.: Rutgers University Press, 1990).

4. Ellen Moers, *Literary Women: The Great Writers* (New York and Oxford: Oxford University Press, 1976), 244; Walker, *The Nightingale's Burden*; Lionel Johnson's "Nihilism" appears in Beckson, *Aesthetes and Decadents*, 120–21.

5. Ruth McKenney, "Satire and Tragedy," review of *Here Lies*, *Saturday Review of Literature* (29 Apr. 1939): 7; Herbert Marshall McLuhan, "The New York Wits," *Kenyon Review* 7 (1945): 20–21.

6. See Laity, "H. D. and A. C. Swinburne," 461–84; Kaplan, *Katherine Mansfield*, 19–35; Kannenstine, *The Art of Djuna Barnes*, 100; and Farr, *The Life and Art of Elinor Wylie*, 61–74.

7. "Convalescent," *The Portable Dorothy Parker*, 77; "A Pig's Eye View of Literature," *The Portable Dorothy Parker*, 220; "Oscar Wilde: An Ideal Husband," *The Portable Dorothy Parker*, 417–18; Arthur Symons, "On the Value of a Lie: The Intellectual Somersaults of Oscar Wilde," *Vanity Fair* (Nov. 1916):49; "Vampire Women: Eight Pen Portraits, from Life," *Vanity Fair* (July 1915):35; "The Hokku: A New Verse Form," *Vanity Fair* (Aug. 1915):46; Kwaw Li, Ya, "The Prize Winners of the Hokku Contest," *Vanity Fair* (Oct. 1915):70.

8. R. K. R. Thornton, "'Decadence' in Later 19th Century England," in Ian Fletcher, ed., *Decadence and the 1890s* (London: Arnold, 1979), 27.

9. "Somebody's Song," and "Summary," *The Portable Dorothy Parker*, 81 and 313, respectively.

10. Whissen, *The Devil's Advocates*, 20.

11. "A Telephone Call," "Chant for the Dark Hours,""Threnody," and "Requiscat," *The Portable Dorothy Parker*, 119–24, 95, 74, and 314, respectively.

12. Taggard, "You Might as Well Live," 7. *The Portable Dorothy Parker* does not indicate the section break found in *Enough Rope*. Part 2 begins with "Portrait of the Artist," 94.

13. Capron, "Dorothy Parker," 75.

14. "Threnody," "Epitaph," "Wail," and "Testament," *The Portable Dorothy Parker*, 74, 79, 80, and 92, respectively.

15. "The Satin Dress," *The Portable Dorothy Parker*, 81. Sandra M. Gilbert discusses this poem in terms of Parker as a "female female impersonator"; see "Directions for Using the Empress: Millay's Supreme Fiction(s)," in Diane P. Freedman, ed., *Millay at 100: A Critical Reappraisal* (Carbondale: Southern Illinois University Press, 1995), 163–81, especially 168–70.

16. Susan Gubar, "Blessings in Disguise: Cross-Dressing as Re-Dressing for Female Modernists," *Massachusetts Review* 22 (Autumn 1981): 477–508.

17. "Epitaph for a Darling Lady," *The Portable Dorothy Parker*, 83.

18. "The White Lady," *The Portable Dorothy Parker*, 90. In both *Enough Rope* and *Not So Deep as a Well*, the last line of the poem reads: "Who hate the *drowsy* dead."

19. Quoted in Farr, *The Life and Art of Elinor Wylie*, 63.

20. "Godspeed," "Love Song," "Indian Summer," "Philosophy," "Observation," and "Neither Bloody Nor Bowed," *The Portable Dorothy Parker*, 103, 106, 107, 107, 112, and 117, respectively. "Ballade of Big Plans," *Enough Rope*, 97.

21. Quoted in Beckson, *Aesthetes and Decadents*, xxxii. Parker's poems appear in *The Portable Dorothy Parker*, 111, 112, 114, 115, and 116, respectively.

22. "Fragment," Silverstein, *Not Much Fun*, 104.

23. Thornton, "'Decadence,'" 26.

24. "The Wonderful Old Gentlemen," *The Portable Dorothy Parker*, 52.

25. Ibid.

26. Ibid, 52–54.

27. Van Doren, "Dorothy Parker," 536.

28. See Oscar Wilde's phrase, "Those who see any difference between soul and body have neither" in "Phrases and Philosophies for the Use of the Young," initially published in the first and only issue of the *Chameleon* (1894), an English journal concerned in part with homosexuality. It is reprinted in Beckson, *Aesthetes and Decadents*, 238–40.

29. Beckson, *Aesthetes and Decadents*, 34.

30. William Butler Yeats, "Modern Poetry," in *Essays and Introductions*, by W. B. Yeats (1936; reprinted, New York: Collier Books, 1961), 497; Kinney, 1978, *Dorothy Parker*, 103, 105–6.

31. Kinney, 1978, *Dorothy Parker*, 100, 107.

32. Parker's triolets can be found in Silverstein, *Not Much Fun*, 119, 149, 156.

33. "Inventory," and "News Item," *The Portable Dorothy Parker*, 96 and 109, respectively.

34. Clare Hanson, *Short Stories and Short Fictions, 1880–1980* (London: Macmillan, 1981), 35.

35. George Egerton, "The Lost Masterpiece," in *The Yellow Book: Quintessence of the Nineties*, ed. Stanley Weintraub (New York: Anchor Books, 1964), 57–63.

36. "The Waltz," "A Telephone Call," "The Little Hours," "Sentiment," and "New

York to Detroit," *The Portable Dorothy Parker*, 47, 119, 254, 354, and 291, respectively; "The Garter" and "But the One on the Right," *Complete Stories* , 99–101 and 132–35, respectively.

37. "The Road Home," and "The Mantle of Whistler," *Complete Stories*, 96–98 and 213–17, respectively.

38. Treichler, "Verbal Subversions in Dorothy Parker,"46–61; "Here We Are," and "Too Bad," *The Portable Dorothy Parker*, 125–34 and 170–81.

39. James McNeill Whistler, *The Gentle Art of Making Enemies* (1892; reprint, New York: G. P. Putnam, 1904).

40. "The Last Tea," *The Portable Dorothy Parker*, 183, 185, 183, 185. For an etymology of the slang use of "baby," see Robert L. Chapman, ed., with Barbara Ann Kipfer, *Dictionary of American Slang* 3^d ed. (New York: HarperCollins, 1995), 11. Mary Ritchie Key discusses the use of baby-talk by adults in both Marathi and English languages in *Male/Female Language* (Metuchen, N. J.: Scarecrow Press, 1975), 94.

41. "Too Bad" and "Horsie," *The Portable Dorothy Parker*, 175 and 267, 271, respectively.

42. "Travelogue," *Complete Stories*, 57–60.

43. The following four stories appear in *The Portable Dorothy Parker*: "Lady with a Lamp," 246–53; "The Bolt Behind the Blue," 394–415; "Glory in the Daytime," 276–90; "The Little Hours," 260–75. "Directions for Finding the Bard," *Sunset Gun*, 68. In his introduction to *Not Much Fun*, Stuart Silverstein briefly discusses Parker's use of slang in her poetry, noting that in some cases hers is the first known use; see pp. 64–65. With respect to Parker's critique of women, Ann Douglas argues that modernists maintained a matricidal impulse in their works, wishing to kill off the influence of the Victorian Lady whose conservative values regarding sexuality and race impeded cultural progress. Parker's satiric portraits of women may well fit into this matrix, though other factors and influences are undoubtedly at work as well. Many of her female protagonists were derived from women she knew or observed—society women or flappers who considered themselves "modern." And of course, her treatment of men in her works is no more flattering than that of women. See Ann Douglas, *Terrible Honesty*, 3–28.

44. "The Sexes," "Arrangement in Black and White," and "The Last Tea," *The Portable Dorothy Parker*, 24–28, 47–48, and 182–86, respectively; "Dialogue at Three in the Morning," "A Terrible Day Tomorrow," "A Young Woman in Green Lace," *Complete Stories*, 47–48, 86–91, and 165–69, respectively.

45. Vincent P. Pecora, *Self and Form in Modern Narrative* (Baltimore: Johns Hopkins University Press, 1989), 260.

46. "Cousin Larry," *Portable*, 333–38; "The Cradle of Civilization," *Complete Stories*, 129–31. Karl Beckson, ed. *London in the 1890s: A Cultural History* (New York: Norton, 1992), 63.

47. Oscar Wilde, "The Priority of Art" (1889) in Ellmann and Feidelson, 23.

48. "Song of the Open Country" and "Woodland Song" can be found in Silverstein, *Not Much Fun*, 87 and 129, respectively.

49. Jessica Feldman, *Gender on the Divide: The Dandy in Modern Literature* (Ithaca: Cornell University Press, 1992), 3.

50. Beckson, *Aesthetes and Decadents*, xxxvi–xxxvii.

51. Calhoun, *Dorothy Parker*, 14; Frank Crowninshield, "The Cub's Den," *Vogue*, 15 Sept. 1944, 162–63, 197–201; Walker and Dresner, *Redressing the Balance*, 133. The three French figures punned in Parker's pseudonym Henriette Rousseau include

Henri Rousseau, the late nineteenth-century French painter (primitivist and surreal) whose work was exhibited by Alfred Steiglitz at his 291 gallery; Jean Baptiste Rousseau, the late seventeeth-/early eighteenth-century poet known for lampooning his friends in verse; and Jean Jacques Rousseau, the eighteenth-century philosopher known for his frank and narcissistic volume, *Confessions*. Randall Calhoun's observation regarding Helen Wells occurred in a private conversation I had with him.

52. Feldman offers an interesting reading of Gautier's female dandy in *Gender on the Divide*, 33–38.

53. Crowninshield, "The Cub's Den," 197.

54. "Are You a Glossy?" 57, 90.

55. "How to Know the Glossies," 59, 89.

56. "The Custard Heart," *The Portable Dorothy Parker*, 319–27.

57. Farr, *The Life and Art of Elinor Wylie*, 46.

58. "Optimism and the Drama," a review (with others) of *The Famous Mrs. Fair*, by James Forbes, *Vanity Fair*, Mar. 1920, 41; "Let 'er Go," a review (with others) of *Shore Leave*, by Hubert Osborne, *Ainslee's*, Nov. 1922, 156–59; "Nights Off," a review (with others) of *Nice People*, by Rachel Crothers, *Ainslee's*, June 1921, 157–59.

59. "Such a Pretty Little Picture," *Complete Stories*, 3–12.

60. "Little Curtis," *The Portable Dorothy Parker*, 339–53.

61. "I Live on Your Visits," *The Portable Dorothy Parker*, 374.

62. Ibid., 380, 383.

63. Ibid., 375.

64. Lois W. Banner, *Women in Modern America: A Brief History* (New York: Harcourt Brace Jovanovich, 1974), 217. Parker's "Lolita," published in the *New Yorker* on 27 August 1955, shares a curious timing with Vladimir Nabokov's famous novel by the same title. According to textual notes by Brian Boyd in the Library of America edition of *Lolita*, Nabokov completed his novel in 1953 but couldn't find an American publisher; it first appeared in France in 1955. Excerpts appeared in an American magazine in 1957, and it was published in book form on 18 August 1958. Parker very favorably reviewed the novel for *Esquire* in October 1958.

65. "Story of Mrs. W —", *The Portable Dorothy Parker*, 89.

66. "Day-Dreams," *Enough Rope*, 63.

67. "The Whistling Girl," *The Portable Dorothy Parker*, 230.

68. Judith Kegan Gardiner, "On Female Identity and Writing by Women," in Elizabeth Abel, ed. *Writing and Sexual Difference* (Chicago: University of Chicago Press, 1982), 185.

69. "A Well-Worn Story," *The Portable Dorothy Parker*, 77; "Directions for Finding the Bard," *Sunset Gun*, 68.

70. "The Flaw in Paganism," *The Portable Dorothy Parker*, 248.

71. Ostriker, *Stealing the Language*, 216, 213.

72. Of the poems mentioned, the following appear in the *The Portable Dorothy Parker*: "Reuben's Children," 216; "Rainy Night," 86; "Renunciation," 100; "Song of One of the Girls," 109; "Partial Comfort," 219; "Words of Comfort to be Scratched on a Mirror," 108. "Cassandra Drops into Verse" appears in Silverstein, *Not Much Fun*, 165.

73. Ruthmarie H. Mitsch, "Parker's 'Iseult of Brittany,'" *Explicator* 44:2 (Winter 1986): 37–40.

74. "Guinevere at Her Fireside," *The Portable Dorothy Parker*, 306.

75. Ibid. Parker's poem also responds to Tennyson's "The Lady of Shalott."

76. "Salome's Dancing Lesson," *The Portable Dorothy Parker*, 298.

77. Edna St. Vincent Millay, "An Ancient Gesture," in *Collected Poems*, ed. Norma Millay (New York: Harper and Row, 1956), 501.

78. "Penelope," *The Portable Dorothy Parker*, 222.

79. Peter Whigham, trans., *The Poems of Catullus* (New York: Penguin Classics, 1984), 52.

80. "From a Letter from Lesbia," *The Portable Dorothy Parker*, 308. Parker's use of the word "queer" deserves notice here; it undoubtedly referred to both oddness and homosexuality. The use of the word "queer" to refer to homosexuals developed between World War I and World War II, according to Tony Thorne in *The Dictionary of Contemporary Slang* (New York: Pantheon, 1990), 413. Parker's relationship to homosexuality was complicated; she befriended and mocked homosexuals. See Meade, *Dorothy Parker*, 227, 300–301, 352, 354–55, 382. Also, in *Death and Taxes*, the first line of the poem reads: ". . . So, praise the gods, at last he's away!"

81. Ibid.

82. Whigham, *The Poems of Catullus*.

83. Ostriker, *Stealing the Language*, 194–98.

84. Arguing that "decadents suffer from a debilitating failure of nerve" and that "lack of conviction has rendered the decadents morally impotent," Thomas Reed Whissen claims that Eliot's Prufrock, Kafka's Gregor Samsa, and E. M. Forster's Tibby suffer the same malady (Whissen, *The Devil's Advocates*, xxv).

CODA

1. Nancy Walker mentions Parker throughout her study, *A Very Serious Thing: Women's Humor and American Culture* (Minneapolis: University of Minnesota Press, 1988); see especially chap. 4, "The Humor of the 'Minority,'" 101–38. Sondra Melzer's analysis appears in *The Rhetoric of Rage: Women in Dorothy Parker* (New York: Peter Lang, 1997). Gloria Steinem interviewed Parker, Nora Ephron and Norman Mailer wrote articles about her, and Steinem and Fran Lebowitz discuss her in a television production about Parker, "'Would You Kindly Direct Me to Hell?': The Infamous Dorothy Parker," *Stage*, produced by Arts & Entertainment, 1994. See also Steinem, "Dorothy Parker," *New York Journal*, 1965, 118e, 118n, 118o; Ephron, "Women," *Esquire*, Nov. 1973, 58, 86; Mailer, "Of Small and Modest Malignancy, Wicked and Bristling with Dots," *Esquire*, Nov. 1977, 125–48. Emily Toth links Parker with Jong in "Dorothy Parker, Erica Jong, and New Feminist Humor," *Regionalism and the Female Imagination* 3 (1977/78): 70–85.

2. Parker's influence on Smith is briefly discussed in Jack Barbera and William McBrien, *Stevie: A Biography of Stevie Smith* (New York and Oxford: Oxford University Press, 1985), 75; Stevie Smith, *Novel on Yellow Paper* (London: Jonathan Cape, 1936; London: Virago, 1980).

3. Laura Severin, *Stevie Smith's Resistant Antics* (Madison: University of Wisconsin Press, 1997).

Bibliography

For convenience, this bibliography is divided into sections: Primary Works of Dorothy Parker, Reviews of Dorothy Parker's Poetry, Reviews of Dorothy Parker's Fiction, Reviews of *The Portable Dorothy Parker*, General Criticism of Dorothy Parker, and General Criticism and Other Primary Sources. Individual poems and stories by Parker used in this study that can be found in the published editions of her work are not listed here, but are included in the Notes section. Since her play reviews typically covered several plays in one review, the individual play titles she reviewed are not included here; these also are found in the Notes section. For additional source material, see Randall Calhoun's *Dorothy Parker: A Bio-Bibliography*, cited below.

PRIMARY WORKS OF DOROTHY PARKER

"The Actors' Demands." [Helen Wells, pseud.] *Vanity Fair* (Oct. 1919): 47, 118.

After Such Pleasures (1933). New York: Sun Dial Press, 1940.

"The Anglo-American Drama: British Playwrights Do Much to Strengthen the Entente Cordiale." *Vanity Fair* (Feb. 1920): 41, 102.

"Are You a Glossy?" *Vanity Fair* (Apr. 1918): 57, 90.

"In Broadway Playhouses: For Auld Lang Syne." *Ainslee's* (Mar. 1922): 155–59.

"In Broadway Playhouses: The Comedy Blues." *Ainslee's* (July 1922): 155–59.

"In Broadway Playhouses: Comic Relief." *Ainslee's* (Nov. 1921): 154–59.

"In Broadway Playhouses: The Force of Example." *Ainslee's* (May 1922): 155–57.

"In Broadway Playhouses: Hard Times." *Ainslee's* (Feb. 1922): 155–59.

"In Broadway Playhouses: Laurels and Raspberries." *Ainslee's* (Dec. 1920): 155–59.

"In Broadway Playhouses: Let 'er Go." *Ainslee's* (Nov. 1922): 156–59.

"In Broadway Playhouses: National Institutions." *Ainslee's* (Sept. 1920): 156–59.

"In Broadway Playhouses: Nights Off." *Ainslee's* (June 1921): 157–59.

"In Broadway Playhouses: Plays in the Past and Present Tense." *Ainslee's* (Aug. 1920):155–59.

"In Broadway Playhouses: The Season's Greetings." *Ainslee's* (Nov. 1920): 155–59.

"In Broadway Playhouses: Standing Room Only, and Very Little of That." *Ainslee's* (Mar. 1921): 154–59.

"In Broadway Playhouses: Take Them or Leave Them." *Ainslee's* (Jan. 1922): 155–59.

"In Broadway Playhouses: Words and Music." *Ainslee's* (Oct. 1920): 154–58.

Brownlow, S. T., ed. *The Sayings of Dorothy Parker*. London: Duckworth, 1992.

"The Christmas Magazines." *Vanity Fair* (Dec. 1916): 83.

Complete Stories. Edited by Colleen Breese, with an introduction by Regina Barreca. New York: Penguin Books, 1995.

Constant Reader. New York: Viking Press, 1970.

Death and Taxes. New York: Viking Press, 1931.

"The Dramas that Gloom in the Spring." *Vanity Fair* (June 1918): 37, 84.

Enough Rope (1926). New York: Sun Dial Press, 1940.

"The Fall Crop of War Plays." *Vanity Fair* (Oct. 1918): 56, 104, 106.

"The First Hundred Plays Are the Hardest." *Vanity Fair* 13:4 (Dec. 1919): 37, 108, 110.

"Good Souls." *Vanity Fair* (June 1919): 47, 94.

Here Lies: The Collected Stories of Dorothy Parker. New York: Viking Press, 1939.

"How to Know the Glossies." *Vanity Fair* (May 1918): 59, 89.

"Incredible, Fantastic . . . and True." *New Masses* (23 Nov. 1937): 15–16.

An Informal Hour with Dorothy Parker, read by the author. New York: Westminster Spoken Arts, 1956. Audiotape.

"Is Your Little Girl Safe?" *Vanity Fair* (Sept. 1918): 46, 86.

Laments for the Living. New York: Viking Press, 1930.

"The New Order of Musical Comedies." *Vanity Fair* (May 1918): 49.

"The New Plays." *Vanity Fair* (Dec. 1918): 39, 84.

"The New Plays — If Any." *Vanity Fair* (Oct. 1919): 41, 112.

"Not Enough." *New Masses* (14 Mar. 1939): 3–4.

Not Much Fun: The Lost Poems of Dorothy Parker. Compiled and with an introduction by Stuart Y. Silverstein. New York: Scribner, 1996.

Not So Deep as a Well: Collected Poems. New York: Viking Press, 1938.

"Optimism and the Drama." *Vanity Fair* (Mar. 1920): 41.

"A Piece about Christmas." *Life* (1 Dec. 1927): 56.

The Poetry and Short Stories of Dorothy Parker. New York: Modern Library, 1994.

The Portable Dorothy Parker (1944). New York: Viking Press, 1973.

"Sophisticated Poetry—and the Hell with It." *New Masses* (27 June 1939): 21.

"'Sorry, the Line Is Busy.'" *Life* 77:2007 (21 Apr. 1921): 560.

"Standing Room Only, and Very Little of That." *Ainslee's* (Mar. 1921): 154–59.

"The Star-Spangled Drama." *Vanity Fair* (Aug. 1918): 29, 66.

Sunset Gun. New York: Boni and Liveright, 1928.

"The Union Forever!" [Helen Wells, pseud.]. *Vanity Fair* (Nov. 1919): 37, 84.

"Who Might Be Interested." In *Voices Against Tyranny: Writing of the Spanish Civil War.* Edited by John Miller. New York: Scribner's, 1986. 192–97.

"Words and Music." *Ainslee's* (Oct. 1920): 154–18.

REVIEWS OF DOROTHY PARKER'S POETRY

Adams, Franklin Pierce. Review of *Death and Taxes*, by Dorothy Parker. *New York Herald Tribune Books* (14 June 1931): 7.

Benét, William Rose. "New Moon Madness." Review of *Sunset Gun*, by Dorothy Parker. *Saturday Review of Literature* (9 June 1928): 943.

———. "Deep, at That." Review of *Not So Deep as a Well*, by Dorothy Parker. *Saturday Review of Literature* (12 Dec. 1936): 5.

"Book Notes." Review of *Death and Taxes*, by Dorothy Parker. *New Republic* 67 (1931): 348–49.

"Books in Brief." Review of *Death and Taxes*, by Dorothy Parker. *Forum* 86 (Aug. 1931): xii.

"Books in Brief." Review of *Death and Taxes*, by Dorothy Parker. *Nation* 133 (23 Sept. 1931): 315.

Brickell, Herschel. Review of *Sunset Gun*, by Dorothy Parker. *North American Review* 226:adv (Aug. 1928).

Busey, Garreta. "A Procupine's View." Review of *Sunset Gun*, by Dorothy Parker. *New York Herald Tribune Books* (15 July 1928): 7.

Canby, Henry Seidel. "Belle Dame sans Merci." Review of *Death and Taxes*, by Dorothy Parker. *Saturday Review of Literature* (13 June 1931): 91.

Clark, Edwin. "Six Rhymsters in Cap and Bells." Review of *Sunset Gun*, by Dorothy Parker. *New York Times Book Review* (1 July 1928): 10.

"Dorothy Parker's Poems." Review of *Death and Taxes*, by Dorothy Parker. *Springfield Republican* (21 June 1931): 7e.

Edman, Irwin. "Well, Not So Deep." Review of *Not So Deep as a Well*, by Dorothy Parker. *Nation* 143:736 (19 Dec. 1936): 736–38.

Gregory, Horace. "Dorothy Parker, Lady Wit." Review of *Death and Taxes*, by Dorothy Parker. *New York Evening Post* (20 June 1931): 12.

Hutchison, Percy. "Satire and Epigram in Dorothy Parker's Versicles." Review of *Death and Taxes*, by Dorothy Parker. *New York Times Book Review* (14 June 1931): 4.

J. F. Review of *Enough Rope*, by Dorothy Parker. *Bookman* (Mar. 1927): 80.

Kronenberger, Louis. "The Rueful, Frostbitten Laughter of Dorothy Parker." Review of *Not So Deep as a Well*, by Dorothy Parker. *New York Times Book Review* (13 Dec. 1936): 2, 28.

Luhrs, Marie. "Fashionable Poetry." Review of *Enough Rope*, by Dorothy Parker. *Poetry* 30.1 (Apr. 1927): 52–54.

"The Phoenix Nest." Review of *Enough Rope*, by Dorothy Parker. *Saturday Review of Literature* (1 Jan. 1927): 492.

Review of *Enough Rope*, by Dorothy Parker. *Nation* (25 May 1927): 589.

Robinson, H. M. Review of *Sunset Gun*, by Dorothy Parker. *Bookman* (Sept. 1928): 96.

Rosenberg, Harold. "Nor Rosemary nor Rue." Review of *Death and Taxes*, by Dorothy Parker. *Poetry* (Dec. 1939): 159–61.

Simon, R. A. Review of *Sunset Gun*, by Dorothy Parker. *New York Evening Post* (2 June 1928): 8.

"Six Rhymsters in Cap and Bells." Review of *Sunset Gun*, by Dorothy Parker. *New York Times Book Review* (1 July 1928): 10.

Taggard, Genevieve. "You Might as Well Live." Review of *Enough Rope*, by Dorothy Parker. *New York Herald Tribune Books* (27 Mar. 1927): 7.

"Three Poets Who Openly Prefer Laughter to Tears." Review of *Enough Rope*, by Dorothy Parker. *New York Times Book Review* (27 Mar. 1927): 6.

Walton, Edith. "New York Wits." Review of *Sunset Gun*, by Dorothy Parker. *New Republic* (27 June 1928): 155.

Wilson, Edmund. "Dorothy Parker's Poems." Review of *Enough Rope*, by Dorothy Parker. *New Republic* (19 Jan. 1927): 256.

Reviews of Dorothy Parker's Fiction

"Books in Brief." Review of *Laments for the Living*, by Dorothy Parker. *Nation* 131:75 (16 July 1930): 150.

Brickell, Herschel. "Hemingway and Parker." Review of *Winner Take All*, by Ernest Hemingway, and *After Such Pleasures*, by Dorothy Parker. *North American Review* (Jan. 1934): 94.

Britten, Florence Haxton. "Devastating, Tender and Witty." Review of *Here Lies*, by Dorothy Parker. *New York Herald Tribune Books* (7 May 1939): 3.

Butcher, Fanny. "Dorothy Parker's Stories Given Praise as Book." Review of *Laments for the Living*, by Dorothy Parker. *Chicago Tribune* (21 June 1930): 6.

————. "Short Stories Still Live as Works of Art." Review of *After Such Pleasures*, by Dorothy Parker. *Chicago Tribune* (28 Oct. 1933): 16.

Curtiss, Mina. "Dorothy Parker's Idle Rich." Review of *Here Lies*, by Dorothy Parker. *Nation* (15 July 1939): 76–78.

"Dorothy Parker's Art." Review of *After Such Pleasures*, by Dorothy Parker. *Springfield* [Mass.] *Sunday Union and Republican* (24 Dec. 1933): 7e.

"Dorothy Parker's *Laments for the Living*." Review of *Laments for the Living*, by Dorothy Parker. *New York Times Book Review* (15 June 1930): 7.

"Dorothy Parker's Stories and Other Recent Works of Fiction." Review of *After Such Pleasures*, by Dorothy Parker. *New York Times Book Review* (29 Oct. 1933): 6.

Graham, Gladys. "Cut–Outs from Life." Review of *Laments for the Living*, by Dorothy Parker. *Saturday Review of Literature* (5 July 1930): 1172.

Hensen, Harry. "The First Reader." Review of *Laments for the Living*, by Dorothy Parker. *New York World* (13 June 1930): 13.

"Irony and Sympathy." Review of *Laments for the Living*, by Dorothy Parker. *Springfield Sunday Union and Republican* (21 Sept. 1930): 7e.

Johnson, Edgar. "Technique and Tantrum." Review of *Here Lies*, by Dorothy Parker. *Kenyon Review* 1.3 (Summer 1939): 348–51.

L. A. S. "With Pity and Anger." Review of *Here Lies*, by Dorothy Parker. *Christian Science Monitor* (17 June 1939): 10.

McCarty, Norma. "Dorothy Parker's Short Stories and Other Recent Works of Fiction." Review of *Here Lies*, by Dorothy Parker. *New York Times Book Review* (30 Apr. 1939): 6.

McKenney, Ruth. "Satire and Tragedy." Review of *Here Lies*, by Dorothy Parker. *Saturday Review of Literature* (29 Apr. 1939): 7.

Mair, John. "New Novels." Review of *Here Lies*, by Dorothy Parker. *New Statesman and Nation* (21 Oct. 1939): 583–84.

Matthews, T. S. "Curses Not Loud but Deep." Review of *Laments for the Living*, by Dorothy Parker. *New Republic* 64 (1930): 133.

————— "Fiction by Young and Old." Review of *After Such Pleasures*, by Dorothy Parker. *New Republic* (15 Nov. 1933): 24–25.

M. F. B. "After Such Pleasures." Review of *After Such Pleasures*, by Dorothy Parker. *Boston Evening Transcript* (20 Jan. 1934): 3.

Nash, Ogden. "The Pleasure Is Ours." Review of *After Such Pleasures*, by Dorothy Parker. *Saturday Review of Literature* (4 Nov. 1933): 231.

Plomer, William. Review of *Here Lies*, by Dorothy Parker. *Spectator* 163 (17 Nov. 1939): 708.

Rascoe, Burton. "Among the New Books." Review of *Laments for the Living*, by Dorothy Parker. *Arts and Decoration* (Sept. 1930): 71, 101–2.

Review of *After Such Pleasures*, by Dorothy Parker. *Forum* (Jan. 1934): 5. Review of *Here Lies*, by Dorothy Parker. *Times (London) Literary Supplement* (25 Nov. 1939): 687.

Review of *Laments for the Living*, by Dorothy Parker. *New Statesman* 36 (22 Nov. 1930): 218.

Review of *Laments for the Living*, by Dorothy Parker. *Times (London) Literary Supplement* (23 Oct. 1930): 860.

Ross, Mary. "Thirteen Manhattans." Review of *Laments for the Living*, by Dorothy Parker. *New York Herald Tribune Books* (15 June 1930): 7.

Ryskind, Morrie. "Man's Words, Woman's Voice." Review of *After Such Pleasures*, by Dorothy Parker. *New York Herald Tribune Books* (12 Nov. 1933): 7.

"Shorter Notices." Review of *After Such Pleasures*, by Dorothy Parker. *Nation* 137 (20 Dec. 1933): 715.

Springer, Ann. Review of *Here Lies*, by Dorothy Parker. *Boston Evening Transcript* (27 May 1939): 2.

REVIEWS OF *THE PORTABLE DOROTHY PARKER*
(PUBLISHED IN LONDON AS *THE COLLECTED DOROTHY PARKER*)
1944 AND 1973 EDITIONS

Fearing, Kenneth. "Review of Distinctive New Fiction." Review of *The Portable Dorothy Parker* (1944), edited by Dorothy Parker. *New York Herald Tribune Weekly Book Review* (6 June 1944): 6.

James, Clive. "Nickel and Ivory." Review of *The Collected Dorothy Parker*, by Dorothy Parker. *New Statesman* (27 Apr. 1973): 623–24.

"Low Spirits." Review of *The Collected Dorothy Parker*, by Dorothy Parker. *Times (London) Literary Supplement* (6 Apr. 1973): 395.

O'Hara, John. "Dorothy Parker, Hip Pocket Size." Review of *The Portable Dorothy Parker* (1944), by Dorothy Parker." *New York Times Book Review* (28 May 1944): 5, 29.

Review of *The Portable Dorothy Parker* (1944), by Dorothy Parker. *Kirkus Reviews* (1 May 1944): 202.

Weeks, Edward. "*The Portable Dorothy Parker*." Review of *The Portable Dorothy Parker* (1944), by Dorothy Parker. *Atlantic* (July 1944): 125.

Wilson, Edmund. "A Toast and a Tear for Dorothy Parker." Review of *The Portable Dorothy Parker* (1944), by Dorothy Parker. *New Yorker* (20 May 1944): 67–68.

GENERAL CRITICISM OF DOROTHY PARKER

Bloom, Lynn Z. "Dorothy Parker." In *Critical Survey of Poetry*, Vol. 5. Edited by Frank N. Magill. Englewood Cliffs, N. J.: Salem Press, 1982.

———. "Dorothy Parker." In *Critical Survey of Short Fiction*, Vol. 5. Edited by Frank N. Magill. Englewood Cliffs, N. J.: Salem Press, 1982, 2052–56.

Bone, Martha Denham. "Dorothy Parker and *New Yorker* Satire." Diss., Middle Tennessee State University, 1985.

Bryan, Joseph, III. "Bittersweet." In *Merry Gentlemen (and One Lady)*. New York: Atheneum, 1985. 99–118. Reprinted in Calhoun, 151–61.

Bunkers, Suzanne. "'I Am Outraged Womanhood': Dorothy Parker as Feminist and Social Critic." *Regionalism and the Female Imagination* 4.2 (1978): 25–34.

Calhoun, Randall. *Dorothy Parker: A Bio-Bibliography*. Westport, Conn.: Greenwood Press, 1993.

Capron, Marion. "Dorothy Parker." In *Writers at Work: The Paris Review Interviews*. Edited by Malcolm Cowley. New York: Viking Press, 1958, 72–87.

Cooper, Wyatt. "Whatever You Think Dorothy Parker Was Like, She Wasn't." *Esquire* (July 1968): 56–57, 61, 110–14. Reprint in Calhoun, 131–50.

Cope, Wendy. *Serious Concerns*. London and Boston: Faber and Faber, 1992.

Daniels, Earl. *The Art of Reading Poetry*. New York: Farrar and Rinehart, 1941.

Drennan, Robert E. *The Algonquin Wits*. New York: The Citadel Press, 1968.

Finch, Annie, ed. *A Formal Feeling Comes: Poems in Form by Contemporary Women*. Brownsville, Ore.: Story Line Press, 1994.

Ford, Corey. *The Time of Laughter*. Boston: Little, Brown, 1967.

Frewin, Leslie. *The Late Mrs. Dorothy Parker*. New York: Macmillan, 1986.

Gaines, James R. *Wit's End: Days and Nights of the Algonquin Round Table*. New York: Harcourt Brace Jovanovich, 1977.

Gill, Brendan. "Introduction" *The Portable Dorothy Parker*. Edited by Brendan Gill. New York: Viking Press, 1973.

Gray, James. *On Second Thought*. Minneapolis: University of Minnesota Press, 1946.

Grimes, William. "Wit at the Round Table: Was It, Er, Um, Square?" *New York Times* (28 June 1944): B1.

———. "The Two Dorothy Parkers at Breakfast," *New York Times* (15 Oct. 1994): B12.

Harriman, Margaret Case. *The Vicious Circle: The Story of the Algonquin Round Table*. New York: Rinehart, 1951.

Hellman, Lillian. *An Unfinished Woman: A Memoir*. Boston: Little, Brown, 1969.

Herrman, Dorothy. *With Malice Toward All*. New York: G. P. Putnam's Sons, 1982.

Johnson, Diane. *Dashiell Hammett: A Life*. New York: Random House, 1983.

Kaufman, George S., and Moss Hart. "Merrily We Roll Along." In *Six Plays by Kaufman and Hart*. New York: Modern Library, 1942. 123–32.

Keats, John. *You Might as Well Live: The Life and Times of Dorothy Parker*. New York: Simon and Schuster, 1970; reprint, New York: Paragon House, 1986.

Kinney, Arthur F. *Dorothy Parker*. Boston: Twayne, 1978.

———. *Dorothy Parker, Revised*. New York: Twayne, 1998.

———. "Dorothy Parker's Letters to Alexander Woollcott." *Massachusetts Review* 30:3 (Autumn 1989): 487–15.

Kline, Virginia. "Dorothy Parker." In *Encyclopedia of American Humorists*. Edited by Steven H. Gale. New York: Garland, 1988, 344–49.

Labrie, Ross. "Dorothy Parker Revisited." *Canadian Review of American Studies* 7 (1976): 48–56.

Lane, Anthony. "Etherized." *New Yorker* (Dec. 1994): 128.

Lauterbach, Richard E. "The Legend of Dorothy Parker." *Esquire* (Oct. 1944): 93, 139–44. Reprinted in Calhoun, 123–29.

McLuhan, Herbert Marshall. "The New York Wits." *Kenyon Review* 7 (1945): 12–28.

Maslin, Janet. "So Witty, So Sophisticated, and So Very Lonely." *New York Times* (23 Nov. 1994): B3.

Meade, Marion. *Dorothy Parker: What Fresh Hell Is This?* New York: Villard Books, 1988.

Melzer, Sondra. *The Rhetoric of Rage: Women in Dorothy Parker*. New York: Peger Lang, 1997.

Mitsch, Ruthmarie, H. "Parker's 'Iseult of Brittany.'" *Explicator* 44:2 (Winter 1986): 37–40.

Orvis, Mary Burchard. *The Art of Writing Fiction.* New York: Prentice-Hall, 1948.

Richart, Bette. "The Light Touch." *Commonweal* (Dec. 1960): 277–79.

Rudolph, Alan, dir. *Mrs. Parker and the Vicious Circle.* Fine Line Features, 1994.

Shanahan, William. "Robert Benchley and Dorothy Parker: Punch and Judy in Formal Dress." *Rendezvous* 3 (1968): 23–24.

Slesin, Aviva, dir. *The Ten-Year Lunch: The Wit and Legend of the Algonquin Round Table.* PBS American Masters, 1987.

Smith, Stevie. *Novel on Yellow Paper.* London: Jonathan Cape, 1936; London: Virago, 1980.

Stewart, Donald Ogden, ed. *Fighting Words.* New York: Harcourt Brace, 1940.

Tighe, Dixie. "Dorothy Parker Returns from Spain with Tears in Her Soul." *New York Post* (22 Oct. 1937): 17.

Toth, Emily. "Dorothy Parker, Erica Jong, and New Feminist Humor." *Regionalism and the Female Imagination* 3 (1977/78): 70–85.

Treichler, Paula. "Verbal Subversions in Dorothy Parker: 'Trapped Like a Trap in a Trap.'" *Language and Style* 13 (1980): 46–61.

Van Doren, Mark. "Dorothy Parker." *English Journal* 23:7 (Sept. 1934): 535–43.

Woollcott, Alexander. "Our Mrs. Parker." In *While Rome Burns.* New York: Viking Press, 1934, 142–52.

"'Would You Kindly Direct Me to Hell?': The Infamous Dorothy Parker." *Stage*, Arts and Entertainment, 1994

GENERAL CRITICISM AND OTHER PRIMARY SOURCES

Abel, Elizabeth, ed. *Writing and Sexual Difference.* Chicago: University of Chicago Press, 1982.

Abrams, M.H., et al., eds. *The Norton Anthology of English Literature*, Vol. 1. New York: Norton, 1993.

Achebe, Chinua. *Hopes and Impediments: Selected Essays.* 1988. Reprint, New York: Anchor Books, 1990.

Altick, Richard D. *Victorian Ideas and People.* New York: Norton, 1973.

Ammons, Elizabeth. *Conflicting Stories; American Women Writers at the Turn into the Twentieth Century.* New York and London: Oxford University Press, 1991.

———. "Edith Wharton's Hard-Working Lily: *The House of Mirth* and the Marrriage Market." In Edith Wharton, *The House of Mirth.* 1905. Reprint, Norton Critical Edition, 1990.

———. Introduction to *"How Celia Changed Her Mind" and Other Stories,* by Rose Terry Cooke. Edited by Elizabeth Ammons. New Brunswick, N. J.: Rutgers University Press, 1986.

Amory, Cleveland, and Frederic Bradlee, eds. *Vanity Fair: A Cavalcade of the 1920s and 1930s.* New York: Viking Press, 1960.

Ardis, Ann. *New Woman, New Novels: Feminism and Early Modernism.* New Brunswick, N. J.: Rutgers University Press, 1990.

Armstrong, Nancy. *Desire and Domestic Fiction: A Political History of the Novel.* New York and London: Oxford University Press, 1987.

Atkinson, Brooks. *Broadway.* New York: Macmillan, 1970.

Baker, Houston, Jr. *Modernism and the Harlem Renaissance.* Chicago: University of Chicago Press, 1987.

Banner, Lois. *Women in Modern America: A Brief History.* New York: Harcourt Brace Jovanovich, Inc., 1974.

Barbera, Jack and William McBrien. *Stevie: A Biography of Stevie Smith.* Oxford and New York: Oxford University Press, 1985.

Baym, Nina. "Reinventing Lydia Sigourney." In *The (Other) American Traditions: Nineteenth-Century Women Writers.* Edited by Joyce W. Warren. New Brunswick, N. J.: Rutgers University Press, 1993. 54–72.

————. *Women's Fiction: A Guide to Novels by and about Women in America, 1820–1870.* Ithaca and London: Cornell University Press, 1978.

Beckson, Karl, ed. *Aesthetes and Decadents of the 1890s.* Chicago: Academy Chicago, 1981.

————. *London in the 1890s: A Cultural History.* New York: Norton, 1992.

Benstock, Shari. *Women of the Left Bank.* Austin: University of Texas Press, 1986.

Bloom, Harold. *The Anxiety of Influence.* Oxford and New York: Oxford University Press, 1973.

Bogan, Louise. *Achievement in American Poetry, 1900–1950.* Chicago: Regnery, 1951.

Bradbury, Malcolm and James McFarlane, eds. *Modernism: A Guide to European Literature, 1890–1930.* New York: Penguin Books, 1976.

Brissenden, R. F. *Virtue in Distress.* New York: Macmillan, 1974.

Broe, Mary Lynn. "Djuna Barnes." In *The Gender of Modernism.* Edited by Bonnie Kime Scott. Bloomington: Indiana University Press, 1990. 19–29.

Bryer, Jackson R., ed. *Conversations with Lillian Hellman.* Jackson: University Press of Mississippi, 1986.

Bush, Ronald. "Ezra Pound." In *The Gender of Modernism.* Edited by Bonnie Kime Scott. Bloomington: Indiana University Press, 1990. 353–59.

Carey, Gary. *Anita Loos: A Biography.* New York: Knopf, 1988.

Christ, Carol T. *Victorian and Modern Poetics.* Chicago: University of Chicago Press, 1984.

Churchill, Allen. *The Literary Decade.* Englewood Cliffs, N. J.: Prentice Hall, 1971.

Clark, Suzanne. *Sentimental Modernism: Women Writers and the Revolution of the Word.* Bloomington: Indiana University Press, 1991.

————. "Uncanny Millay." *Millay at 100: A Critical Appraisal.* Edited by Diane P. Freedman. Carbondale: Southern Illinois University Press, 1995, 3–26.

Cott, Nancy F. *The Grounding of Modern Feminism.* New Haven: Yale University Press, 1987.

————. Introduction to *Root of Bitterness: Documents of the Social History of American Women*. New York: Dutton, 1972.

Davis, Angela Y. *Women, Race, and Class*. New York: Vintage Books, 1983.

Davison, Dennis, ed. *The Penguin Book of Eighteenth Century Verse*. New York: Penguin Books, 1973.

Dobson, Joanne. "The American Renaissance Reenvisioned." *The (Other) American Traditions: Nineteenth-Century Women Writers*. Edited by Joyce W. Warren. New Brunswick, N. J.: Rutgers University Press, 1993. 164–82.

Dolmetsch, Carl R. *The Smart Set: A History and Anthology*. New York: Dial Press, 1966.

Donovan, Josephine. *New England Local Color Literature*. New York: Frederick Ungar, 1983.

Douglas, Ann. *The Feminization of American Culture*. 1977. Reprint, New York: Anchor Press, 1988.

————. *Terrible Honesty: Mongrel Manhattan in the 1920s*. New York: Noonday Press/ Farrar, Straus and Giroux, 1995.

Dowling, Linda. Introduction to *Aestheticism and Decadence: A Selected Annotated Bibliography*. New York: Garland, 1977.

Drabble, Margaret, ed. *The Oxford Companion to English Literature*, 5th ed. Oxford and New York: Oxford University Press, 1985.

Drake, William. *The First Wave: Women Poets in America, 1915–1945*. New York: Collier Books, 1987.

DuPlessis, Rachel Blau. *Writing beyond the Ending: Narrative Strategies of Twentieth-Century Women Writers*. Bloomington: Indiana University Press, 1985.

Eliot, T. S. *Collected Poems, 1909–1962*. New York: Harcourt Brace Jovanovich, 1963.

Ellmann, Richard, and Charles Feidelson, eds. *The Modern Tradition*. Oxford and New York: Oxford University Press, 1965.

Emery, Edwin. *The Press and America* 2[d] ed. Englewood Cliffs, N. J.: Prentice-Hall, 1962.

Eysteinsson, Astradur. *The Concept of Modernism*. Ithaca: Cornell University Press, 1990.

Farr, Judith. *The Life and Art of Elinor Wylie*. Baton Rouge: Louisiana State University Press, 1983.

Feinstein, Sascha. *Jazz Poetry from the 1920s to the Present*. Westport, Conn.: Praeger, 1997.

Feldman, Jessica. *Gender on the Divide: The Dandy in Modern Literature*. Ithaca: Cornell University Press, 1992.

Fetterley, Judith, ed. *Provisions: A Reader from Nineteenth-Century American Women*. Bloomington: Indiana University Press, 1985, 1–40.

Fetterley, Judith, and Marjorie Pryse, eds. *American Women Regionalists, 1850–1910*. New York: Norton, 1992.

Fiedler, Leslie A. *Love and Death in the American Novel*. New York: Criterion Books, 1960.

Fletcher, Ian, ed. *Decadence and the 1890s*. London: Arnold, 1979.

Forster, E. M. *Commonplace Book.* Edited by Philip Gardner. Stanford, Calif.: Stanford University Press, 1985.

Freedman, Diane P., ed. *Millay at 100: A Critical Appraisal.* Carbondale: Southern Illinois University Press, 1995.

Friedman, Norman. "E. E. Cummings and the Modernist Movement." In *Critical Essays on E. E. Cummings.* Edited by Guy Rotella. Boston: G. K. Hall, 1984. 39–46.

Friedman, Susan Stanford. *Psyche Reborn: The Emergence of H. D.* Bloomington: Indiana University Press, 1981.

Fulweiler, Howard W. *"Here a Captive Heart Busted": Studies in the Sentimental Journey of Modern Literature.* New York: Fordham University Press, 1993.

Furia, Philip. *Ira Gershwin: The Art of the Lyricist.* Oxford and New York: Oxford University Press, 1996.

Gardiner, Judith Kegan. "On Female Identity and Writing by Women." In *Writing and Sexual Difference.* Edited by Elizabeth Abel. Chicago: University of Chicago Press, 1982, 177–91.

Gilbert, Sandra M. "Directions for Using the Empress: Millay's Supreme Fiction(s)." In *Millay at 100: A Critical Reappraisal.* Edited by Diane P. Freedman. Carbondale: Southern Illinois University Press, 1995, 163–81.

Gilbert, Sandra and Susan Gubar. *No Man's Land: The War of the Words.* New Haven and London: Yale University Press, 1987.

———. The *Madwoman in the Attic: The Woman Writer and the Nineteenth-Century Literary Imagination.* New Haven: Yale University Press, 1979.

Goldman, Emma. *"The Traffic in Women" and Other Essays on Feminism.* Introduction by Alix Kates Shulman. New York: Times Change Press, 1970.

Gregory, Eileen. "Rose Cut in Rock: Sappho and H. D.'s *Sea Garden*." In *Signets: Reading H. D.* Edited by Susan Stanford Friedman and Rachel Blau DuPlessis. Madison: University of Wisconsin Press, 1990. 129–54.

Griswold, Rufus, ed. *The Female Poets of America.* Philadelphia: Carey and Hart, 1849.

Gubar, Susan. "Blessings in Disguise: Cross-Dressing as Re-Dressing for Female Modernists." *Massachusetts Review* 22 (Autumn 1981): 477–508.

Guilason, Thomas A. "The Lesser Renaissance: The American Short Story in the 1920s." In *The American Short Story, 1900–1945.* Edited by Philip Sterick. Boston: Twayne, 1984. 71–102.

Gummere, Francis B., ed. *Old English Ballads.* Boston: Ginn, 1894.

H. D. (Hilda Doolittle). *Collected Poems, 1912–1944.* Edited by Louis L. Martz. New York: New Directions, 1983.

Hanson, Clare. *Short Stories and Short Fictions, 1880–1980.* London: Macmillan, 1981.

Harris, Susan K. "'But is it any good?': Evaluating Nineteenth-Century American Women's Fiction." *The (Other) American Traditions: Nineteenth-Century Women Writers.* . Edited by Joyce W. Warren. New Brunswick, N. J.: Rutgers University Press, 1993. 267–79.

Hemingway, Ernest. *88 Poems.* Edited by Nicholas Gerogiannis. New York: Harcourt Brace Jovanovich, 1979.

Hoffman, Frederick J. *The Twenties.* New York: Macmillan, 1962

Hoffman, Frederick J., Charles Allen, and Carolyn F. Ulrich. *The Little Magazines.* Princeton: Princeton University Press, 1947.

Hoffman, Michael J., and Patrick D. Murphy. Introduction to *Critical Essays on American Modernism.* Edited by Michael J. Hoffman and Patrick D. Murphy. New York: G. K. Hall, 1992, 1–16.

Hogeland, Lisa Maria. *Feminism and Its Fictions: The Consciousness-Raising Novel and the Women's Liberation Movement.* Philadelphia: University of Pennsylvania Press, 1998.

Honey, Maureen. Introduction to *Shadowed Dreams: Women's Poetry of the Harlem Renaissance.* Edited by Maureen Honey. New Brunswick, N. J.: Rutgers University Press, 1989.

Housman, A. E. *A Shropshire Lad.* 1896. New York: Dover, 1990, 2.

Hull, Gloria. "Afro-American Women Poets: A Bio-Critical Survey." In *Shakespeare's Sisters: Feminist Essays on Women Poets.* Edited by Sandra Gilbert and Susan Gubar. Bloomington: Indiana University Press, 1979, 165–82.

Huyssen, Andreas. *After the Great Divide.* Bloomington: Indiana University Press, 1986.

Jehlen, Myra. "Archimedes and the Paradox of Feminist Criticism." 1981. In *Feminisms.* Edited by Robyn R. Warhol and Diane Price Herndl. New Brunswick, N. J.: Rutgers University Press, 1991. 75–96.

Johnson, Diane. *Dashiell Hammett: A Life.* New York: Random House, 1983.

Juhasz, Suzanne. *Naked and Firey Forms, Modern American Poetry by Women: A New Tradition.* New York: Colophon Books, 1976.

Kannenstine, Louis F. *The Art of Djuna Barnes: Duality and Damnation.* New York: New York University Press, 1977.

Kaplan, Amy. *The Social Construction of American Realism.* Chicago: University of Chicago Press, 1988.

Kaplan, Fred. *Sacred Tears: Sentimentality in Victorian Literature.* Princeton: Princeton University Press, 1987.

Kaplan, Sydney Janet. *Katherine Mansfield and the Origins of Modernist Fiction.* Ithaca: Cornell University Press, 1991.

Kelley, Mary. *Private Woman, Public Stage: Literary Domesticity in Nineteenth- Century America.* New York and Oxford: Oxford University Press, 1984.

Kertesz, Louise. *The Poetic Vision of Muriel Rukeyser.* Baton Rouge: Louisiana State University Press, 1980.

Key, Mary Ritchie. *Male/Female Language.* Metuchen, N. J.: Scarecrow Press, 1975.

Laity, Cassandra. "H. D. and A. C. Swinburne: Decadence and Modernist Women's Writing." *Feminist Studies* 15:3 (Fall 1989): 461–84.

Lakoff, Robin. *Language and Woman's Place.* New York: Harper, 1975.

Lauter, Paul. "Race and Gender in the Shaping of the American Literary Canon: A Case Study from the Twenties." In *Feminist Criticism and Social Change: Sex, Class, and Race in Literature and Culture.* Edited by Judith Newton and Deborah Rosenfelt. New York: Methuen, 1985. 19–43.

Lawrence, Margaret. *The School of Femininity.* 1936. Reprint, Port Washington, N.Y.: Kennikat Press, 1966.

Leighton, Angela and Margaret Reynolds. *Victorian Women Poets: An Anthology*. Oxford: Blackwell, 1995.

Lerner, Gerda. *The Majority Finds Its Past: Placing Women in History*. Oxford and New York: Oxford University Press, 1979.

Levenson, Michael. *A Genealogy of Modernism: A Study of English Literary Doctrine, 1908–1922*. New York: Cambridge University Press, 1984.

———. *Modernism and the Fate of Individuality*. Cambridge: Cambridge University Press, 1991.

Lewis, David Levering. *When Harlem Was in Vogue*. New York: Oxford University Press, 1982.

Locke, Alain, ed. *The New Negro*. 1925. Reprint, New York: Antheneum, 1968.

Locke, Alain, and Montgomery Gregory, eds. *Plays of Negro Life*. 1927. Reprint, Westport, Conn.: Negro Universities Press, 1970.

Longfellow, Henry Wadsworth. *The Poetical Works of Henry Wadsworth Longfellow*. Cambridge ed. Boston: Houghton Mifflin, 1975.

Loos, Anita. *Gentlemen Prefer Blondes*. 1925. Reprint, New York: Penguin Books, 1992.

MacDermott, Kathy. "Light Humor and the Dark Underside of Wish Fulfillment: Conservative Anti-Realism." *Studies in Popular Culture* 10:2 (1987): 37–53.

McDowell, Deborah. "New Directions for Black Feminist Criticism." In *The New Feminist Criticism*. Edited by Elaine Showalter. New York: Pantheon, 1985, 186–99.

May, Caroline, ed. *The American Female Poets*. Philadelphia: Lindsay and Blakiston, 1848.

Millay, Edna St. Vincent. *Collected Poems*. Edited by Norma Millay. New York: Harper and Row, 1956.

Millett, Kate. *Sexual Politics*. New York: Avon, 1971.

Moers, Ellen. *Literary Women: The Great Writers*. Oxford and New York: Oxford University Press, 1976.

Mott, Frank Luther. *A History of America Magazines, 1885–1905*. Cambridge: Harvard University Press, 1957.

Nekola, Charlotte and Paula Rabinowitz, eds. *Writing Red: An Anthology of American Women Writers, 1930–1940*. New York: Feminist Press, 1987.

Nelson, Cary. *Repression and Recovery: Modern American Poetry and the Politics of Cultural Memory, 1910–1945*. Madison: University of Wisconsin Press, 1989.

Nims, John Frederick. *Western Wind: An Introduction to Poetry*. New York: Random House, 1974.

———, ed. *The Harper Anthology of Poetry*. New York: Harper and Row, 1981.

Ostriker, Alicia Suskin. *Stealing the Language: The Emergence of Women's Poetry in America*. Boston: Beacon Press, 1986.

Paulson, Ronald. *Satire and the Novel in Eighteenth-Century England*. New Haven: Yale University Press, 1967.

Pecora, Vincent P. *Self and Form in Modern Narrative*. Baltimore: Johns Hopkins University Press, 1989.

Perkins, David. *A History of Modern Poetry from the 1890s to the High Modernist Mode*. Vol. 1. Cambridge: Belknap/Harvard University Press, 1976.

———, ed. *English Romantic Writers*. 2ᵈ ed. New York: Harcourt Brace College Publishers, 1995.

Pinsky, Robert. "Tidings of Comfort and Dread: Poetry and the Dark Beauty of Christmas." *New York Times Book Review* (4 Dec. 1994): 37–38.

Preminger, Alex, ed. *Princeton Encyclopedia of Poetry and Poetics*, enlarged ed. Princeton: Princeton University Press, 1974.

Procter, Adelaide Ann. *Legends and Lyrics*. 2 Vols. London: Bell and Daldy, 1865.

Quiller-Couch, Arthur, ed. *The Oxford Book of English Verse, 1250–1900*. Oxford: Oxford University Press, 1900; reprint 1931.

Ransom, John Crowe. "The Poet as Woman." In *The World's Body*, 1938. Reprint, Port Washington, NY: Kennikat Press, 1964.

Rascoe, Burton and Groff Conklin. *The Smart Set Anthology of World Famous Authors*. New York: Halcyon House, 1934.

Rich, Adrienne. "When We Dead Awaken: Writing as Re-Vision." *On Lies, Secrets and Silence: Selected Prose, 1966–1978*. New York: Norton, 1979, 33–49.

Richards, I. A. *Practical Criticism*. London, 1929.

Rose, Gillian. *Feminism and Geography: The Limits of Geographical Knowledge*. Minneapolis: University of Minnesota Press, 1993.

Rosenberg, Carroll Smith. *Disorderly Conduct*. New York: Knopf, 1985.

Scott, Anne Firor. *The Southern Lady: From Pedestal to Politics, 1830–1930*. Chicago: University of Chicago Press, 1970.

Scott, Bonnie Kime, ed. *The Gender of Modernism*. Bloomington: Indiana University Press, 1990.

Seidman, Steven. *Romantic Longings: Love in America, 1830–1980*. New York and London: Routledge, 1991.

Severin, Laura. *Stevie Smith's Resistant Antics*. Madison: University of Wisconsin Press, 1997.

Showalter, Elaine. "Feminist Criticism in the Wilderness." In *The New Feminist Criticism*. Edited by Elaine Showalter. New York: Pantheon, 1985. 243–70.

———. *Daughters of Decadence: Women Writers of the Fin-de-Siècle*. New Brunswick, N. J.: Rutgers University Press, 1993.

Stedman, E. C., ed. *An American Anthology, 1787–1900*. Boston: Houghton Mifflin, 1900.

Thornton, R. K. R. "'Decadence' in Later Nineteenth-Century England." In *Decadence and the 1890s*. Edited by Ian Fletcher. London: Arnold, 1979, 15–29.

Todd, Janet. *Sensibility: An Introduction*. London and New York: Methuen, 1986.

Tompkins, Jane. *Sensational Designs*. Oxford and New York: Oxford University Press, 1985.

Trilling, Lionel. *The Liberal Imagination*. New York: Viking Press, 1950.

Walker, Cheryl, ed. *American Women Poets of the Nineteenth Century: An Anthology*. New Brunswick, N. J.: Rutgers University Press, 1992.

————. *Masks Outrageous and Austere: Culture, Psyche, and Persona in Modern Women Poets.* Bloomington: Indiana University Press, 1991.

————. *The Nightingale's Burden: Women Poets and American Culture before 1900.* Bloomington: Indiana University Press, 1982.

Walker, Nancy. "The Remarkable Constant Reader: Dorothy Parker as Book Reviewer." *Studies in American Humor,* New Series 3:4 (1997):1–14.

————. *A Very Serious Thing: Women's Humor and American Culture.* Minneapolis: University of Minnesota Press, 1988.

Walker, Nancy and Zita Dresner. *Redressing the Balance: American Women's Literary Humor from Colonial Times to the 1980s.* Jackson: University Press of Mississippi , 1988.

Warhol, Robyn R. *Gendered Interventions: Narrative Discourse in the Victorian Novel.* New Brunswick, N. J.: Rutgers University Press, 1989.

Warren, Joyce W. "Canons and Canon Fodder." *The (Other) American Traditions: Nineteenth Century Women Writers.* Edited by Joyce W. Warren. New Brunswick, N. J.: Rutgers University Press, 1993, 1–25.

————. *The (Other) American Traditions: Nineteenth-Century Women Writers.* Edited by Joyce W. Warren. New Brunswick, N. J.: Rutgers University Press, 1993.

Washington, Mary Helen. "'The Darkened Eye Restored': Notes Toward a Literary History of Black Women." In *Reading Black, Reading Feminist.* Edited by Henry Louis Gates, Jr. New York: Meridian, 1990, 30–43.

Watts, Emily Stipes. *The Poetry of American Women from 1632 to 1945.* Austin: University of Texas Press, 1977.

Weintraub, Stanley, ed. *The Yellow Book: Quintessence of the Nineties.* New York: Anchor Books, 1964.

Weiss, Andrea. *Paris Was a Woman: Portraits from the Left Bank.* San Francisco: HarperSanFrancisco, 1995.

Wharton, Edith. *The House of Mirth.* 1905. Reprint, New York: Norton Critical Edition, 1990.

Whigham, Peter, trans. *The Poems of Catullus.* New York: Penguin Books Classics, 1984.

Whissen, Thomas Reed. *The Devil's Advocates: Decadence in Modern Literature.* New York: Greenwood Press, 1989.

Whistler, James MacNeill. *The Gentle Art of Making Enemies.* 1892. Reprint, New York: G. P. Putnam, 1904.

Wylie, Elinor. *Collected Poems of Elinor Wylie.* New York: Knopf. 1934.

Yeats, William Butler. "Modern Poetry. " In *Essays and Introductions,* by W. B. Yeats. 1936. Reprint, New York: Collier Books, 1961, 497–98.

Zagarell, Sandra A. "The Conscience of Her Age." Review of *Harriet Beecher Stowe: A Life,* by Joan D. Hendrick. *Women's Review of Books* (Apr. 1994): 13–15.

————. "'America' as Community in Three Antebellum Village Sketches." *The (Other) American Traditions: Nineteenth-Century Women Writers.* Edited by Joyce W. Warren. New Brunswick, N. J.: Rutgers University Press, 1993, 143–63.

————. Introduction to *A New Home, Who'll Follow? or Glimpses of Western Life,* by Caroline M. Kirkland. Edited by Sandra Zagarell. New Brunswick, N. J.: Rutgers University Press, 1990.

Index

235